Jerusalem EasyWalks

by

Aviva Bar-Am

With Gershon Rechtman

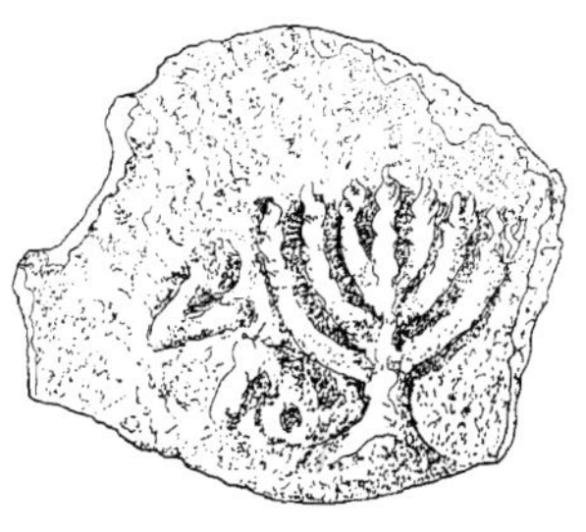

Ingeborg Rennert Center for Jerusalem Studies

ISBN 965-90048-6-9

Front cover photos (clockwise from top left): Menorah at the Knesset, Tower of David Museum, Old City marketplace, Orde Wingate Square, Mahane Yehuda Market
Back cover photos (clockwise from top left): Jaffa Gate, the Western Wall, Damascus Gate, Church of St. Mary Magdalene, Dome of the Rock, Via Dolorosa procession, Old City domes and towers, El Aksa and the Ophel, the Valley of Kidron at night

Other Books by Aviva Bar-Am

Guide to the Golan Heights by Aviva Bar-Am and Yisrael Shalem
Israel's Southern Landscapes: Your Guide to Eilat and the Negev
    by Aviva Bar-Am and Yisrael Shalem
EasyWalks in Israel: Sites & Stories by Aviva Bar-Am
Beyond the Walls: Churches of Jerusalem by Aviva Bar-Am

About Aviva Bar-Am

A native of Minnesota, Aviva Bar-Am immigrated to Israel in 1968 and has lived in Jerusalem ever since. She holds a degree in social work from the Hebrew University, and during her years as a staff correspondent at the *Jerusalem Post* published articles on social issues, opened a newspaper hot-line for English speakers and had her own Consuming Interest column. But the highlight of her work at the *Post* was a weekly two-page travel column called "Landscapes" that appeared in the *Jerusalem Post Magazine* until 1995.

Since that time Aviva has written and produced five guides to Israel, engrossing volumes that blend history, nature and folklore together with a light, journalistic touch. Aviva's Israeli-born husband Shmuel accompanied her on thousands of material-gathering trips around the country and took the brilliant photos that enliven all five books.

Aviva and Shmuel have two strapping sabra offspring: Guy and Na'ama.

About Gershon Rechtman

Talented tour guide Gershon Rechtman was born in Pretoria, South Africa and immigrated to Israel in 1985. While studying at Yeshivat Bet El near Jerusalem he developed a love of Jewish history and spent his free time hiking the country. After serving in an elite reconnaissance unit in the Israel Defense Forces, Gershon received a degree in Land of Israel Studies from Bar Ilan University. At this writing he was studying for a Masters Degree in Jewish History and Philosophy. He lives and works in Jerusalem.

Acknowledgments

It's done! I finally completed the book about Jerusalem that I carried in my heart for so many years. I take this opportunity to thank those wonderful people who gave freely of their advice, their expertise and their support to make my dream come true …

I owe a huge debt of gratitude to the Society for the Protection of Nature in Israel (SPNI) and to those outstanding SPNI guides who led me through many of the sites described in *Jerusalem EasyWalks*: Adi Eshed, Penina Ein Mor, Baruch Gian, Itai HaCohen, Orna Shapira and Alona Vardi. A special thanks to Peretz Reuven, who patiently answered my seemingly endless questions no matter what time of day or night I called!

My sincere thanks to other excellent tour guides who helped me with this book: Constantine Neno, from Shepherds Tours and Travel, and Hanna Kessler.

I am immensely grateful to Dr. Randall D. Smith, International Director of Christian Travel Study Programs, who has been a tremendous source of practical assistance and encouragement.

A number of people gave freely of their time and their knowledge. I can't thank them enough! They are: Dr. Michael Avishai, Director of the Botanical Gardens; Ayelet Hallel, Director of the First Temple Period Museum; Father Michael Sellors, Dean of St. George's Cathedral; Yoram Tamir, Assistant Director of Ammunition Hill; Sister Miriam and Sister Pat of St. Peter's Church.

Thank you to my two favorite Mikes — Horton and Hillel — for their wonderful maps, to Mike Horton for this book's terrific cover, to Judie Fattal for her great layout, and to tour guide Madeleine Lavine — for all her help.

I am grateful to: Miriam Oren, Events Coordinator at the Bible Lands Museum; Public Relations staff at the Tisch Family Zoological Gardens; Haim Ohayon, Egged Transportation Department; architect Mike Turner; Yoel Marinov and Sara Malka, Director and Deputy Director of the East Jerusalem Development Co.; Elly Dlin, Director of the Valley of the Communities at Yad VaShem. Thank you to Noam Morad for material on Israel's Karaite community.

I am indebted to Terri Morgan, my American web site designer, confidante and very, very dear friend. And I am grateful to Larry Blieberg for always being there when my computer fails (or I don't know how to use it!)

Thank you to my husband Shmuel for his wonderful photographs. And finally, a super-special thanks to my parents, Barbara and Irv Schermer. My mother proofread at each stage of production, offering boundless encouragement and practical suggestions; my author/father edited *Jerusalem EasyWalks* and added some of the most interesting material in the book!

Table of Contents

Uniquely Jerusalem Historical Sites and Attractions

Other sites, museums and Jerusalem attractions appear in the walking tours:

Tips for Tourists
and How to Use this Book

We once spent two weeks in England visiting one lovely site after another. But it was only as we were leaving the grounds of the last castle on our itinerary that a friendly lady asked us to become members of the National Trust. Turns out that had we known about the Trust at the beginning of our trip we could have bought a membership that would have saved us a significant amount of money!

In Israel, museums and other attractions that charge entry fees offer a variety of discounts. *Never be afraid to ask* — about discounts, memberships and combination tickets for other sites under the same management. Bring all the cards you can find when you visit one of these sites, including student cards, senior citizen cards, and Visa gold cards. People confined to wheelchairs are eligible for large discounts.

Commercial enterprises are open in Israel from Sunday to Friday. Friday is the Sabbath eve, and by 14:00 almost every store, museum and restaurant has shut down. Many reopen on Saturday morning; others do not; hours of sites described in this book are given at the end of every chapter. Opening and closing hours for Jewish religious holidays and holiday eves correspond to those of the Sabbath and Friday afternoons. Buses do not run on religious holidays. Most banks and post office branches close for afternoon siesta and reopen later on.

Several of the walks in this book take you next to or within unique and fascinating ultra-orthodox neighborhoods. Some residents of these neighborhoods object to women in shorts, mini-skirts and sleeveless blouses and on rare occasion may even become hostile when they are worn. If any part of your walk takes you near or through such a neighborhood, I have drawn your attention to that fact at the beginning of the chapter. Please take this into account and avoid a potentially unpleasant encounter.

Wheelchair access: At the end of the 20th century wheelchair accessibility was greatly improved in Jerusalem. Look for a special logo on signs next to wheelchair accessible sites. Wheelchair-accessible restrooms can be found at most museums, near the Western Wall, at St. Peter's Church and in the Ophel Gardens.

Driving in Jerusalem — Survival Tips: Fortunately for the tourist, excellent signs lead to practically every significant site in Israel. When in doubt, don't hesitate to ask for help; Israelis *love* to give advice. Despite the signs, roads in Jerusalem are hazardous for lanes weave back and forth and so do the drivers.

City traffic jams may cause even the most patient driver to speed whenever he gets the chance — and Israeli drivers are *not* known for their patience. Take this into account and <u>drive defensively</u>! Even when it is yours — give the other guy the right of way. When you park your car, make sure you have left nothing of any value in plain sight.

At the end of the 20th century a wonderfully modern tunnel system appeared in the city. It is named for former Prime Minister Menachem Begin — so if you see a sign that reads Begin Tunnels, it does not mean that there will also be another leading you to Tunnels End!

If you park next to sidewalks marked in blue and white stripes you must either pay the meter (if there is one) or use a parking ticket. Parking tickets are available at the post office, shops posting a relevant sign and sometimes on the curb itself. Parking is free before 8:00 in the morning, Sunday through Thursday after 19:00 and Friday after 13:00 until Sunday morning.

Although readers of this book won't be doing any strenuous hiking, the climate in Jerusalem is very very dry. Therefore, you should take water with you on every walk. And please wear a hat!

Stop in at one of the city's information centers for maps and brochures advising you of current Jerusalem events. You may find the centers very difficult to reach by phone, but it doesn't hurt to try ...

Jaffa Gate Information [628-0382]: Sun.-Thurs., 8:00-16:00; Fri., 8:00-13:00; may also be open Saturdays

Safra Square (municipal complex) [625-8844]: Sun.-Thurs., 9:00-16:00; Fri., 9:00-12:30

Christian Information Center (Jaffa Gate) [627-2692]: Mon.-Sat., 8:30-13:00

Money: Israeli currency is called shekels, and there are 100 agoras to a shekel. Most tourist enterprises honor major credit cards or travelers' checks but not personal checks.

Transportation: (a) Buses — Israel has first-rate, inexpensive public transportation. You don't need exact change to purchase a ticket on the bus. If you will be riding a number of buses on your visit, buy a bus card from your first driver and get a discount. (b) Taxis — Taxi drivers are required by law to turn on their meters. If they refuse to do so, tell them you wish to leave the cab. This will generally do the trick.

Bus 99, like other circular lines in major cities, takes you past a number of major sites and you can get on and off as much as you want. There are one-day tickets and two-day tickets available. The bus runs from Sunday (10:00-16:00) to Friday (10:00-14:00). Get your brochures at an Information Center or on the bus. The bus's first stop is at Jaffa Gate at 10:00, 12:00 and 14:00. For details call Egged Bus Information 530-4704 or 530-4422.

Telephones: Almost all public phones are operated by inserting magnetic telephone cards that can be bought at all post offices. *Information, (144) and the overseas operator (188) do not require a card.* Shops and restaurants often have coin-operated phones that take only shekel coins. Use of these phones is generally double the cost of a telecard.

Shopping: Jerusalem has a large and noisy shopping mall in Malha (western Jerusalem), a picturesque shopping area in Nahalat Shiv'a (downtown) and a long street filled with shops (Emek Refaim, part of the German Colony). Other places to shop or hang out: Talpiot (southern Jerusalem) and the Ben Yehuda Pedestrian Mall (downtown). An added value tax (VAT) of 17% is already included in any shekel price that you are quoted.

How to use this book:

1. Many circular walks described in the book close with an area side trip or two. Thus, a short walk may turn into a half-day jaunt.

2. You may wonder why some place names have been put into Capital Letters within the text. When this occurs, it means that this specific site appears as a separate chapter in the book (check the index or table of contents to find out where.)

Additional material on a number of the sites or individuals in this book can be found in two of my earlier volumes. Extra information on the churches included in *Jerusalem EasyWalks* is available in my fourth book, *Beyond the Walls: Churches of Jerusalem. Beyond the Walls* also takes you to practically every church on the Mount of Olives.

HaNevi'im Street, only touched on here, has its own chapter in *EasyWalks in Israel: Sites and Stories.* In *EasyWalks in Israel* you will also find further material on the market neighborhoods and a whole chapter describing Jerusalem's extraordinary municipal complex.

Aviva Bar-Am

Jerusalem scene

My Jerusalem

As I was driving toward my home near Mount Scopus on one of Jerusalem's rare gloomy afternoons, the sun suddenly peeked out from behind the clouds and shed its rays upon my beloved mountain. Each and every building — all constructed out of Jerusalem stone — turned a shimmering golden sheen.

Over the years my travels have taken me to some of the world's most enchanting cities. Yet to my mind not one holds a candle to the splendor that is Jerusalem, where historic hills and vales offer ever-changing landscapes, unparalleled views and a spiritual uplift that will tug at your heartstrings forever.

Readers of this book can visit Jerusalem not only by foot or by car, but also from their comfortable armchairs thousands of kilometers away. You will read tales as old as the dawn of history and as modern as the Six-Day War. With this book you can visit, among other sights, the wealthy suburb of Talbieh, the century-old Bukhara neighborhood, and Jerusalem's ancient Jewish quarter.

Let *Jerusalem EasyWalks* lead you along charming Yemin Moshe lanes. From the historic Windmill gaze down into the Valley of Hinnom, where children were burned as offerings to the evil god Moloch. View the excavations near the Temple Mount; learn about the contributions that the American Colony made to the Holy City, and roam through the pastoral setting of Ein Kerem.

My Jerusalem is a magical city, a place of wonder and delight. Enjoy your walks through its enchanted streets and historical sites — and please! Come back again and again.

Aviva Bar-Am

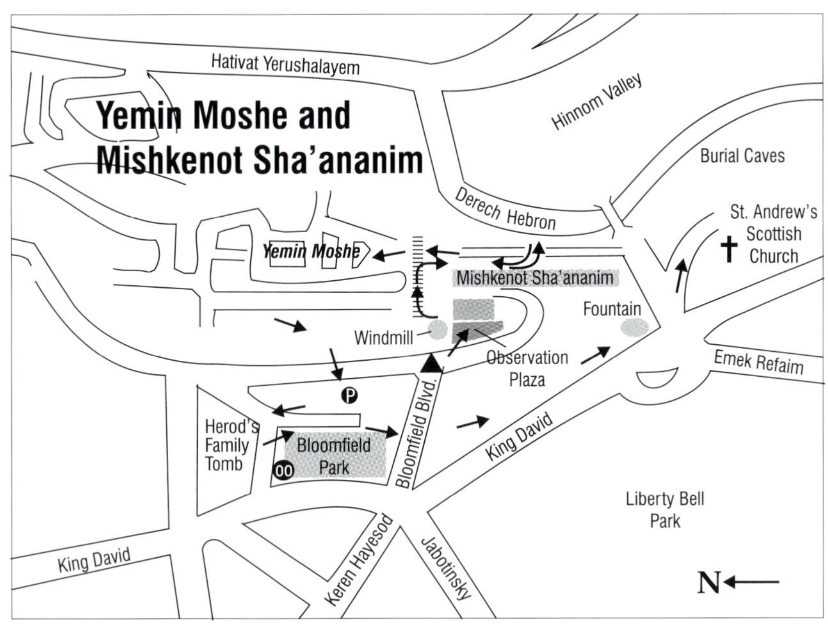

The roofs of Mishkenot Sha'anamim are crenellated like the Old City ramparts.

Yemin Moshe and Mishkenot Sha'ananim

- **Begin and end**: at the Windmill above Mishkenot Sha'ananim
- **Take bus**: 7, 8, 21, 48
- **Park your car**: in the lot at the site
- **Time frame**: 1-2 hours

Judah Touro was a distinguished 19th-century Jewish merchant who made his fortune in New Orleans. During the American-British War of 1812 Touro was seriously wounded and his recovery was slow and painful. But he continued to work and his various businesses and investments paid off handsomely. His financial resources enabled him to contribute heavily to both Jewish and Christian charities.

Touro bequeathed $60,000 to the Jews of the Holy Land in his will — a legacy that would have startling, long-range consequences. Indeed, as a result of his generosity, and because Touro chose Sir Moses Montefiore as executor of his estate, the situation of Jerusalem's Jews was to improve beyond recognition. A small group of Jews moved into houses that Montefiore built for them outside the congested Old City. And, in time, a whole New Jerusalem grew up outside the walls.

Begin at the Windmill near the entrance to the parking lot. You are about to visit two tiny but picturesque neighborhoods: Mishkenot Sha'ananim and Yemin Moshe. The former was the first Jewish community to be established outside of the Old City walls and translates as "dwellings of tranquility." The latter name honors the neighborhoods' founder: Sir Moses (Moshe, in Hebrew) Montefiore.

Tall and dignified, Montefiore made a fortune in the stock market while still a very young man. At the age of 40 he retired and devoted himself to good works. And by the time he died, at the ripe old age of 101, he had helped countless numbers of Jews in the land of Israel.

In 1855 he paid his fourth visit to Jerusalem, setting up his tent in what we know today as the Russian Compound. Armed with the money left by Judah Touro, he began looking for land on which to build a hospital for the Jews of Jerusalem. Eventually he bought a plot across from Mount Zion and surrounded it with a high stone wall. Although the hospital was never built, the land became the locale for the first modern Jewish neighborhood outside of the Old City walls.

Montefiore laid the cornerstone for this neighborhood — Mishkenot Sha'ananim — in 1857. He then erected an 18-meter-high ultra-modern windmill for grinding grain into flour. And despite the curses of local Arabs not happy with the competition, it continued to spin until steam-powered mills made it obsolete.

If you are here on a weekday, walk inside the mill to view an interesting museum dedicated to Montefiore. You will learn that Sir Moses Montefiore was active not only on behalf of the Jews of Israel, but also the Jewish communities of Syria, Iran, Romania, Morocco and Russia!

Take a good look at Montefiore's coat of arms, displayed above the entrance. How many British knights do you know of who proudly wrote the word Jerusalem in Hebrew on their coats of arms? Perhaps Montefiore, an observant Jew, wanted to carry out the biblical injunction: *"Let my tongue cling to the roof of my mouth if I do not remember you, if I do not raise Jerusalem at the height of my joy"* (Psalms 137:6).

For many years the carriage in which Montefiore rode during his travels in Israel was on display next to the Windmill. Vandals set it on fire in 1986 and the carriage was completely destroyed. Pieces of wood found in the rubble were incorporated into the reconstructed carriage that you see here today.

Now visit the lovely Observation Plaza. Mount Zion is directly across from you. You can identify the impressive Dormition Abbey by its adjacent clock tower and, directly below the Abbey, you will see the large and stately Greek Orthodox Seminary. The Jerusalem University College stands just below the Seminary and to your right. Originally a school for Arab boys, the structure was built in 1853 by Anglican Bishop Samuel Gobat.

In 1964 Pope Paul VI visited Mount Zion. The road that winds around the right side of the mountain was built especially for the car that drove him to Dormition Abbey and to the Cenacle — site of the Last Supper.

To your right on the other side of the valley is the mixed Arab-Jewish neighborhood of Abu Tor, and at its edge a Scottish flag flies above St. Andrew's Church. In front of you and to your left are the walls of the Old City: at their edge stands the minaret that is mistakenly referred to as the Tower of David.

Descend the steps next to the museum entrance. Pass through an ironwork gate, then stop and look around. To your left is the residential area of Yemin Moshe, built in 1892. On your right, below the plaza, are the two buildings that make up Mishkenot Sha'ananim. The Jerusalem Music Center is located in the upper building, while the second, lower structure has been turned into a hotel for visiting writers, musicians and artists.

Yemin Moshe is one of Jerusalem's most picturesque neighborhoods.

By 1860 the first building in Mishkenot Sha'ananim was complete. It contained 28 one-and-a-half room apartments. Also included in the compound were a water cistern complete with a revolutionary iron pump, a ritual bath, and an oven. The second, smaller building was constructed in 1866 about the same time that a cholera epidemic raged inside the Old City.

Until that time, moving outside of the Old City walls seemed foolish at best. Indeed, some of the people who maintained homes in Montefiore's brand-new neighborhood refused to stay in them overnight. But that year, the residents apparently decided that robbers and wild animals were less menacing than the deadly cholera and finally moved into their homes outside the walls.

Continue walking down the steps, pass under a vine-covered trellis, and turn right just above the Mishkenot Sha'ananim restaurant. You are now on a lovely, shaded path directly below the elongated building which is the historic first edifice of Mishkenot Sha'ananim. Note the roof, which is crenellated like the ramparts on the other side of the valley. Above each door is a Hebrew letter — one letter for each family that lived there. Much of the pretty metal work decoration was produced in Ramsgate, Montefiore's hometown.

Directly in front of you, at the end of the walkway, is the old guard house. It was so frightening to live outside of the walls that the residents requested a live-in guard! **The original wooden gate is to your left. Open it, walk through it, cross the asphalt slightly to the left and descend 18 steps. Look left to see the blocked-up entrance to a tunnel.**

During the course of the War of Independence Israel conquered Mount Zion. But there was no safe way to get supplies and troops up the mountain and to evacuate the wounded. Even after the armistice, vehicles and people moving below the Old City walls were potential Jordanian targets.

Finally, the Israelis burrowed out the tunnel that you have reached. The exit, also blocked, is visible across the road just beyond the traffic light. But the tunnel was too narrow to handle much traffic and included far too many bends to make it practical, so Officer Uriel Hefetz came up with the idea for a cable car. The cable car was put into operation in December of '48, and while it was used for only a short time it was kept ready — along with the tunnel — for any emergency. So secret was the cable car that until it was revealed to the public in 1972 few people in the country knew of its existence!

Yemin Moshe was restored after the Six-Day War.

See if you can find the cable. It stretches between the Jerusalem University College on Mount Zion and an early 20th-century Ophthalmic Hospital on the other side of the valley not far from where you are standing. You should be able to make out the cable car just below the window of the former hospital.

Below you and to the right lies the notorious Hinnom Valley. In ancient times pagans and some Israelites worshipped in the valley, using it as a sacrificial site. It was here that parents offered the lives of their children to appease the monstrous god Moloch. *"They built high places for Baal in the Valley of Ben Hinnom to sacrifice their sons and daughters to Moloch, though I never commanded, nor did it enter my mind, that they should do such a detestable thing and so make Judah sin"* (Jeremiah 32:35).

Now retrace your steps and walk back through the wooden gate. As you pass through, look toward the top of the building in front of you. It is decorated with an eight-sided star and a Hebrew inscription describing the contributions of both Montefiore and Judah Touro.

Stroll almost all the way back to the ironwork gate. Now it is time to visit Yemin Moshe, the group of dwellings on your right. What a beautiful sight — gorgeous houses and handsome gardens in a serenely peaceful setting. Yet until the city was unified in 1967 the neighborhood was anything but peaceful!

First, in the 1920's, Arab riots shattered the tranquility here. Later, in the months before the British evacuated Palestine, Arab snipers repeatedly threatened residents from their positions atop the Old City walls. In February of 1948 Arab forces staged a massive attack on the neighborhood. Although the Arabs were repulsed, most of the inhabitants abandoned their homes.

During the 19 years when the city was divided, part of the border between Jordan and Israel was located just below Yemin Moshe. The government crowded immigrant families, mainly impoverished refugees from Turkey and Kurdistan, into the deserted apartments. Jordanian snipers were a constant menace, living conditions deteriorated and the historic neighborhood turned into a slum.

Following extensive urban renewal after the Six-Day War, the residents were re-located to other sites. Artists and the very affluent moved in after promising to restore the buildings. **Today the little lanes are charming so take a walk through the neighborhood stopping in at any art galleries that are open. Then return to the parking lot.**

Side Trip One: Herod's Family Tomb

and more … especially for families with children!

Walk to the far end of the parking lot. Ascend just over a dozen steps on your left and turn right on the stone walkway. Within seconds you will reach a large burial cave complex that was uncovered in 1892 in which, apparently, members of King Herod's family were entombed.

Walk around the tomb to the right to discover another part of the complex. Here you will find the rolling stone common to Second Temple period tombs: *"… and they asked each other, 'Who will roll the stone away from the entrance of the tomb?' But when they looked up, they saw that the stone, which was very large, had been rolled away"* (Mark 16:3-4).

Follow the stone path back in the direction of the steps. The walkway you are on curves around to one of Bloomfield Park's little playgrounds, located next to a fountain and restrooms (which may or may not be open.) Look to your left to see a stone-encased structure surrounding a stone staircase. You can descend the steps to reach the closed entrance to a Second Temple period aqueduct.

Children will have fun climbing a curious ear-shaped structure and playing in sandboxes next to the fountain. **When they tire of this playground, follow the stone path to Bloomfield Boulevard. Cross the narrow road and immediately descend a flight of stairs on your right to view another blocked-up water channel.** This is thought to be part of an aqueduct that transported water from the south of the city to the area of Jaffa Gate during the Second Temple period and the centuries that followed.

Return to the path, and continue all the way down to the bottom of King David Street. You will be strolling through beautiful landscaped terrain laced with sandboxes and rock formations that are excellent for childish play. At the very bottom of the street is one of Jerusalem's strangest attractions: — a (sometimes) dancing fountain, decorated with sculpted animals.

Side Trip Two: St. Andrew's Church

Before returning to your cars or getting back on the bus, take a walk to one of Jerusalem's most interesting landmarks. It is St. Andrew's Church, and is only a hop, skip and a jump away from the dancing fountain at the bottom of King David Street. Simply cross the road (see map) and walk up the hill.

The white-domed Scottish Church, flying a blue flag, is visible from many parts of Jerusalem. Located on a hill across from Mount Zion, the church was built in 1927 of white limestone with simple, straight lines and modern colored windows. A charming guest house adjoins the church and between the two stands a tall dome-covered belfry topped with a stone cross.

St. Andrew's Church honors hundreds of Scottish troops who died wresting the Holy Land from the Ottoman Turks during World War I. Tribute is paid here to another outstanding Scottish soldier as well. He was Sir Robert the Bruce, a war hero who secured Scottish independence from England against heavy odds in 1314 and subsequently took up his rightful position as King of Scotland. Although it was a wish that has not yet been granted, a plaque on the floor pays tribute to the king's deathbed request that his heart be buried in Jerusalem.

Decorative stained-glass windows in varying shades of blue dominate otherwise unadorned white stone walls. The clean lines of the unpretentious arched ceiling suggest purity, and there is a feeling of spaciousness to the nave. Each seat in the modest wooden pews has the name of a Scottish regiment, town or district inscribed on its back.

St. Andrew's church was on the front line during the War of Independence. It survived shellfire and the raking of Arab machine guns at that time, and again during the Six-Day War of 1967.

Historic archeological finds were unearthed on the slope just beneath the church. They include burial caves from the First Temple period, a Second Temple period quarry and the ruins of a large Byzantine sanctuary.

It was the discovery of two thin small silver tablets rolled into scrolls that made the most news, however. Dating back to the 7th century B.C.E., they are written in ancient Hebrew script and the priestly benedictions engraved upon them are almost identical to the verses found in the Bible: *"May the Lord bless you and keep you; may the Lord cause His face to shine upon you and be gracious unto you; may the Lord turn His face toward you and grant you peace"* (Numbers 6:24-26). Look for these tablets in the Israel Museum.

Hours: **WINDMILL MUSEUM:** Sun.-Thurs., 9:00-16:00;
                    Fri., 9:00-13:00; Sat., closed
                    ST. ANDREW'S CHURCH [673-2401]: open all week long,
                    just ring the bell at the Scottish Center — the guest house that
                    is annexed to the Church
Restrooms: The Scottish Church, and in summer, next to the sandbox near
                    Herod's Family Tomb

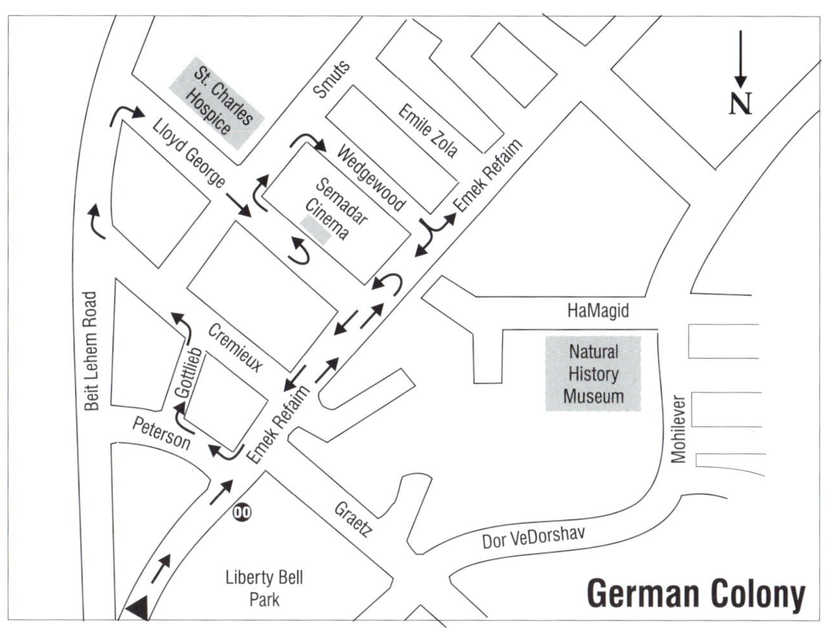

Beit Ha-Am, the Templers' Community House, is simple and unpretentious.

German Colony

- **Begin and end**: at the junction of Beit Lehem Road and Emek Refaim Street
- **Take bus**: 4, 14, 18
- **Park your car**: in the lot at Liberty Bell Park
- **Time frame**: $1^1/2$ hours

In 1978 a family residing in Jerusalem's calm and tranquil German Colony found a Nazi cache hidden away in a long-abandoned attic. Probably secreted there in 1939 during a British search for German sympathizers, the Nazi gear included a steel knife inscribed in German with the slogan "Blood and Honor." A hat and patent leather belt carried the name of one Erich Imberger, a third-generation Templer. Since the majority of German Templers living in Palestine during World War II were eventually deported to Australia, it is likely that Eric Imberger met the same fate.

Find a shady spot across from the junction. This is the northern boundary of the German Colony, populated for almost 80 years by members of the Templer movement.

You may have heard of Templars before. But there is no connection between the 12th-century Templar Crusaders and the German Templers. The German Templer movement, a splinter group that seceded from the Lutheran Church, was established in 1854. An evangelical sect, the Templers believed that the Day of Judgment was near and favored Jewish settlement in the land of Israel.

Templer leaders Christoff Hoffman and George David Hardegg, persecuted and even excommunicated in their native Southern Germany, decided to take their followers and settle in the Holy Land. Not missionaries in any sense, they hoped to establish a spiritual Kingdom of God together with the People of the Book. They believed that the ideal society they wanted to create would set an example for the local population.

The first large group of settlers landed in Haifa in 1868. (I described that bunch of colorful eccentrics in my book *Easy Walks in Israel: Sites and Stories*.) A second wave arrived in 1871: their agricultural settlement of Sharona would later become the site of Israel's very first official government offices (HaKiriya, in Tel Aviv). Jerusalem's quietly elegant German Colony, generally considered the most important community of all, followed a few years later. Interestingly, the Templer movement in Germany eventually disappeared — and its only remaining members were those living in the land of Israel.

Unlike the German Colony in Haifa and that of Sharona, the Jerusalem neighborhood is quite well preserved. In fact, many of the houses still retain their original look. As a result the whole effect — if you can ignore the traffic — is that of a quiet German village.

Jerusalem's German Colony was founded in 1873 on land located fairly close to the revered Temple Mount. Houses were of a style hitherto unknown in Jerusalem, for they were at the same time both spacious and modest. The vast majority were one-family homes although a few were built for two-family occupancy. Metal fences generally surrounded the dwellings; inscriptions in Gothic German were often carved above the doors.

In Jerusalem, the German design generally found among wooden structures was modified by the use of local materials — stone instead of wood — and by the artistry of local Arab builders. Of particular interest is a light-colored stone edging on many of the corners and windows.

The Colony's main street was called Emek Refaim, probably because it was located along what the Templers believed to have been the Valley of Refaim mentioned eight separate times in the Bible. Use of this name was just one more piece of evidence connecting them to the Scriptures.

Shaded by the Colony's tall cypress and pine trees, begin your walk. Cross the road and stand opposite #1 Emek Refaim Street. This will enable you to get a good look at the Templers' Beit Ha'am (Community House). Strong believers in simplicity and brotherly love, the Templers shunned the trappings of more conventional religion and worshipped here, inside one of the village houses.

Unpretentious though it was, this house does have a decorative gabled entrance and a belfry. The bell called Templers to worship on Sunday mornings. One of the elders would preach a sermon at the conclusion of the prayer service and an organ accompanied the singing that followed. Today the building belongs to the Armenian Church.

Next are the Colony's two schools, today part of the Israel Fiber Institute. The structure furthest from Beit Ha'am, at **#5**, was constructed in 1878. Templers added the edifice at **#3** to the Colony in 1882.

You are now going to visit a house on your side of the street, at # 6 Emek Refaim Street. Mattheus Frank erected this, the Colony's earliest edifice. It was also called the Miller's House, because of the steam-powered mill (and bakery) located on the property. But it differed from many of the later structures. Not only was it two stories high and built on a large area of five dunams, but it boasted a private swimming pool! The original wooden shutters on the ground floor are still intact.

Like so many of the houses this one is graced with an attractive facade. Above the front door are the words Eben-Ezer (literally translated as "helping stone"). The name apparently comes from the biblical verse *"Then Samuel took a stone and set it up between Mizpah and Shen. He named it Even-Ha'Ezer, saying, 'Thus far has the Lord helped us'"* (1 Samuel 7:12). Look for the date of this historic dwelling (1873) over the entrance.

House-owners in the German Colony took wise advantage of their land, and so did Mattheus Frank. Cellars were used for storage and attics provided additional living space. This house's side wings are far more elegant than those on the former schools across the street.

Built in stages by a rich and well-connected family that imported German goods, the sprawling house at **#10** has a gable-topped attic. The year of its construction is displayed over the door and the inscription is from Psalms: *"the Lord loves the gates of Zion more than all the dwellings of Jacob"* (Psalms 87:2).

Two sisters and their families lived together in the house at **#12**. Constructed in 1875, the house is divided by a Roman-style column with each family residing in half of the dwelling. Feast your eyes on the original wooden balcony, topped by an oval window and attractive gable; look for the double arches at the entrance.

The homes at **#14** and **#16** belonged to the extensive Imberger family. Built in 1877, the dwelling in front (**#16**) is engraved with the following prophetic

The beautiful residence at #16 was built in 1877.

This delightful dwelling, built by Templer architect Gottlieb Bauerle, contains all kinds of decorative elements (p. 24).

words -in German, like other inscriptions in the Colony: "*Arise, shine, for your light has come, and the glory of the Lord rises upon you*" (Isaiah 60:1). The beautiful entrance is slightly reminiscent of a Greek temple. To the rear of the building is late-comer **#14**, constructed 49 years later.

Next door is a quietly attractive residence built in 1878 and shaped very much like its neighbor. It belonged to Paula Paulus, the granddaughter of Templer founder Christoff Hoffman.

Now cross the street and walk back on Emek Refaim. Cross Lloyd George Street and you will reach the house at #15 Emek Refaim. A typical German Colony residence, it contains a basement (the service floor) and attic. Although it is a simple home it has an unusual side entrance. If you walk around the house to its left you will be able to see the attic windows and a quaint little garden.

Continue strolling toward the first houses of Emek Refaim. Don't miss the building at **#9**, the entrance of which is embellished with a sculpted lion's head resting on its paws. This was the Sandel home; a lion was the symbol of the family's chain of pharmacies back in Germany.

The man who put up this house, Theodore Sandel, was an architect who was at least partially responsible for all kinds of famous Jerusalem institutions. Among them: the Sha'arei Tzedek Hospital (the 19th-century hospital on Jaffa Road, not the hospital that is used today) Lamel School, Dormition Abbey and the Anglican School on HaNevi'im Street.

Turn into Peterson Road, located just past #7. During the early decades of the 20th century there were only two pubs in Jerusalem — and the house at #7 was one of them! Enjoy the trees, a lovely fragrance, and the quiet ambience.

Head right at a tiny alley called Maurycy Gottlieb Street. Follow it to the end, then turn left on Cremieux to see the corner dwelling at #7. It was built by Abraham Fast in 1891. Fast was to become famous as the proprietor of a fancy hotel across from Jaffa Gate.

Prior to the establishment of the Fast Hotel, overnight lodgers stayed in his home, giving him the hotel experience that he would need for the future! He had plenty of business, as 1892 was the year in which a French company built the railroad that ran from Jaffa to Jerusalem. French surveyors and engineers needed lodgings and a place to eat, both of which Fast was able to supply.

Continue up Cremieux, walking all the way to Beit Lehem (Bethlehem) Road and turning right. As you stroll, take a good look at the extraordinary corner house at #22. It boasts a strange and unusual gable, lovely gardens, decorative windows and a round corner tower. The Ehmann family lived here until they moved to Haifa during the 1920's.

Turn right at the next street, which is Lloyd George. To your left is the St. Charles' Hospice, a beautiful building dating back to the late 19th century. Contained within its walls are a school and orphanage run by nuns of the German Catholic Borromean Order.

The order is named for 16th-century saint Charles Borromeo, who was nephew to Pope Pius IV. Deeply involved in the realization of ideals put forth during the Catholic Counter-Reformation, Archbishop (and later Cardinal) Borromeo actively encouraged Church involvement in charitable works.

When you reach Smuts Street the corner residence at #6 Lloyd George will undoubtedly catch your eye. Gottlieb Bauerle, another Templer architect, built this delightful dwelling. All kinds of novel elements are incorporated into this house: a covered entrance, several decorative balconies, circular windows in the attic and designer balcony supports.

Adjacent to this house is the building at **#4A**, constructed in 1927 by Bauerle Junior. Originally called the Orient Cinema, it was later renamed the Semadar and was restored in the early 1990's. My husband and I often went to the movies at the pre-renovated early Semadar, and I remember with nostalgia that the antiquated wooden chairs were *very* simple and fastened together. As a result, when one person sneezed, a whole row of theatergoers would jump!

Retrace your steps to Smuts Street and turn right. A top story was added to the stunning old house at **#10**. The dwelling at **#9** belonged to Abraham Fast's architect son Theodore, who was thrown out of Palestine with his father during World War II because of their German sympathies. The house, already distinct from other Templer homes since it was built in 1929, was completely altered in later years.

Despite differences in venue, and variations in the characters of their colonies, all of the Templers in Israel came to the same sad end. The founders were practically Zionistic in their belief that the Chosen People should live in the land of Israel, and they vehemently opposed German nationalism. But when German Emperor Wilhelm II visited the Holy Land in 1898, the second generation flew German flags and sang the German anthem. And, incredibly, the native-born third generation turned into enthusiastic Nazi sympathizers, setting up a branch of the Nazi movement within the Colony! Some of these Templers voluntarily left Palestine for Germany, while almost all of the rest were evicted from this country during World War II.

You can rest in the little park next to #9 if you wish, then backtrack a few meters to Wedgwood Street and follow it all the way back to Emek Refaim. If you turn right when you get there you will end up at Liberty Bell Park, a terrific combination of sports fields, rinks, playgrounds and rest areas. Before you do so, you might want to turn left instead to visit one of the Colony's numerous coffee shops and restaurants.

Side Trip: Natural History Museum

When they were young our offspring spent many of their afternoons at the Natural History Museum, on 6 Mohaliver Street. The museum, with its enthralling stuffed animals and birds and hands-on exhibits is at least partly responsible for both of our children's strong interest in biology and zoology. **To get there, ascend Graetz Street, located between #6 Emek Refaim and #8. Then, just follow the signs.**

Hours:	**NATURAL HISTORY MUSEUM** [563-1116]: Sun., Tue., Thurs., 8:30-13:00; Mon., Wed., 8:30-18:00; **Entrance fee**
Restrooms:	Liberty Bell Park, in restaurants and at the Natural History Museum

Talbieh and Rehavia

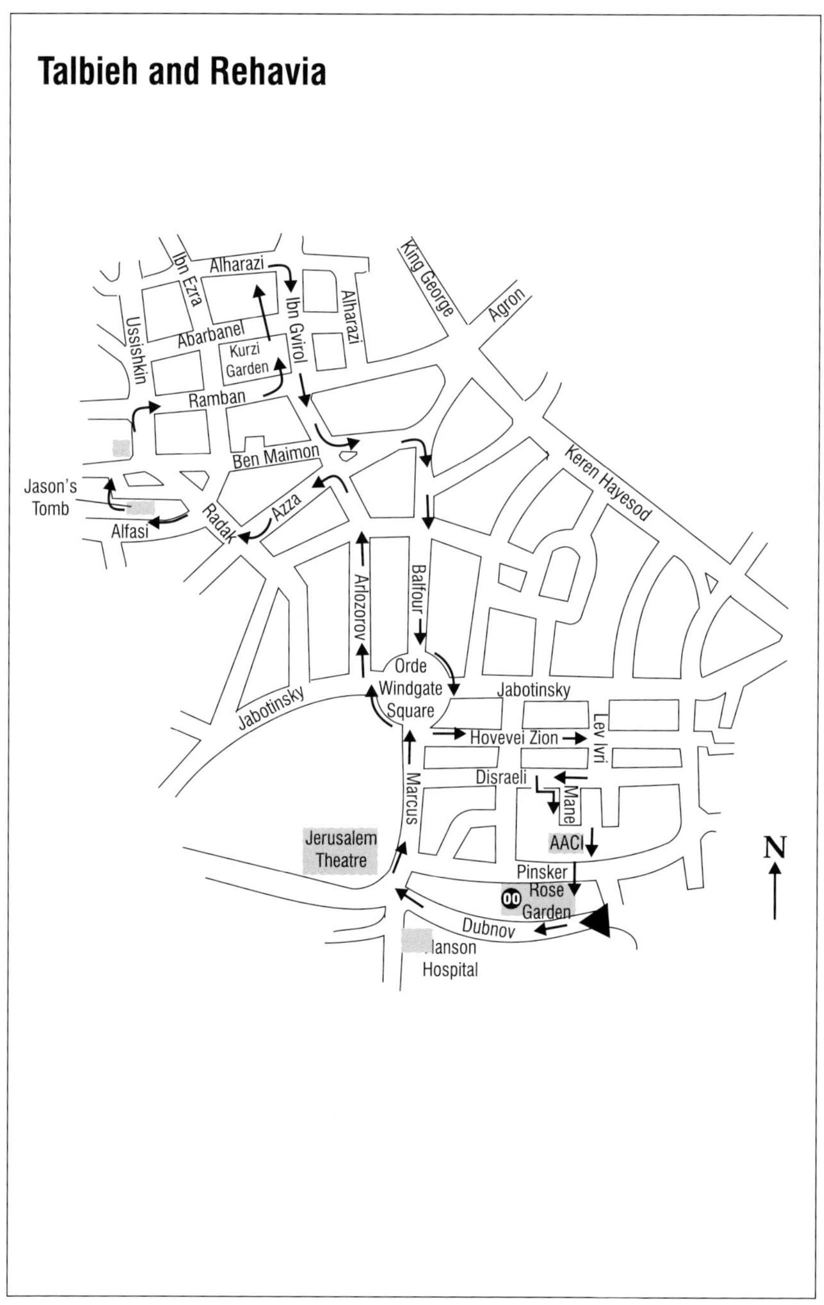

Talbieh and Rehavia

- **Begin and end**: at the Rose Garden, Dubnov Street entrance
- **Take bus**: 15
- **Park your car**: on the street, next to the Rose Garden
- **Time frame**: 2-3 hours

Until I took a guided tour through the Jerusalem suburbs of Rehavia and Talbieh, I never really paid attention to the houses that line their streets. But as I walked through the neighborhoods and heard tales of the people who resided here during one of Israel's most exciting eras, the houses and their inhabitants suddenly came alive. For the first time street names with which I had been familiar for decades became as real as if those famous and colorful figures were standing next to me in flesh and blood!

You can almost cover both neighborhoods in a circular walking tour that starts and ends in Talbieh. Begin at the main entrance to Talbieh's Rose Garden, located at the eastern end of Dubnov Street (near #13). Walk slightly downhill in the direction of the Jerusalem Theater. On your left there are no houses, only trees and a fine view of southern Jerusalem. To your right are some of the newest and most fashionable homes in Talbieh.

Like its next-door neighbor Rehavia, Talbieh was developed in the 1920's and 1930's. But the very large edifice you see to your left, which reaches to the corner of Dubnov and Marcus Streets, appeared in the 1880's. This is the Hansen Government Hospital for the Treatment and Prevention of Leprosy, originally a German institution called *Jesus Hilfe* (with the help of Jesus). Designed by renowned German-Christian architect Conrad Schick, it was constructed around an inner courtyard and graced with a beautiful garden.

Walls surround the once magnificent edifice, which was built of large, beautiful stones. Modern for the times, every room in the hospital was heated by a cast iron, wood or coal burning stove imported from Germany. A German evangelist planted trees and flowers here at the beginning of the 20th century. Most of the foliage is mentioned in the Bible.

One of Jerusalem's most revered and colorful figures, Rabbi Arye Levin, was a frequent visitor to the hospital. Long before he became known as the "prisoners' rabbi" because of his devotion to Jews locked up in the Jerusalem Central Prison, he was already paying regular calls on patients at the city's lepers' hospital.

"Reb" Arye's interest in the hospital began one day when he was praying at the Western Wall. Approaching a woman who was crying pitifully, he asked her the meaning of such sorrow. She replied that her son was an incurable leper tucked away in an institution and forever lost. Having made up his mind to visit the boy, the rabbi was shocked to find 12 Jewish patients living amidst a crowd of Arabs, and to learn that all were cared for by German nuns. The Jews were ecstatic at his visit — apparently it been years since anyone had come to call on them! Then and there Reb Arye decided to return every week, when he would read from the Bible and speak to each patient.

Nuns cared for the sick here until the 1950's, when they moved with their Arab patients to Ramallah. At the end of the 20th century only a handful of Jewish patients remained in the hospital.

Turn right on Marcus Street. David "Mickey" Marcus, a Jewish colonel in the American army, was summoned to Palestine before the declaration of the State to help shape the Haganah into a modern fighting force. Known here by the pseudonym of "Stone," Marcus had never been an active Zionist. Nevertheless he was delighted when asked to use his military expertise for the good of the Jewish people.

Marcus threw himself into the struggle. His experience and initiative made him such an invaluable asset to the war effort that he was named a Brigadier General and Commander of the Jerusalem Front on May 28, 1948.

Less than two weeks after his appointment, and after an exhausting day of battle, Marcus took a night walk just outside of his camp near Abu Gosh. Still unversed in Hebrew, he didn't reply with the password when challenged by a cautious sentry. Two more calls went unanswered before the guard nervously fired his gun. Marcus died from a bullet wound in the chest, shot by a Jewish guard only a few hours before the first Arab-Israeli truce went into effect.

The modern structure on your left is the Jerusalem Theater, completed in 1971. Much of it was funded by the wealthy Sherover family, the owner of the decorative villa at **#2** Pinsker Street on the corner of Marcus. Pinsker Street was also named for a famous figure: Leon Pinsker, a forerunner of the Zionist movement. Written in 1882, his book *Auto-Emancipation* advocated Jewish emigration to a national homeland.

Now you begin to see the houses of early Talbieh. Constructed by wealthy Christian Arabs, these magnificent dwellings were designed with dignified lines and superb gardens. The imposing Villa Haron El Rashid at **#18,** built in 1926, is a perfect example. Notice the fancy garden and ceramic tiles, then walk through the side entrance. The building's name is written above the door in both English and Arabic.

Former Prime Minister Golda Meir lived here in the 1960's when she was the country's Foreign Minister. Legend has it that before United Nations

Secretary Dag Hammerschild came to visit, she had her security men cover the sign — supposedly to hide the fact that the house had belonged to an Arab.

During the British Mandate the British purchased the house for their Air Force Command. Because Villa Haron El Rashid towered over the rest of the buildings in the neighborhood, both the Haganah and the Iraqi troops occupying the Arab Katamon district nearby wanted to use it as a lookout post. On the eve of the British evacuation of Jerusalem on March 14, 1948, their officials agreed that the Haganah could have the keys if they could get in without Iraqi knowledge. Thus, as the British vacated the house from the front door, the Jews came in through the back!

The house at **#11** belonged to Reuven Mass, who transferred his publishing house from Germany to this building in Talbieh in 1936. Mass's son Danny was killed in a rescue mission that subsequently became known by the number of volunteers who took part — ("HaLamed Hay" — The Thirty-Five).

He had been sent to lift the Arab siege on the Etzion Bloc, four small Jewish settlements located in the Hebron mountains to the south of Jerusalem. Local Arabs had severed the settlers' connection to the rest of Jewish Palestine after the United Nations announced the Partition Plan in November of 1947. The isolated settlers soon began to run out of food and ammunition, and rescue attempts met with tough Arab resistance. By mid-January, 1948, the situation was critical.

With several dozen other young men, most of them students at the Hebrew University, Danny Mass was sent to the aid of these besieged settlers. During their attempt to reach the Bloc by a roundabout route the troops were discovered by hundreds of well-armed local Arabs. The entire group was cut down in battle; some people believe that the last three soldiers to remain alive blew themselves up with a remaining hand grenade. The Bloc fell to the Arabs on May 13, 1948.

Continue walking up Marcus Street. When the beautiful apartment building at **#4** was built in the 1930's, it was only two stories high and belonged to a Spanish Benedictine monastery named Montserrat. Staff here engaged in biblical research, and was responsible for translating the Bible into the Catalan language. On the first floor balcony an M for Montserrat is woven into the ironwork.

At the top of the street you come to Salameh Square. Although it was renamed for Orde Wingate, the fundamentalist Christian and British officer whose highly trained Jewish "Night Squads" broke the back of Arab terrorism in Palestine in 1938, Jerusalemites stubbornly persist in calling it by its original name.

Tranquil Rose Garden, on the edge of Talbieh.

Constantine Salameh was a Christian Arab who owned all the buildings that surrounded the square. Besides dealing in real estate, and maintaining close connections with the Jews, Salameh made a fortune supplying the British army with fruits and vegetables.

Salameh rented out the elegant buildings situated around the square. The one exception was the structure in which he made his home, an impressive three-story dwelling surrounded by a handsome garden. Near the end of the British Mandate Salameh left Jerusalem, after entrusting his house keys to the Belgian consul.

Turn left at the square, then turn right at Arlozorov (the first street you reach). Salameh's mansion will be on your right, giving you a surprise view of some tall, stately palm trees that were planted in the villa's garden.

As you walk along Arlozorov, the tone of the neighborhood will change and the houses may seem less interesting. This means that you have entered Rehavia which, although built in exactly the same period as Talbieh, was designed in a completely different style. Home to some of Israel's most famous personalities and political leaders, Rehavia was populated only by Jews and was constructed with Jewish labor. Each house had a garden encompassing an area twice as large as the house itself.

The architect who designed Rehavia was a German Jew named Ricard Kaufmann. Kaufmann also planned Beit HaKerem, Talpiot, Kiryat Moshe, Makor Haim and Bayit VeGan, Jerusalem's other European-style garden neighborhoods.

Part of a path which was supposed to run straight through the neighborhood was appropriated on behalf of Yitzhak Ben-Zvi. Ben-Zvi needed the space for garden parties when he was President of Israel and lived on the corner of Rehavia's Alharizi Street. That portion of the path was never returned to Rehavia residents. You will view Ben-Zvi's home later on in this walk.

Look through the gate of **#10**. This is a housing development called "workers' homes, B," built in 1934. Each apartment had a private entrance, its own garden, and special childproof railings. During construction, two "*sliks*" (camouflaged hiding places for weapons illegally possessed by the Jews during the British Mandate) were dug into the ground.

Turn left on Azza Street (the Hebrew for "Gaza"), then turn right at the first street you come to: Radak Street at Rafael Rafi Weiss Square. Ascend

The magnificent Haron El Rashid.

to Alfasi, and turn left. Jerusalemites are used to having millennia-old artifacts incorporated into their neighborhoods — this *is* the Holy City, after all! If you are from out of town, however, you may be surprised by what you see opposite **#15** — a Jewish burial cave from the Hasmonean period (2nd-1st century B.C.E.) It was discovered during the neighborhood's construction and restored with stones found at the site. With its pyramid-shaped top it strongly resembles Zechariah's Tomb in the Kidron Valley. Walk right up to it. The name "Jason" was inscribed on one of the walls, so of course it is known locally as Jason's tomb.

When you finish viewing the tomb, don't return to the sidewalk; instead, climb up the stone stairs along the side of the cave. Cross the square and stop at the corner of Ben Maimon and Ussishkin (the ascending street). Turn left on Ben Maimon, walk a few meters, then turn into the first opening you see.

Peek through the gate. Believe it or not, this dry, overgrown garden and shabby-looking deserted residence housed the first four prime ministers of Israel: David Ben-Gurion, then Moshe Sharett, Levi Eshkol and Golda Meir. The structure was built in 1933 by an English Jew named Julius Jacobs, who served in the British army during World War I. When Jacobs became interested in Zionism, he obtained a high-placed job with the British Civil Administration in Palestine. But because Jacobs was an unusually honest and straightforward man, he found himself torn by conflicting loyalties. He couldn't bring himself to reveal to the British the important secrets he learned from his Haganah friends. And his position in the British Civil Administration made him privy to highly confidential material that could have been helpful to the Haganah.

Finally, Jacobs asked for a less sensitive job, thereby avoiding any conflict of interests. His new office was in the King David Hotel. Jacobs was killed while working at the hotel when it was blown up by the Jewish underground on July 22, 1946.

Jacob's family was devastated. Perhaps in order to forget unhappy memories, they transferred ownership of the house to the Jewish Agency. In 1950, when Israel's brand-new government needed a suitable residence for Prime Minister David Ben-Gurion, this two-storied edifice was chosen.

Ben-Gurion was a most remarkable individual. One of the most famous Ben-Gurion stories — so characteristic that it is probably completely true — relates that the great man looked out the window one day and caught a glimpse of the guard who was permanently stationed outside this house. Since it was raining, the Prime Minister asked the guard inside for a cup of tea and a chance to dry out. The guard demurred, unwilling to leave his post. With that Ben-Gurion took the rifle off the guard's shoulder and told him "You go in. I'll guard the house for awhile." (Tour guides tell a similar tale about President Yitzhak Ben-Zvi, man of the people, near his house on Alharizi Street.)

The Prime Minister's complex contained six bedrooms, a living room, a kitchen, a garage and a garden. It was here that major government decisions were taken, including plans for the Sinai Campaign of 1956. Later, Golda Meir held her "kitchen cabinet" (a small group of handpicked statesmen who met together in the kitchen) in this residence. Eventually the building deteriorated and when Yitzhak Rabin became Prime Minister for the first time in 1974, he and his wife Leah decided to live elsewhere.

Jason's Tomb — antiquity in the center of the Jerusalem metropolis.

Walk back to Ussishkin and ascend to Ramban Street. Cross to the other side and stop at the corner house — #32 Ramban. It belonged to Menachem Ussishkin, one of the giants of the Zionist world and the chairman of the Jewish National Fund (JNF) for almost 20 years. A very strong, single-minded personality who was dedicated to the idea of settlement in Palestine, Ussishkin was the driving force behind the purchase of the swamps in the Jezreel valley, which the JNF then transformed into wonderfully fertile land.

When he became chairman of the JNF in 1922, Ussishkin was put up in an exquisite two-story villa in MUSRARA that contained over 40 rooms. The house was built in 1885 by Swiss missionary banker Jacob Johannes Frutiger, who called it "Mahanaim" for the biblical verse *"When Jacob saw them, he said, "This is the camp of God!" So he named that place Mahanaim"* (Genesis 32:2).

After Frutiger's bank collapsed in 1896, the handsome villa was sold and eventually purchased by the Anglo-Jewish Association. Ussishkin was housed within its walls until 1927. Then, following a Jerusalem earthquake in which the British High Commissioner's residence was damaged, the British commandeered Mahanaim and replaced Ussishkin with the commissioner. Ussishkin never forgot this "insult" and that is why, it is said, he called his new home "Mahanaim." You will see the name, written in Hebrew, over the door.

On Ussishkin's 70th birthday, the street on which he resided was given his name. Gossips liked to say that if you got up early enough in the morning you would find Ussishkin — not known for his modesty — busy polishing the street sign. **Turn right on Ramban Street.**

The three-story modern house at **#30** was the home of Arthur Ruppin, who dedicated most of his life to the establishment of Jewish settlement in the land of Israel. Later residents added the top two floors and part of the western wing, but you can still observe the beauty of the original style and stones utilized in the bottom story. See if you can find the gardener's residence — a small, yellow, covered rotunda around the building to it's left (your right).

Built in 1924, the dwelling on the corner of Ramban and **#22 Ibn Ezra Street** belonged to Gad Frumkin, the only Jewish Supreme Court justice to serve during the British Mandate. The sign "Havatzelet" (lily) over the door was a gesture to his father, who published a historic newspaper of that name for over 40 years.

Further along Ramban you reach the Kurzi garden, originally designed as the playground it is today. But in the beginning, when there were few children in the neighborhood, Rehavia's tennis players decided to use the site for their games. Time passed, and eventually the toddlers of Rehavia needed a place to play. Many of the people on the neighborhood committee were sports enthusiasts, and they decided to let the tennis players continue. In protest against the fact that the youngsters were being deprived of their playground, committee chairman Judge Gad Frumkin resigned.

Walk through the playground all the way to Yad Yitzhak Ben-Zvi (the lettering is in Hebrew but the signs are huge and there is a big *menorah* — the symbol of the State of Israel — on one of the exterior walls). An institution dedicated to Land of Israel Studies, it served as the home of this country's second president, Yitzhak Ben-Zvi, in 1953.

Continue along a shady path to a narrow street called Alharizi. Turn right. In 1920, the first British governor of Jerusalem decreed that all new buildings must be faced with lovely Jerusalem stone — thus laying the groundwork for the city's harmonious architectural style. The tall, ornate, cream-colored building at **#22**, however, was constructed in Spanish Colonial style with nary a hint of the characteristic stone. Tour guides joke that the illustrious owner of this edifice must have either been unaware of Governor Storrs' new rule, or believed that it applied only to houses visible from the Old City!

This was the home of Dr. Dov Yosef, a Canadian-born Jewish lawyer who immigrated to Israel in 1921. This luminary is said to have saved Israel twice: first, during the siege of Jerusalem, when he was in charge of handing out food and was so meticulous that everyone got an equal share. And a second time in the early 1950's, when he was Minister of Rationing and Supply. Although paid for with his own private funds, the grandeur of this villa comes as quite a shock — considering the positions that Dov Yosef held!

During Dov Yosef's lifetime the house was a center for distinguished writers, diplomats and artists and it is said that this is where the city's most famous society parties were held. In 1980 the house was sold and a few years later the new owners doubled its area. Nevertheless, the original design of the building remains.

At the first intersection with Ibn Gvirol Street, turn right and descend all the way back to Ramban. Cross Ramban and walk down Arlozorov to Ben Maimon Street. Here take a left.

You are walking up Ben Maimon to the point at which it is joined first by Azza Street and then by Balfour. Pass by the tip of Azza and make a sharp right turn onto Balfour, a street with some lovely houses. You will see the residence of the current Prime Minister at #3 Balfour. Continue straight back into Talbieh as far as Orde Wingate Square. A note on Orde Wingate: Displeased with his services to the Jewish people, the British recalled Wingate to England. During World War II Wingate, by then a Major General, was killed in an airplane crash in Burma where he had been organizing guerrilla warfare against the Japanese.

Cross the square, then walk down Marcus and turn onto Hovevei Zion, the first side street on the left. Noted Jewish philosopher Martin Buber spent the last years of his life in the villa at **#3.** If you look closely you may see roses growing out of a Roman column in the garden.

All of the homes on Hovevei Zion Street are a delight and you will be able to observe some fascinating elements. Enter the passage between **#9** and **#11** to see an original hand pump used to raise water from the cistern beneath. Especially unusual is **#16**, an eclectic mixture of colors, building materials and designs. The house at **#21**, on the corner of Lev Ivri Street, resembles a castle.

Turn right on Lev Ivri, and right again on Disraeli. Note the staircase at **#13,** which was the setting for a best-selling Israeli mystery novel by author Batya Gur — *A Saturday Morning Murder*. Then stop to observe the villa at **#12,** one of four splendid houses built in Talbieh by the wealthy Jamal family.

The intriguing Beit Jaled edifice at **#7** incorporates all kinds of colors, tiles, crenellations, arches, and stone railings. This is where the Peel Commission worked in 1937 and came up with the first plan to partition Palestine. However this plan pleased no one, and was subsequently dropped. In 1948 this fine edifice became the Motza Children's Home.

Beit Jaled hosted the Peel Commission deliberations on Palestine.

An unusual staircase leads to #4 Mane Street.

Backtrack a bit on Disraeli. Although it looks more like a driveway, the paved road across from #13 is the entrance to Maneh Street. The dwelling at **#4**, another Jamal house, is perhaps the most elegant of them all. While perhaps smaller than some other homes in Talbieh, it boasts an imposing staircase that gradually narrows near the top.

The grand edifice at **#6** houses the offices of the Association for Americans and Canadians in Israel. **Walk around the building and cross Pinsker Street. You will be back at the Rose Garden, this time at its northern entrance.**

Unlike Jewish neighborhoods, the cosmopolitan Talbieh was not planned with community services in mind. Indeed, the Rose Garden seems to be an afterthought: this may be why it is located on Talbieh's outskirts. **As you walk through the garden to the other side, enjoy the antics of children and dogs at play on the beautiful landscaped lawns.**

Restrooms: In the Jerusalem Theater (open during the week and on Saturday nights) near the Rose Garden's northern entrance (sometimes the garden restrooms are locked)

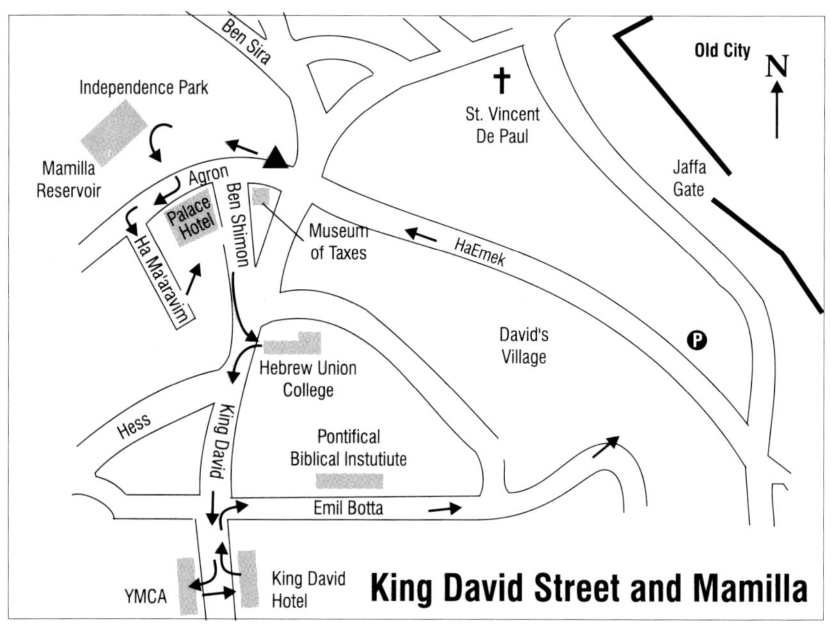

Ben Sira
Old City
N
Independence Park
St. Vincent
De Paul
Jaffa
Gate
Mamilla
Reservoir
Agron
Palace
Hotel
Ben Shimon
Museum
of Taxes
HaEmek
Ha Ma'aravim
David's
Village
P
Hebrew Union
College
Hess
King David
Pontifical
Biblical Instutiute
Emil Botta
King David
Hotel
YMCA
King David Street and Mamilla

King David Street and Mamilla

- **Begin and end**: at 32 Agron Street
- **Take bus**: 6,18, 20, 21, 30
- **Park your car**: on Agron Street or anywhere nearby
- **Time frame**: 2-3 hours

Black Saturday — June 1946. Palestine's British rulers decide to crack down on the Jews and take away their defensive weapons. In a hitherto unprecedented move, soldiers and policemen carry out mass arrests and herd thousands of Jews into internment camps without trial. While ferreting out weapons, the British smash open office safes, break down walls, tear up floors and storm through Jewish collective settlements ...

Etzel was an underground Jewish military force organized in 1937 to fight Arab terror and to engage in retaliatory attacks against the British Mandatory authorities. On July 22, 1946, furious Etzel soldiers planted explosives in milk containers. Then, disguised as Arab workers, they delivered the churns to the King David Hotel — site of the British Military and Administrative Headquarters. Scores of people were killed or wounded in the ensuing blast despite the Etzel's multiple warnings to evacuate the building.

The King David Hotel is only one of a dozen historic sites you will visit on a stroll along four fascinating streets: Agron, Emil Botta, Mamilla and King David. Your jaunt includes three museums, some stunning architecture, and one of Jerusalem's very oldest neighborhoods!

Begin at the Customs Administration Building at #32 Agron. If you are here during opening hours you can take a tour of the Jerusalem Museum of Taxes. This delightful little showcase acquaints you with the history and development of taxation both in Israel and in a few other countries. You may want to peruse a booklet of "modern" tax decrees from Mantova, Italy — published in 1695. Or read a shocking document written in 1723, describing how England's Jews were stoned at Easter if they didn't pay protection fees. Be sure to look through the fascinating collection of fiscal stamps.

What do vests, a relief of the Last Supper, sandals and a leather belt have in common? At one time or another all of them were used for bringing diamonds, gold and other undeclared goods into the country. The walking stick, on the other hand, carried smuggled narcotics into the Holy Land. Additional curious items include a long sword that was toted by the person who walked in front of the Turkish Customs Director.

Did you step on someone's foot? Before you say "excuse me," take a closer look. Ten gets you one that it was the foot of a costumed mannequin, one of several so lifelike that it is hard to tell them apart from human beings.

When you finish, or if you do this tour on days when the museum is closed, cross the street and stand on the steps. You are situated at the edge of Independence Park and next to two historical sites: the Mamilla Moslem Cemetery, and the Mamilla Reservoir.

Dating back to the 13th century, the Moslem Cemetery was filled, at first, with Mameluke tombs. Mamelukes — former slaves who managed to over-throw their Egyptian masters — ruled Israel from 1268 to 1517.

The most impressive tomb holds the remains of the Mameluke Emir who governed Safed during that period. **Walk around the tomb to the other side to see the ornamental entrance, above which Arabic scholars will make out the Emir's name (Aydugdi) and the date of his demise (1289).**

Now mosey over to the Mamilla Reservoir, off to your right and surrounded by a fence. During the Second Temple period Solomon's Pools, south of Jerusalem, provided the city with water. Two aqueducts transported the water: one led directly to the Temple reservoir and the other apparently to Mamilla. Rumor has it that when the Persians conquered Israel in the 7th century they martyred Christians and tossed them into the Mamilla Pool.

The name Mamilla may come from the Arabic for "water from God" — *ma'e meen Allah*. Rainwater that collected in this reservoir helped slake the thirst of Jerusalemites who were under siege during the War of Independence.

Back on the sidewalk, take a look at the strangely shaped building at #30 across the street. Construction on this grandiose structure was begun in 1928 and was completed in 1929. Originally a luxurious hotel called the Palace, it was the brainchild of the Supreme Moslem Council and meant to counter Jewish expansion outside the Old City walls.

Built in medieval Spanish style, the Palace Hotel has horseshoe-like arches above the windows. Observe the decorative, rounded facade and note that the inscription on the top of the building is written only in Arabic.

Jerusalem Mufti Haj Amin El Husseini, the city's most influential Moslem, put out a tender for construction. It was taken up by an Arab contractor and two Jewish architects. One of the architects was Chaim Weizmann's brother-in-law Tuvia Donia; the other was Haganah member Baruch Katinka.

In his book, *From Then 'till Now*, Katinka described the conditions of the tender. It stipulated that whoever took on the project had to finish it within

This Mameluke tomb dates back hundreds of years.

13 months or pay a penalty of 1,000 liras a day until it was complete! Other conditions included a seven-day workweek and a preference for Arab workers, in this way insuring a high ratio of Arabs to Jews.

The Palace was finished before the deadline despite a short setback in August of 1929 when Arab laborers took 10 days off work. During that period Arabs rioted all over the country; in Jerusalem they destroyed several neighborhoods and massacred some of the city's residents.

Considering that the Mufti visited daily and that most of the laborers were Arabs, it is astounding that the Palace walls contained two built-in hiding places for Jewish-held weapons. Forbidden by the British to bear arms of any kind, the Jews had no choice but to prepare secret caches for weapons that they could use in self-defense. Called *sliks*, these ingenious hideaways were located all over the country: the two at the Palace were designed by Katinka.

When the British Peel Commission came to Jerusalem in 1936 to discuss the "Palestine problem," they held a number of their meetings at the fabulous Palace Hotel. But while some of the doors were kept open, there were others tightly shut. How, then, were the Jews to hear what was going on? Incredibly,

Katinka managed to plant microphones in some of the electric wires so that the Jews could keep abreast of current events.

Do go inside to view the ex-hotel's impressive interior. Four stories high, the building shines with restored marble floors, pillars and lovely grillwork on the railings. There are 140 rooms and when it operated as a hotel its ultra-modern services included an elevator, a restaurant, and central heating!

Following the bomb blast at the King David Hotel and other acts of Jewish resistance, the British evacuated shop-owners and residents from the center of Jerusalem and turned much of the city into a fortified ghetto surrounded by barbed wire. Locally the area was known as Bevingrad, for the unpopular British foreign minister who ruthlessly turned Holocaust survivors away from Palestine's shores. Look for portions of the barbed wire on pipes outside of the building.

Exiting the Palace, turn left up Agron street and then take the first left into a little alley: Rehov HaMa'aravim. Believe it or not, this unpretentious lane was part of a pioneer neighborhood. Called Mahane Yisrael, this was the second Jewish neighborhood outside the Old City walls.

One of the founders was Rabbi David Ben-Shimon, a leader of the Moroccan community. Although his North African flock was very poor, they managed to establish this neighborhood in 1868. From here you will note that the backside of the Palace Hotel is devoid of ornamentation — one way of saving money during construction! **Walk through the minuscule neighborhood. Then turn left, again left and finally right to a little thoroughfare paralleling King David Street (Ben Shimon).**

Immediately to your right is the striking Gesher Center. The lovely edifice was constructed on top of a historic building from the Mahane Yisrael neighborhood. **If you like, you can walk inside to see what has been preserved of the original.**

Back on the sidewalk, turn right and ascend King David Street. Located across the road, at **#13,** is the Hebrew Union College. The HUC houses the superbly designed Skirball Museum, which is a showcase for excavations of the Nelson Glueck School of Biblical Archeology. Not only are there artifacts and models on display, but you will also find descriptions of the process of excavation. Thus you can see exactly how the unique 3,800-year-old triple-arched gate at Tel Dan was uncovered.

One of the country's most significant finds was unearthed at Tel Dan in 1993, and contains the first extra-biblical mention of the Davidic Dynasty. It is an Aramean victory stele (inscribed standing stone) from the 9th century B.C.E. that refers to Joram King of Israel and Ahaziah King of the House of

David. A replica of the stele is on display here at Skirball near other Tel Dan discoveries: the original is located in the Israel Museum.

Most of the exhibits relate to finds from three different archeological sites: the ancient cities of Dan-Laish (northern Israel), Gezer (in the center of the country) and Aroer (located in the northern Negev). Themes center on burial customs, cult practices, and fortifications; among the finds are sarcophagi from the biblical period and burial urns for infants and children. Among the unusual artifacts are an enormous bathtub from the 9th century B.C.E., horns from an altar and signs written in the earliest alphabet known in Israel (16th century B.C.E.).

Alongside large-scale models and big color photographs of the excavations are interesting period tables. Written both in English and Hebrew, they provide biblical quotes that connect these finds to the Jewish heritage.

Exit the Hebrew Union College and cross the street. You have reached a side road named for German-born political activist and writer, Moses Hess. One of Hess's works, "Rome and Jerusalem," called for the renewal of a Jewish state. Although it received scant notice when published in 1862, this Zionist classic later served as a source of inspiration to Theodore Herzl. Together with other Zionist works, Hess's book also helped motivate early Jewish settlement in Palestine. On your right are houses that were part of the pioneer Mahane Yisrael neighborhood.

Jerusalemites were once asked what, in their opinion, was the city's most distinguished edifice. First choice for that honor was the Dome of the Rock; the exquisite runner-up will be the next stop on your tour. It is the Young Men's Christian Association building — probably the world's most magnificent YMCA. **You will find it up the main road, at 26 King David Street.**

No other site in Jerusalem is as laden with symbols as this YMCA. Reflected on its walls, ceilings, stones and pillars are manifestations of the world's three greatest faiths, a statement of unity that remains stable in a city too often shattered by war. The international YMCA theme in which a triangle represents the body, the mind and the soul is repeated throughout the building.

As you approach the YMCA you see 12 cypress trees, a symbolic number representing Jesus' disciples, the Israelite tribes and the followers of Mohammed. Forty pillars in its courtyard and portico symbolize the Jews' 40 years in the desert and Jesus' 40 days of temptation. Each column is topped by an ornamental capital sculpted to illustrate biblical fauna and flora.

On the floor of the outer entrance is a copy of the mosaic Madeba Map (another is on display at the Roman Cardo in the Jewish Quarter). Over the door which leads into the building is a glass window decorated with an olive branch. In order to keep this symbol of peace from shattering during the War of

Splendid by day, the YMCA is even more glorious at night.

Independence, the window was removed each time there was violence in the city. One day, in 1948, a shell flew through the hole where the window had been and hit the ceiling. Fortunately it didn't explode and the ceiling was later repaired.

At the end of World War I the Greek Orthodox Patriarchate began selling some of its Jerusalem property. Land was sold to the Jews — who built in REHAVIA; land was sold to the Arabs, who built in TALBIEH; and land was sold to the YMCA, so that the organization could build a monument to peace. So impressed with the idea were the Jews of Manchester, England, that they contributed to its construction!

It was Dr. Archibald C. Harte, General Secretary of the International YMCA, who had the vision. He wanted to serve people of all faiths and nationalities in the Holy Land, and impressed millionaire James Jarvie of New Jersey with his ideas. On Christmas Eve of 1924, Harte found $400,000 in his Christmas stocking — a gift from Jarvie. Jarvie was eventually to add another $600,000 to this sum, dying before he saw the end result of this largess. The architect was Arthur Louis Harmon, whose firm designed New York's world-famous Empire State Building.

Far more modern than other contemporary Jerusalem buildings, the YMCA had the city's first heated swimming pool and its first real gymnasium — complete with a wooden floor. The first concerts broadcast from the Jewish radio station (the Voice of Israel) were transmitted from its stunning auditorium.

For a small fee you can ride an elevator up to the 50-meter central tower for four outstanding panoramic views of the city. Alternatively you walk up 220 steps. (Please note — there are a few steps to climb at the end of the elevator ride as well).

Leave the YMCA, cross the street and stand in front of the King David Hotel. You will find that its only exterior decorations are the rosettes typical of the period in which it was built. Inside, you will find a warm and elegant lobby, always adorned by elaborate, fresh floral arrangements.

If you plop yourself down on one of the comfortable chairs, you will be relaxing in what is known as the "People Watching Lobby." Some people say that if you sit here long enough you will see everyone who is anyone! Famous figures that have visited the King David Hotel include Heads of State Menachem

A renewed Mamilla. In the back: the majestic King David Hotel and the YMCA tower.

Begin and Anwar Sadat, Prince Philip, his son Charles, actor Ben Kingsly and pugilist Muhammad Ali.

When constructed in 1931 the enormous hotel contained 200 rooms with an adjacent bath, some even with hot running water. It vied with the Palace for the title of finest hotel in the city. At the time waiters at the elegant King David wore white waistcoats and long baggy pants, and sported fez hats.

In 1938 the British took over a large portion of the building, turning its lavish rooms into offices. When the Federmann family bought the King David Hotel in 1958, they rebuilt the damaged southern wing, put in a swimming pool and added two additional stories. Like the original floors, the additions are made of a lovely pink stone quarried in Hebron. Decorations in the lobby are meant to represent the biblical era by evoking an ancient Semitic style. The lounge is decorated in a mode supposedly reminiscent of King David and the Hittite influence; the reading room reflects a style its designers considered worthy of King Solomon.

Look for Ambassador Hall (the name is on the wall). Here you see numerous abstract Stars of David above the lintel and on the mirrors. Note the lights on the wall: they are shaped like small candelabra resembling the *Menorah* that stood in the Temple.

On the other side of the lobby doors open onto the Reading Room. Its distinctive entrance is decorated with a pomegranate relief. The room is quite historic: not only are you stepping on the original parquet floor, but the wall lighting and tapestries also remain from the early King David Hotel. The large table in the Reading Room was loaned to Beit Gavriel (on the banks of the Sea of Galilee) in 1994. It was around this table that Israeli Prime Minister Yitzhak Rabin (1922-1995) and Jordan's King Hussein (1935-1999) participated in a historic peace-signing ceremony.

Exit the Reading Room into the hall. In the past the hotel's general manager worked in the Oak Room, located on the other side of the hall. Today used for family parties and small events, it is covered in wood and looks for all the world like a British men's club! Posh-looking books on the shelf are fake, but the superb Armenian vases and plates are very real.

You can visit the Presidents' Hall by turning left as you leave the Oak Room, passing the lobby, and walking all the way to the end of the hotel. Although the interior decorations here have been repainted over the years, the decor looks exactly as it did when the hotel was built.

Coming out of the King David, look straight ahead for a panoramic view of the YMCA in all its glory. Then turn right and at the first street on your right turn again. You are on Emil Botta Street. Next stop is a gem of a museum,

located at 3 Emil Botta Street and housed in two rooms of the massively grand Pontifical Biblical Institute.

On display in this beautiful little museum are artifacts from Jordan's Teleilat Ghassul which date back 6,000 years. You will see burial jars containing infant bones from the Chalcolithic Period (4000 B.C.E.). Look for animal bones which appear to have been split and filed into pins, belt buckles, pottery, needles and fishermen's tools. The earliest spoons and ladles known to this area are also on exhibit.

A beautiful box made of hippopotamus tusk, pottery with designs in red ocher and something that resembles an egg cup are also on exhibit. There are pot bases with impressions from the woven mats on which they were set to dry and also pottery decorated with snake appliques. Note animal figurines that once decorated cup rims — perhaps used for children.

Unique artifacts are the norm at this museum, including the earliest oil lamp found in the Middle East. But what will really catch your eye is an Egyptian mummy, the oldest on display in Israel. The mummy is that of a 15-16 year old Egyptian boy buried 2,300 years ago; you can see his toes peeking through the wrapping. At one time museum staff called the boy Alex, for the city of Alexandria where he was discovered. Later, however, an Egyptologist visiting the museum deciphered the hieroglyphics on his sarcophagus and determined that his name was the Egyptian equivalent of "Under the Protection of the God Horus."

Continue along Emil Botta Street, pass the stunning French Consulate and walk to the bottom of the road. When the street ends descend a few steps and turn left: you have reached the late 20th-century residential complex called David's Village. Across from you is a landscaped parking lot.

Walk past David's Village to the road. Until the middle of the 20th century, Mamilla was a thriving commercial center and business district full of lovely homes, shops, restaurants, and even the first Cadillac agency in the Middle East. Then, in November of 1947, the United Nations decided that Palestine should be divided into one Jewish and one Arab state. Enraged that the Jews were going to have their own country, angry Arab mobs stormed Mamilla and torched over 100 Jewish-owned stores. That, in effect, was the end of Mamilla as a commercial center. Instead, and after Jerusalem was divided in 1948, Mamilla found itself on the front line between Israel and Jordan.

On your left is a wall with the words Tannous Bros carved out of the stone. Incredibly, this is all that remains of a huge shopping mall and residential complex which flourished here in the 1930's.

As you near the corner of King David and Agron, look right to see a stunning complex — the St. Vincent de Paul Convent. Its courtyard is decorated

St. Vincent's Convent helped shape early Mamilla.

with palm trees. Constructed at the end of the 19th century, the convent was the first building to appear on this street. It is run by the Daughters (Sisters) of Charity, an order of mainly French nuns founded by St. Vincent de Paul in 1633.

Convent heads showed excellent business acumen. They put up a row of stores in front of the church and convent, on the border of Mamilla Street, and rented them out. Not only did the rent help them finance their charitable works, but the clergy at St. Vincent's can also be credited with helping to shape the commercial character of Mamilla.

<table>
<tr><td>Hours:</td><td>SKIRBALL MUSEUM [620-3261]: Sun.-Thurs-, 10:00-16:00; Sat., 10:00-14:00; wheelchair accessible
PONTIFICAL INSTITUTE MUSEUM [625-2843]: Mon., Wed., Fri., call to ask about changes; Entrance fee
YMCA TOWER [569-2692]: Mon.-Fri., 9:00-13:00; 15:00-dark; Sat., 9-13:00; closed Sun.; Fee for the tower
CUSTOMS MUSEUM [670-3201]: Official hours: Sun.-Thurs., 9:00-15:00; on occasion the museum is closed at that time — phone in advance if possible; Entrance fee</td></tr>
<tr><td>Restrooms:</td><td>King David Hotel, YMCA, Skirball Museum</td></tr>
</table>

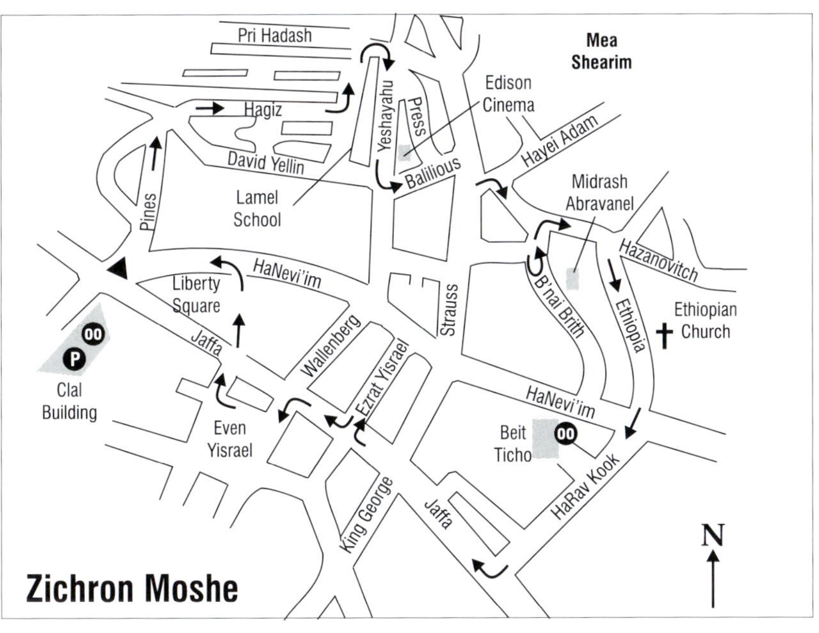

Liberty Square and its famous Davidka (p. 50).

Zichron Moshe
to Jaffa Road

- **Begin and end**: at Liberty (or Davidka) Square
- **Take bus**: 6, 13, 18, 20, 23 (alight on Jaffa Road)
- **Park your car**: in the market lot, or on a side street
- **Time frame**: 1-2 hours
- **Take note**: Part of this walk takes you through ultra-orthodox neighborhoods. Modest dress recommended.

In the early days of this century, land meant to house an unusually modern Jerusalem neighborhood was purchased on a hill 812 meters above sea level. Money for the property came from a special fund established in 1874 by friends of renowned English philanthropist Sir Moses Montefiore. The occasion: Montefiore's 90th birthday.

Intended to help Jews in the Holy Land expand their settlement and to build their own homes, the fund supplied the capital for a number of Jerusalem communities. They included this neighborhood — Zichron Moshe — as well as Yemin Moshe, Mazkeret Moshe, Ohel Moshe and Kiryat Moshe.

Residents of Zichron Moshe were an educated bunch. Indeed, many of them were intellectuals whose presence helped create what would become a hotbed of liberal thought. David Yellin, one of pre-State Israel's most enlightened educators and a leading figure of the period, lived almost next door to historian Yeshayahu Press. Nearby, on a side street, Eliezer Ben-Yehuda wrote the definitive dictionary of ancient and modern Hebrew.

Begin your circular tour of Zichron Moshe and other area neighborhoods at Liberty Square, located on the corner of Pines Street, Jaffa Road and HaNevi'im (also called Street of the Prophets). Known to the locals as Davidka Square, the plaza holds a monument to one of Israel's noisiest weapons.

In the period before the War of Independence Jewish troops suffered from a severe shortage of long-range weapons. Engineer David Leibowitch, a member of the Haganah defense forces, spent his evenings in a secret hideout upgrading those arms that the Haganah had somehow managed to acquire. Fortunately for the Jewish effort, Leibowitch's experience also enabled him to produce a new and unusual mortar.

Later to be called the Davidka, the mortar was anything but reliable. But what made it such a momentous addition to the weapons stock was its noise: when it did manage to land and actually explode, it emitted a dreadfully frightening shriek. Some Arabs apparently thought that the Jews had obtained the atomic bomb, for they fled in panic from the sound!

A Davidka was brought to Jerusalem during the War of Independence and proved essential in the Israeli capture of Mount Zion, Katamon and the Allenby camp. The inscription you see is part of a phrase from the Bible: *"I will defend this city and save it ... [for my sake and for the sake of David my servant]"* (Kings 2:19:34).

Now stroll down Pines Street. You are walking through a tiny neighborhood called Ruchama, established in 1921. The Central Hotel, frequented mainly by religious guests, will be on your right.

Turn right at the third street (Moshe HaGiz), and stop at the entrance to the very first building on your right. Following the fall of the Second Temple, sages of the period declared that every new building must carry a reminder of that destruction. That reminder was to be an unpainted area one cubit by one cubit (46 centimeters by 46 centimeters) in size. Owners of this corner house took the edict literally. Look inside the entrance to see a black square that measures exactly one cubit by one cubit!

Continue along this tree-shaded street, which borders the neighborhood of Zichron Moshe. The houses, albeit often dilapidated, are delightfully old-fashioned. If you feel you are in a country even more foreign than Israel, that's because the children playing in the streets call out to each other in Yiddish.

At the very end of HaGiz Street turn left into an alley. As you continue to stroll, peer into the quaint little streets to your left. The alley ends at Pri Hadash, a street that is parallel to HaGiz. Turn right and follow your nose to the Avichail Bakery across the street at #8. We gravitate to the bakery nearly every Thursday night to buy fresh *challah* — braided Sabbath bread — and delicious, inexpensive coffee cakes. Pri Hadash runs into Yeshayahu Street, which is Zichron Moshe's main thoroughfare.

Founded in 1906, Zichron Moshe was planned for middle-class families whose homes would be both spacious and attractive. Much thought was put into the planning. David Yellin wrote to directors of the Montefiore fund in London that the middle classes were no longer satisfied with one-room houses and were demanding at least two chambers! And they didn't want their rooms one on top of the other, but side by side instead. Other modern improvements suggested by Yellin included toilets and a cistern for every one-to-two houses.

Zichron Moshe's population was considered religiously liberal and the neighborhood was integrated and cohesive. Most of the families were originally from other New Jerusalem neighborhoods or had previously lived in the Old City, and residents included a large number of Sephardic Jews. Unlike

Neighborhood youngsters at play.

some of the other communities in Jerusalem in which the population was either all Ashkenazic or completely Sephardic, here the two groups were brought together. That is how Montefiore, who wholeheartedly encouraged ethnic mixing, would have wanted it to be.

As you will see when you walk through Zichron Moshe, the population has changed. Today it is dotted with ultra-orthodox schools built by the extremely religious population that gravitated to the neighborhood as earlier residents moved out. Thus, despite its liberal origins, Zichron Moshe today is part of and surrounded by a network of ultra-orthodox communities: Mea She'arim, Geula and Makor Baruch.

Turn right and ascend Yeshayahu Street as far as the Lamel School at #13. The first modern educational facility in the country, Lamel was built in 1853 and originally stood inside the Old City walls. It was established as a memorial to Austrian-Jewish nobleman Simon Von Lamel.

The present building was constructed in 1903 on an isolated hill, well before the first houses of Zichron Moshe appeared on the scene. Located in the middle of total wilderness, Lamel School sat an equal distance from Jerusalem's two main byways: Jaffa Road and Mea She'arim Street. Prolific author Avraham

Moshe Luncz once wrote that the view from the school's windows included a sight of the Judean Hills, MOUNT SCOPUS, the Mount of Olives and new Jerusalem. In spite of the buildings that block most of the view nowadays, the hill is so high that even today you can still see some of Jerusalem's hills from the sidewalk.

Designed by architect Theodore Sandel of Jerusalem's GERMAN COLONY, the Lamel school was one of the city's finest edifices and had a large hall which doubled as a synagogue and a meeting place. Note the encircled Star of David under the upper windows, and a clock on which time is represented by letters of the Hebrew alphabet. The lintel above the door to the school contains a carving of a palm tree shading a well. Chiseled into the background is a view of the Old City. The inscription on the facade of the building reads "Edler Von Lamel Schule."

Immediately across the street, at **#14**, the old Edison movie theater has fallen into disuse. One of the first of its kind in Jerusalem — and the fanciest — the theater was named after the American genius credited with inventing the first movie projector. Yves Montand and other noted performers appeared on its stage; so did Israel's pre-State Philharmonic Orchestra.

The Edison Theater was constructed in 1932 on a vacant tract that hosted open-air performances in earlier years. During bloody Arab riots in 1920, Jews carried out drills and military exercises on the empty lot. Commander of the troops was Ze'ev Jabotinsky, a militant Zionist leader who helped organize the Haganah (pre-State defense forces) soon afterwards. Thus it was here, in Zichron Moshe, that some of the seeds of the Haganah were sown.

Turn left on Balilious Street, just past the Edison Theater. The house at **#10** is unusually lovely. Note its pillars, whose pedestals are each decorated with a Star of David. Yeshayahu Press lived and worked at **#5**, located on the corner of Press Street. A plaque informs Hebrew-readers that Press was not only one of the founders of Zichron Moshe, but also helped set up the Israel Teachers' Union. A respected researcher and historian, Press authored a volume called the *Land of Israel Encyclopedia*.

Jerusalem-born David Yellin, one of the first people to support Eliezer Ben-Yehuda in his obstinate struggle to revive Hebrew as a spoken language, lived at the opposite end of Press (the corner house at **#2** — you passed it as you walked up Yeshayahu Street). Although an important member of the staff at the teachers' seminary connected to Lamel School, he quit in 1914 after a dispute on the language of instruction. Classes were in German — and Yellin insisted that they be taught in Hebrew. Some years later Yellin became director of the Seminary.

Balilious ends on a main street — Strauss. Turn right, then *immediately*
go left on Hayai Adam street and take a sharp right onto the curiously trans-
literated Benei Berite (B'nai Brith) Road. Walk about 50 meters and stop
outside #18 (on your left-hand side). This is Midrash Abravanel.

Over four centuries after the Jews were exiled from Spain, and to mark the
400th anniversary of that expulsion, a historic library was established in Jerusalem. It was named after Don Isaac Abravanel, a child prodigy born in 1437
who became a renowned Talmudic scholar, philosopher and philanthropist. He
was also a respected statesman. Thus upon the death of his father, finance minister
to the King of Portugal, Don Isaac was named to that lofty position.

In 1483 the King's successor accused Abravanel of participating in a con-
spiracy against him. Abravanel fled to Spain, leaving his colossal fortune behind.
There he immersed himself in Jewish literature — and continued to do so even
after he began working for the Queen of Castile. When the Jews of Spain were
forced to leave the country in 1492, despite Abravanel's efforts to annul the
decree, this amazing statesman/scholar led his brethren to safety in Naples.

Called Midrash Abravanel, the handsome two-storied red-roofed edifice
was built in 1902 to house the first Jerusalem Library. It contained thousands
of volumes donated by Dr. Yosef Hazanovitch, who had pushed long and hard
for a central library. Eighteen years later the building officially became Israel's
National Library, remaining so until the impressive collection it now held was
moved to the Hebrew University at Mount Scopus in 1930. Renovated in 1978,
this historic building is still being used as a library. Notice the striking recessed
windows on the second floor.

Now backtrack a few meters to the corner and turn right. Walk on the
right-hand sidewalk to reach Ethiopia Street — one of the city's most beau-
tiful roads. As you saunter to its very end, peek through the fences to get a
glimpse of some wonderful architecture on the other side. The influential Arab
Nashashibi family built most of the houses on this street in the late 19th and
early 20th centuries. Although high walls surround many of the buildings, on
occasion you can get a glimpse of some lovely gardens.

History seems to seep out of the walls of Ethiopia Street dwellings. Between
1928 and 1930 the house at **#15** served as district headquarters for the Haganah;
Eliezer Ben-Yehuda, born Eliezer Yitzhak Perelman, lived at **#11**.

Ben-Yehuda was the undisputed father of modern Hebrew. Over a decade
before Theodore Herzl wrote *The Jewish State* and proposed that the Jews set
up a country in the land of Israel, Ben-Yehuda asserted that the Jewish people
must have their own nation. He advocated the use of Hebrew as a spoken
language in Palestine, and after immigrating in 1881 published several Hebrew

magazines and newspapers. Among them was "Small World," the first children's periodical in Hebrew.

His was the first home in pre-State Israel in which only Hebrew was spoken. And Ben-Yehuda's son was the first child of the times to deliver his first words in Hebrew. That boy, later to become a silver-tongued speechmaker and outstanding journalist, was named Ben-Zion (son of Zion). Later, he adopted the name his mother had preferred — Itamar. And in order to avoid having the same surname as a man so outstanding as his father, he changed his last name to Ben-Avi. This means "son of my father" and is a play on the Hebrew abbreviation of the name Eliezer Ben-Yehuda.

Ben-Yehuda and other enlightened intellectuals waged a bitter battle against Jewish religious extremists who believed that Hebrew may be spoken only in prayer and objected vehemently to its use in daily life. Note some broken bricks in the facade of the building; they once held a sign in place naming this as Ben-Yehuda's house. But individuals who opposed the use of spoken Hebrew continually defaced the sign and it was eventually removed by the authorities.

Directly across from Ben-Yehuda's house is the Ethiopian Church (**#10**). Only a few decades after Jesus' death and resurrection, Philip the Evangelist baptized an Ethiopian eunuch from the royal court (Acts 8:26-38). Enthusiastic Christians, the Ethiopians were among the earliest pilgrims to visit the Holy City. And over the years Jerusalem's Ethiopian community acquired the rights to a great many holy sites.

By the 17th century, however, their financial situation had seriously deteriorated. Because they couldn't afford to pay the property taxes demanded by the Ottoman rulers, the Ethiopians lost their hold on most of the hallowed sites. Indeed, for the next 200 years the Ethiopian Christian population slowly disappeared from Jerusalem; those few who remained here lived huddled together in abject poverty.

Near the end of the 19th century, Ethiopian Emperor Johannes IV decided to better his compatriots' situation. In 1882 he began construction of a monastery and church complex on this, one of the most picturesque streets in Jerusalem. Completed in 1893 by Johannes' successor, Menelik II, the unusual circular church is dedicated to Jesus' mother Mary.

Since Ethiopians trace their royal family to a union between King Solomon and the Queen of Sheba, it shouldn't be surprising to learn that the symbol of the Ethiopian kingdom is the Lion of Judah. That symbol is proudly displayed above both sides of the gate leading to the Ethiopian church. Before stepping on the church floor, which is covered with rugs, you must remove your shoes. It is open most of the day — do go in for a visit.

In 1906 Professor Boris Schatz opened the famous Bezalel Art School in the house at **#8.** Later on, Bezalel was relocated downtown and near the end of the 20th century moved to Mount Scopus.

The splendid two-story edifice at **#3** is typical of statuesque Arab construction. For many years the dwelling of one of Jerusalem's ophthalmologists, it later housed the British Cultural Center.

When you reach HaNevi'im Street turn left and then stop to view the structure at the corner of HaRav Kook Street. Constructed in 1888, this building is regarded as the first Jewish hospital in the new city. The hospital was originally situated in the Old City's Jewish Quarter, founded there in 1854 by scions of the House of Rothschild in memory of family patriarch Mayer Amschel Rothschild. Rothschild Hospital shut down during World War I, and afterwards was taken over by the Hadassah Women's Organization of America to become Israel's first Hadassah Hospital. Despite changes in the 1960's, which ruined much of its outstanding beauty, the Rothschild Hospital is still a very imposing edifice.

Next descend HaRav Kook Street, turning right at a little lane (Ticho Street). Almost immediately to your right is the entrance to Beit David, the fourth Jerusalem neighborhood built outside of the Old City walls. Originally consisting of 10 one-floor apartments built around a central courtyard, the complex is named for Polish immigrant and philanthropist David Reiss. Notice the two cisterns and the base of a hand pump imported from England.

Reiss was getting on in years and in bad health when he moved to the already established neighborhood of Nahalat Shiv'a in 1872. It is said that during Rosh Hashanah (New Year) services in 1873 Reiss was inspired by a sermon on the importance of expanding Nahalat Shiva. When it came his turn to be called up to the Torah, he pledged the money necessary for a new neighborhood close to the existing one. Named for its founder, it was meant for poor Ashkenazic families in which the men were devoted to holy studies. The second stories were added in 1902 to house the offices of a charitable organization.

Beit David's most illustrious tenant was Rabbi Abraham Isaac HaCohen Kook, pre-State Israel's first Chief Ashkenazic Rabbi. Born in Latvia in 1865, a brilliant student and a much sought-after scholar and rabbi, he was a liberal who encouraged settlement in the land of Israel and hoped to spend his life there. Thus, when the tiny Jewish community in Jaffa asked him to lead their congregation in 1904, Rabbi Kook jumped at the chance. No manner of enticements and pleas by congregations all over Europe could change his mind.

Rabbi Kook attempted to bring secular Jews closer to Jewish values without ever belittling their own contribution to Jewish culture. Indeed, he emphasized the need to find a happy medium between modern life and tradition. Upon his appointment as Chief Ashkenazic Rabbi in 1921, Rabbi Kook decided to move to Beit David. With the help of donations from abroad, a special home with ritual bath and study hall was annexed to the tiny complex.

Today Rabbi Kook's dwelling has become a small museum in which the rooms that he occupied have been reconstructed and from its windows you have an excellent view of the Beit David complex. Besides the study the museum includes the most important room in the house — the Yeshiva Hall Synagogue with original furniture and ark. Look for a chair that was a present from Sir Herbert Samuel, the first High Commissioner to rule Palestine during the British Mandate.

Further down the lane you reach Beit Ticho, an elegant building surrounded by lavish gardens, which was built by a wealthy member of Jerusalem's Nashashibi family. At the time it was constructed, in the mid-19th century, there were few other buildings outside of the Old City walls.

One of its most famous occupants was apostate Jew Moses Wilhelm Shapira, who ran an antique shop in the Old City. Tourists who visited the shop must have had a wonderful time, for although he apparently did handle some rare manuscripts, Shapira also planted fake relics that he let them "discover."

Beit David — the fourth Jewish neighborhood outside the Old City walls.

Shapira is notorious for having sold fake artifacts and texts. But by far the most scandalous episode in his career took place when he brought an ancient scroll of Deuteronomy — the earliest ever found — to London. It was apparently on display at the British Museum when French scholar Charles Clermont-Ganneau proved it to be a phony. And it is no wonder the French expert was skeptical. For in the 1880's what scholar in his right mind would have believed that a piece of parchment could hold up for 2,000 years! The distraught and discredited Shapira took his own life in 1884.

Following discovery of the Dead Sea Scrolls in 1947, a few scholars began to wonder if Shapira's ancient manuscript was for real. We may never know for sure, as what may have been a fabulously precious artifact has disappeared.

In 1924 the house was purchased by a prominent Jerusalem ophthalmologist and his world-famous artist wife — Dr. Avraham and Anna Ticho. It was here that Dr. Ticho treated Jews and Arabs alike for the dreaded trachoma.

Dr. Ticho was stabbed in the back by an Arab in 1929, a year in which the city was torn by Arab riots. He was rushed to Hadassah Hospital (originally the Rothschild — across the street) and despite a wound four centimeters wide that reached all the way through to his ribs, he recovered from his injury.

The Ticho home was a center of Jewish culture and during the Mandate Period was a popular meeting place for the city's most famous philosophers, doctors, artists and authors. Avraham Ticho died in 1960; his wife passed away 20 years later. She bequeathed the splendid building to the people of Jerusalem. Today there is a coffeehouse and garden restaurant at Beit Ticho, as well as a library of art books. Galleries are open to visitors: climb to the second floor to view Dr. Ticho's office exactly as it used to be.

Now return to HaRav Kook Street and turn right. The once extraordinarily handsome building across the street on your left was originally Jerusalem's Italian Consulate. Built in 1889, it has housed at least half a dozen different establishments, including a hotel, some offices of *The Jerusalem Post*, living quarters for a religious school and an exclusive clothing store.

Walk down the street to Jaffa Road and turn right. Ascend to the corner of King George Street (on your left), cross the diagonal crosswalk and stand in front of the building at #2. An inscription in three languages marks the establishment of one angle in what is known as the "triangle": Jaffa Road, Ben-Yehuda Street, and King George Street.

King George V Avenue (today "Street") was officially declared open at an unusually festive ceremony held on December 9, 1924. Present at the opening were British High Commissioner Sir Herbert Samuel, Jerusalem Governor Sir Ronald Storrs and Jerusalem Mayor Ragheb Bey El Nashashibi.

After Israel became a State, some of Jerusalem's street names were changed and apparently for a short time Jaffa Road was called Herzl-Jaffa Road. There was talk of changing the name of King George Avenue as well. Tour guides say that Yitzhak Ben-Zvi, who had been present at the monarch's coronation, objected, reminding whoever wanted to make the change that George V had been King at the time of the Balfour Declaration. "Do whatever you like," he is reported to have stated, "but leave King George Avenue alone!"

Cross Jaffa Road and you will be standing in front of Ma'ayan Stub, the first department store in Jerusalem. Turn left, and continue your Jaffa Road ascent. Take the first right onto a tiny lane called Ezrat Yisrael Street, which leads to a charming little neighborhood of the same name founded in 1892. Ezrat Yisrael translates as "Help of Israel" and comes from two different passages in Psalms: *"My help comes from the Lord, the Maker of heaven and earth"* (121:2) and *"May he send you help from the sanctuary and grant you support from Zion"* (20:2). At the lane's end you can see the clean lines of the International Evangelical Church, a building which blocks the neighborhood exit to HaNevi'im street.

Avraham Luncz, who lived across Jaffa Road in the Even Yisrael neighborhood you will be visiting shortly, operated a printing press in a house at the beginning of the street. The Polish-born Luncz came to Jerusalem from Kovna in Poland when he was 14 years of age. He was later thrown out of his yeshiva after he developed an avid interest in secular literature. This is the edifice in which he printed a travel guide to Israel.

A second press in the neighborhood put out the weekly "Unity." Its editors were David Ben-Gurion (later to become Israel's first prime minister), Yitzhak Ben-Zvi (Israel's second president) and Ben-Zvi's wife Rachel Yanait. Famous in her own right, Yanait was an enthusiastic Zionist activist and one of the people who founded the Shomer (the Jewish Guards) in 1909. Together with other young Russian-born radicals, these historic figures all lived for a time in Ezrat Yisrael.

Back on Jaffa Road, stop for a look at #64. Guarded by two lions, the building is known by locals as The House of the Messiah. Mashiah (Messiah) Borochov, whose first name is a common one among Jews from Bukhara, put up the splendid building in 1908.

Walk a few meters to Raoul Wallenberg Street, a narrow byway. Raoul Wallenberg was a Swedish aristocrat — some say a saint — who saved close to 100,000 Hungarian Jews during the holocaust. Although reported to have died in a Soviet prison in 1947 there are those who believe he was still rotting away in a Russian jail as late as 1975.

Walk up Wallenberg just far enough to see the magnificent edifice with pyramidal symmetry and a lovely gabled roof behind #68 Jaffa Road. For a short time in the 1990's it housed one of my favorite restaurants — an English tearoom!

This was originally the home of entrepreneur Yosef Navon, honored with the title "Bey" by the Turks. It was Navon who initiated Israel's first railroad, which began running from Jaffa to Jerusalem in 1892.

An impressive mixture of eastern and western architecture, the building was one of the first Jerusalem homes outside the Old City walls. In its heyday it was surrounded by spectacular gardens; a stable and a carriage house were located at the rear of the grounds.

Next to the Navon residence is an office building. Originally it was a lovely house built by the Greek Orthodox Church and rented out to the Turkish governors of Jerusalem. During receptions the Turkish military orchestra would play concerts in the garden. Later a wealthy Jewish merchant from Aden, Menachem Banin, bought the building.

Continue up Jaffa Road and stop across from #73, a dingy building with a tin-covered gable. Legend has it that this was the house of the Widow Levy, who would watch with envy as the rich merchant courted a Jerusalem girl, bringing her to his home in a fancy carriage. According to the story she probably didn't know that the young woman was in love with another, a comely but impoverished youth and would be forced to wed Banin against her will.

Walk back down to the Wallenberg intersection and cross the street. Look for an opening in the wall of shops at #63 Jaffa Road (just to your left) and walk inside. This will lead you to another enchanting old neighborhood called Even Yisrael. Turn right at the first lane. The sixth neighborhood outside of the Old City walls, it was built in 1875 around a central courtyard and has kept much of its original character. Both Ashkenazic and Sephardic Jews lived in Even Yisrael, and each ethnic group had its own synagogue.

Pass the playground, then turn right to exit onto Jaffa Road. Immediately across the street is a long ugly building at #68. Cross this busy street *with care!* and find the parking lot between #68 and #70. Follow the passageway into the parking lot and look straight ahead at a rather shabby building. Inconceivable as it may seem, this edifice once housed the most elegant hotel in Jerusalem: the Kaminitz. It was built by a German who came to Jerusalem in the mid-19th century, the apostate Jew Paul Bergheim. Bergheim is famous for having established one of the first private banks in Jerusalem and for helping to create the basis for the city's modern commercial era.

The stately residence of Yosef Bey Navon.

In 1883 Eliezer Lipman Kaminitz took over the European-style house built by Bergheim and turned it into a five-star hotel. In addition to expanding the building and planting a lovely garden, Kaminitz prepared a special driveway for carriages.

You return to HaNevi'im Street and the Davidka by walking through the parking lot and past the former hotel. Among the Very Important People who lodged at the Kaminitz were philanthropist Baron Edmund de Rothschild and the father of Zionism — Theodore Herzl. The esteemed Zionist came to Jerusalem in 1898 to meet with Emperor Wilhelm II. Herzl stayed at the Kaminitz for one night only and spent the rest of his visit at the Marx-Stern family home in Mamilla (destroyed during renovations of the neighborhood).

Hours: **BEIT TICHO** [624-5068]: Sun.-Thurs., 10:00 until late afternoon (restaurant until midnight); Fri., 10:00-14:00
BEIT HARAV KOOK [623-2560]: Open most weekdays
Restrooms: Central Hotel, Beit Ticho

Russian Compound and Musrara
Old City
Christian Quarter
Tancred's Tower
Hotel
New Gate
IDF Square
Paratrooper Road
St. Louis Hospital
Jaffa
City Hall
Notre Dame
Safra Square
Ayin Het
Elisha
Museum
Russian Compound
Courthouse
Shivtei Yisrael
Holy Trinity
Police
Jaffa
Park
Natan HaNavi
P
Beit Sergei
Heleni HaMalka
Monbaz
St. Paul's
HaNevi'im
Italian Hospital
N

Russian Compound and Musrara

- **Begin and end**: at Beit Sergei, corner of Monbaz and Heleni HaMalka Streets
- **Take bus**: 6, 13, 18, 20, 21, 23 (alight on Jaffa Road)
- **Park your car**: in the Russian Compound lots or on side streets
- **Time frame**: about two hours
- **Take note**: The latter part of this tour takes you near an ultra-orthodox neighborhood. Modest dress recommended.

While studying social work at the Hebrew University in the early 1970's, I was sent on a home visit to the run-down Jerusalem neighborhood of Musrara. As I walked through the crime-ridden and drug-infested lanes, I confess to literally quaking in my shoes.

I returned to Musrara decades later with a guide from the Society for the Protection of Nature in Israel. As we wandered through the neighborhood's alleys I was astounded by the change. Thoroughfares once drab and wretched are, today, pleasant and clean. Nineteenth-century designer lanterns have replaced Musrara's continually smashed streetlights. Flowers planted in window boxes all through the neighborhood now bloom with color and residents proudly grace their doors with creative nameplates. The Musrara of earlier years has simply disappeared!

A delightful walk that includes a visit to Musrara starts and ends on the outskirts of the Russian Compound. **Begin at the Beit Sergei tower, which stands at one end of land purchased by the Russian Orthodox Church in 1860.** It was in this same landmark year that Jerusalem Jews first tried life outside the Old City walls. In fact, the Jews competed with the Russians for this particular property — and lost! Formerly a Turkish cavalry parade ground, it was originally known as Nuva Yerushalma, or New Jerusalem. Today everyone calls it the Russian Compound.

Russian pilgrims began visiting the Holy Land *en masse* in the middle of the 19th century. To provide for their needs several hospices were constructed inside the Russian Compound within walking distance of the Old City's holy sites. But none of these hostels was fancy enough to house the Russian aristocracy. The nobility preferred the elegance of Beit Sergei, built in 1890 and restored approximately a century later. Today Beit Sergei houses the Jerusalem offices of the Society for the Protection of Nature in Israel and the SPNI's comprehensive bookshop.

Two of the Jerusalem landmarks which are artistically lit up at night: Beit Sergei.

Along with other buildings constructed on land purchased by the Imperial Palestine Russian Orthodox Society, Beit Sergei is marked with an intricate symbol. Look for it on the tower: it contains the intertwined Greek letters "P" and "X" — *chi* and *rho* — and probably had its origins in 312. That was the year in which Roman Emperor Constantine the Great prepared for combat with a dangerous adversary named Maxentius.

A Christian tradition relates that God appeared to Constantine in a vision and promised him victory. All the Emperor had to do in order to win was inscribe an abbreviation of the word Christos (*chi* and *rho)* on his standard. In that decisive battle, which took place at the Milvian Bridge near Rome on Oct. 28, 312, Maxentius was roundly defeated and Constantine was able to consolidate his power. As if to prove the truth of the legend, the formerly pagan Constantine slowly began leaning towards Christianity that very same year. And in 324 Constantine declared Christianity the official religion of the empire.

Notre Dame de Jerusalem.

Also on the symbol are the first and last letters of the Greek alphabet, an alpha and an omega. They refer to a phrase from the New Testament: *"I am the Alpha and the Omega, the First and the Last, the Beginning and the End"* (Rev.

22:13). Written in early Russian script in a circle around the letters is the biblical quotation: *"For Zion's sake I will not keep silent, for Jerusalem's sake I will not remain quiet ..."* (Isaiah 62:1).

Across Heleni HaMalka Street, at the entrance to the Russian Compound's parking lot, stands a 19th-century gatehouse. There were two gatehouses here until the 1980's, at which time the road was widened and the second of the pair was torn down. Carved into the wall is the same symbol you saw on the Beit Sergei tower.

Now walk into the Russian Compound. Directly across from you stands the majestic Cathedral of the Holy Trinity, built with funds donated by the people of Czarist Russia. Construction began in 1860 and the magnificent edifice was inaugurated in 1872. Over the years its bright green domes made this one of Jerusalem's most distinctive churches. For some mysterious reason the domes were repainted a dull gray near the end of the 20th century.

Walk around to the front of the church. If the doors are open, go inside and view a typical Russian church interior. Otherwise feast your eyes on the shiny white stone exterior, the dazzling facade and the octagonal bell-towers.

Continue on the road that bypasses the cathedral. To your right is a long building that was originally a hospice and also hosted the offices of the Russian Mission. For decades this edifice housed all of Jerusalem's courts. The lower courts are still here, but the SUPREME COURT moved to far more impressive lodgings near the end of the 20th century.

Take note of a driveway descending to your left, between a parking lot and the pink-and-white stone building that is Jerusalem's City Hall. The descent leads to the reconstructed Jerusalem Central Prison, originally a Russian hostel. During the British Mandate it held Jews of the Haganah, Etzel, Lehi and Brit HaBiryonim underground forces.

Northern Jewish settlements suffered repeated Arab attacks during the early years of the Mandate. In 1920 Arabs rioted in Jerusalem as well, and in 1921 they attacked Tel Aviv. Dozens of Jews were killed during these assaults and hundreds were wounded.

When it became obvious that the British were either unable or unwilling to defend the Jews from Arab aggression, a clandestine Jewish army of defense was established. The secrecy was necessary because Jews were not allowed to carry arms — even in self-defense! The organization was called the Haganah, and would later form the backbone of the Israel Defense Forces.

Etzel, Lehi and Brit HaBiryonim — smaller, splinter groups — were formed some years later. They were less restrained than the Haganah, and believed in retaliation against the Arabs and actions meant to drive the British out of Israel.

Fifteen members of the underground who were incarcerated at the Jerusalem Central Prison were sentenced to death. Nine sentences were commuted to imprisonment but six men were scheduled to hang.

Although there was a gallows here, and this is where Arab prisoners were executed, the British feared violence on the part of Jewish Jerusalemites. Thus four of the Jews were taken to Acre Prison and executed at dawn on April 17, 1947; they went to the gallows singing HaTikva — the Jewish National Anthem. On April 21, just hours before they were scheduled to hang, the two others blew themselves up with a grenade that had been smuggled into the prison.

On the Sabbath, Jewish inmates congregated together in one of the jail cells. This was then transformed into a makeshift synagogue by rolling up the bedding to make room for benches and for the Holy Ark. Services were led by Rabbi Arye Levin, who never missed a Saturday. Pictures of this saintly man are displayed at the entrance to the reconstructed "synagogue." You can view the rabbi's humble abode when you walk through MAHANE YEHUDA.

Commonly known as the "prisoners' rabbi," Arye Levin was called Reb Arye by one and all. He had a phenomenal memory, which enabled him to pass messages back and forth between people incarcerated in the jail and families whose addresses he was instantly able to recall.

If you are in the Russian Compound from Sunday to Thursday you should definitely stop in at the museum which is located in the old prison. Besides the exercise yards, workshops and showers, you will visit jail cells. One is located above a tunnel: On February 20, 1948, 12 Etzel and Lehi members managed to break out of the jail by digging under their cells and into the sewage system.

Now walk back up to the courthouse and follow the walkway into the Jerusalem municipal complex. Pass City Hall, cross Safra Square (there will be palm trees to your right), stroll under a bridge and continue along the walkway. When the modern municipality was built in 1996, a number of the charming late 19th-century and early 20th-century buildings that stood in different parts of the Russian Compound were restored and added to the municipal complex. The building at **#6 Safra Square** was erected in 1882 by a German banker; that at **#8** was called House of the Bible and constructed in 1926 by the British and Foreign Bible Society.

Stop at #10, located at right angles to the House of the Bible. Established in 1930, this served as Jerusalem's city hall until the new municipality was completed. Engraved on the original cornerstone are the words "Municipal Offices. This stone was laid by Sir Steuart [sic] Spencer Davis ..." Ragheb Bey El Nashashibi was mayor at the time. The city always held a Jewish majority, but the British repeatedly appointed Moslem Arab mayors to run Jerusalem.

Money for the early municipal building was made available by Barclays' Bank. The bank's offices were located in the rounded section of the building, on the side that faces the walls of the Old City. **Continue along the path that you were on until you reach IDF Square, the junction of Shivtei Yisrael Street and Jaffa Road.**

Behind you the rounded facade of the former bank is marred by jagged holes. These are the result of bullets fired by Jordanian soldiers during the War of Independence and during the 19 years that Jerusalem was divided. Despite modern restoration, the holes were left as they were and serve to remind onlookers of Jerusalem's travails.

Across the intersection you will see the Dan Pearl Hotel, constructed in the 1990's atop a hole in the ground on which the famous Fast Hotel was once located. Designed by German Templer Theodore Sandel in 1891, the original three-story hotel was taken over by Abraham Fast at the beginning of the 20th century.

When World War I ended with British control of Israel, and until it returned to German hands, the Fast Hotel became General Allenby's temporary head-quarters. Just before the onset of World War II, at which time Fast and other Templers were deported to Australia, a swastika could be seen hanging from the front of the hotel. The building was torn down in 1975 and replaced by the super-modern Dan Pearl.

You should now be facing the walls of the Old City of Jerusalem built by Suleiman the Magnificent in the 16th century. You can't see it from here but behind the garden, on the corner of the wall directly across from you, are remains of a tower. It is often called Goliath Tower because King David is believed by some to have buried Goliath's head on the site. However most people know it as Tancred's Tower, named for the Norman Crusader commander who attacked the city from this direction on July 15, 1099. At exactly 9:00 the next day, (the hour at which Jesus is believed to have been crucified), Jerusalem's defenses fell and the Crusaders swarmed into the city.

Tancred is said to have promised amnesty for the tens of thousands of men, women and children left in Jerusalem. However, despite his pledge, the Moslems were ruthlessly slaughtered and the Jews burned alive.

Turn left and begin to descend Paratroopers' Road. On your left are two 19th-century buildings which are often called the French Compound. The first building on your left is the French Hospital of St. Louis, which houses termi-nal patients of all faiths; the second is Notre Dame de Jerusalem.

In 1889, during the period in which the French Hospital and Notre Dame were constructed, Turkish ruler Abed El Hamid hewed a gate out of the wall across the street. Called New Gate, it provided French Catholics with easy access in and out of the Christian Quarter. It differs from the Old City's earlier gates because it completely lacks ornamentation and has no strategic curve at the entrance to foil enemy onslaughts.

St. Louis Hospital, founded in the mid-19th century by the Sisters of San Joseph, was originally located inside the Old City walls. But when French count Marie Paul A. de Piellat visited the hospital in 1874 he was appalled by its unsanitary conditions and decided to establish a modern facility outside the walls. Both hospitals were named for Louis IX, crowned King of France at the age of 12 in 1226. King Louis led two Crusades to the Holy Land and was canonized for his piety and righteousness in 1297.

Staff at the hospital does everything possible to help in the recovery of patients who were considered incurable upon admission. And, indeed, there have been terminal patients who have improved so much that they have been sent home. Yet, when there is nothing left to try, the patients are accorded an unparalleled measure of respect and devotion.

During the years that the city was divided, between 1948 and 1967, a terminal patient at the French Hospital leaned out a window, yawned or coughed, and lost her false teeth in the twisted barbed wires of no-man's land below. It took meticulous maneuvering, and the good will of Israel, Jordan

Patients at the French Hospital receive unparalleled care and devotion.

Musrara's House of Windows (p. 71).

and the United Nations. But in the end, and accompanied by representatives of the Mixed Armistice Committee, a nun from the hospital was permitted to search for and retrieve the teeth.

As you walk past the building, look up to see an ancient Atlantic terebinth tree towering over the hospital walls. Believed to be nearly a thousand years old, the tree was already on the site when Count de Piellat built the hospital and it was incorporated into the grounds. Sir Moses Montefiore and entourage are said to have rested in its shade on one of their visits to Jerusalem.

Descend the sidewalk to reach one of the city's most impressive structures: Notre Dame de Jerusalem (originally called Notre Dame de France). Construction on its imposing stone walls and round turrets began in 1884, a time at which French Catholics began thronging to the Holy City. Notre Dame was built by the Assumptionists, who pioneered penitential pilgrimages to the Holy Land. The Assumptionists lodged their pilgrims at Notre Dame and fed them with food grown at a farm on the grounds of St. Peter's Church.

Walk into the courtyard and look up to see an enormous statue: Mary holding the baby Jesus high in the air. The European powers believed that whoever was most visible in Jerusalem would hold the most power. Perhaps that's why the statue is so tall!

The Notre Dame monastery was severely damaged during heavy fighting in 1948, in a battle that prevented the Arab Legion from invading western Jerusalem. From 1948 to 1967 Israeli soldiers guarded Jerusalem from the rooftops of Notre Dame, which faced Jordanian positions on the Walls.

Notre Dame was charmingly restored in the 1970's and has returned to its original objective as a hotel for Catholic pilgrims. You may want to stop in for coffee or to visit the simple but striking chapel.

Continue down the sidewalk to the traffic light and turn left at the strangely named Ayin Het Street (off Abraham Halperin Square). The letter "Ayin" in Hebrew corresponds to the number "70" while "Het" is "eight." In 1948, Arabs massacred a convoy of 78 doctors, nurses, patients, teachers and students who were making their way to Hadassah Hospital on MOUNT SCOPUS. This street takes you deep into Musrara.

When the War of Independence broke out Musrara's Arabs left the neighborhood. The Israeli establishment decided that the empty villas were perfect for housing a flood of new immigrants who had come mainly from North Africa and Iraq. Once beautiful houses were divided into tiny, one-room apartments, each of which housed an entire family: thus every villa was occupied by a number of large immigrant households. To make room for even more immigrants, long dreary rows of little apartments called "blockim" were added to the formerly lovely neighborhood. Life was extremely difficult for the new immigrants and it didn't take long for slum conditions to develop. Musrara became a hotbed of violence and unrest.

Today's population is relatively new. It includes artists, journalists and other strong elements that have renovated and expanded their apartments and opened galleries. The whole atmosphere has changed and the old school is now a community center full of neighborhood activities. At some point, in an attempt to get rid of the stigma attached to the name "Musrara," the neighborhood became officially known as "Morasha." Nevertheless, if you ask directions to Morasha all you will get from the locals are blank stares.

The house at **#18** belongs to the Catholic Salesiane Sisters. It is only one of many Christian institutions that were cut off from most of their flock after the city was divided in 1948. Across the street, on the corner at **#9,** is a beautiful house with a multi-arched portico. In 1949 Israel learned that this striking edifice sat on a sewage system which continued all the way to Damascus Gate. As this was the border and tension was high, Israel decided to prepare for Jordanian attack by mining the entire system with tons of explosives.

Months went by and all was quiet, but Israel began to dread an accidental explosion. Officials spoke to both the United Nations and to the Jordanians about their fears and a curfew was passed in the Old City. Residents were evacuated, and Israel set off a portion of the explosives. This resulted in smoke, noise and a big hole — but at least no one was hurt!

Walk up the little street called Natan HaNavi. The first building on your left as you ascend is **#14 Ayin Het Street**. One good look at the rear of the building will help you understand why it is called the "House of the Windows." Built in 1896, it is covered with over two dozen windows in a variety of shapes.

Continue ascending Natan HaNavi, which is tastefully decorated with old-fashioned street lamps. Walk up the steps, keeping a lookout for the block-shaped apartments built for new immigrants. Located as they were on the border between Jordan and Israel, the residents became unwilling targets for Jordanian cannons for almost two decades. You will see that some of the windows are tiny, planned so that at night when lying in bed inhabitants couldn't be seen by enemy snipers.

After passing through a little park you will be on Shivtei Yisrael Street. Turn right and stop just before the church located at #32. In Hebrew, Shivtei Yisrael means "the tribes of Israel." During the Mandate Period, when Israel was controlled by the British, this was called St. Paul's Street because of the charming Anglican church constructed here in 1873.

Situated only a moment's walk from the Old City's Damascus Gate, St. Paul's Church was one of the very first buildings to be erected on what were then the wastelands of New Jerusalem. It was established by a British organization called the Church Missionary Society, which was founded as a vehicle for converting Jews to Christianity. However, so few Jews answered the call to change their religion that the association began working among the Arabs instead. The sign on the front of the sanctuary is, therefore, written in Arabic. At one time as many as 150 Arab Anglicans worshipped at the church.

When Israel's War of Independence drew to a close in 1948 and cease-fire lines divided Jerusalem in two, St. Paul's was cut off from its Arab congregation. The sanctuary was abandoned and fell into severe disrepair. However in 1973, a few years after the re-unification of Jerusalem that resulted from the Six-Day War, the building was leased to a Pentecostal group called "Focus on Israel" on condition that the new occupants renovate the building.

Twice in 1987 the newly restored sanctuary was torched by arsonists that were apparently displeased with its activities. The interior was severely damaged and again the once-lovely church fell into ruin. Restoration began anew in the mid 1990's.

Topped by a belfry, St. Paul's facade is softened by some attractive decorative elements. Its twin entrances are lined by pilasters and enriched by gabled arches; the roof's pediment is embellished with miniature arches held in place by four very narrow columns. Above the gable is a weather vane that announces the year of the sanctuary's construction. Additions made to the facade during the latest restoration include wrought-iron flag holders, circular stone designs and an old-fashioned lamp.

Most notable is the large round window on the upper part of the facade. During the War of Independence St. Paul's was situated along the Jordanian-Israeli border. One day, I am told, a bullet shot straight through the window — hitting and shattering the black slate of a plaque on the church's back wall. The handsome circular window was boarded up for nearly 50 years but, as part of the '90's renovation, the planks were replaced with colorful stained glass. If the sanctuary is closed, you can enjoy the facade from the sidewalk. Be sure and get a view of the beautiful exterior side wall.

One of the most interesting buildings on this street is located next door, at #34. Today it houses the offices of the Minister of Education, so on work days you can open the gate and step inside the compound. During the British

Renaissance Italy in the center of Jerusalem — the Italian Hospital.

Mandate this was a center of Jerusalem culture and hosted concerts, readings and sing-alongs. Dating back to 1885, the entrance of this stately edifice is graced with two pilasters and a gable. In its heyday the property included a wonderful garden and an enviable collection of archeological artifacts.

The house was built by Jacob Johannes Frutiger, who called it Mahanaim and wrote its name above the door. For it says in the Scriptures: *"When Jacob saw them, he said, "This is the camp of God!" So he named that place Mahanaim"* (Genesis 32:2).

Frutiger was part of a Christian mission that sent tradesman to work alongside the Jews, hoping in this way to have some influence over them. Conrad Schick was another of the missionaries. In the beginning Frutiger worked in a shop and Schick labored as a carpenter and watchmaker.

Schick eventually left the trade to engage in archeology and biblical research and to design many of Jerusalem's finest edifices. His own stunning residence was located only a few blocks from St. Paul's Church.

Frutiger became a banker — one of the richest in the country. But eventually he began acting in such a peculiar manner that he seemed to have lost his mind (today it is assumed that he was suffering from Alzheimer's disease). The Frutiger banking empire eventually collapsed and all of the family's property was lost.

The site was bought by the Anglo-Jewish Association, which established a girl's school named for Evelina de Rothschild. Ultra-orthodox girls who studied here were said to be so well educated in English that they were sought after to become clerks of the Mandatory government. Menachem Ussishkin, director of the Jewish National Fund, lived here from 1922 until 1927 when he was forced out to make room for the British High Commissioner.

Continue down the sidewalk to reach the noisy lower part of HaNevi'im Street. The complex across the street on the left belongs to the Education Ministry but is still known by its original name: The Italian Hospital.

Cross the street, turn left, and then walk to the right into the courtyard *behind the complex.* As you gaze at the monumental structures you well may wonder what a fabulous Italian Renaissance building is doing in the middle of what has become an ultra-orthodox Jerusalem community.

The Italians began erecting buildings in Palestine quite a bit later than the other European powers. But Italy, too, wanted to make its mark. The doors of this hospital, said to resemble the grandest structures of 14th-century Italy, were opened in 1919.

Because the splendor of the Italian Hospital was meant to impress rather than to provide comfort for the patients, it is composed of a number of separate sections. To their undoubted chagrin, patients had to walk in and out of different portions of the hospital in order to reach a specific department.

During World War II the British declared the hospital to be enemy property, and expropriated it for use as Air Force headquarters. Both the Jews and the Arabs considered the hospital a prime strategic site and hoped desperately to get hold of it when the British left in 1948. Because the Haganah was able to learn the exact time of the British exit, the Jews entered first and placed a blue-and-white flag on the tower.

The Italian hospital was on the front line during the War of Independence and therefore became an important frontal position and observation post. Although the Jordanian Legion was responsible for seriously damaging the hospital's roof and tower with shells and mortars, it was from Israel that Italy demanded compensation after the war! Eventually, and after long negotiations, the Italians sold the hospital to the Israeli government.

Cross the street to the other side of HaNevi'im and ascend the sidewalk, in order to return to the Russian Compound where you began your tour. From here you get your best look at **#38-#40 HaNevi'im Street.** The structure was built by a devout Christian Ethiopian, the Empress Zauditu, in 1928. Among the distinctive bright mosaics on its facade you will see a lion — symbol of the Ethiopian royal house. Handsome arched windows and decorative gables made this a delightful addition to an already distinguished street. The elegant 90-room, three-story building served as Israel's Ethiopian Consulate for many years. Today the rooms in this house are rent out to lodgers.

Constructed in 1903, the complex at **#42** is situated on a historic plot. Five years earlier, when he visited the land of Israel, Wilhelm II pitched his tent here on what was then an empty lot. It was here, on November 2, 1898, that Theodore Herzl and the German Emperor discussed the Zionist issue.

Turn left on Monbaz Street. As you approach the Russian Compound, you will pass what looks like a side entrance to Beit Sergei. In fact, although the modern-day entrance is on Heleni HaMalka (Queen Helena) Street, originally it was here, around the corner on Monbaz.

Hours: **UNDERGROUND MUSEUM** [623-3166]: Sun.-Thurs., 8:00-16:00; **Entrance fee**

Guided Tours of the Municipality: Call one of the Tourist Information Offices for details [625-8844 or 628-0382]. *A complete tour of the municipality and its 19th-century buildings is found in my book EasyWalks in Israel: Sites and Stories.*

Restrooms: In the courtyard of Beit Sergei and at the Underground Museum

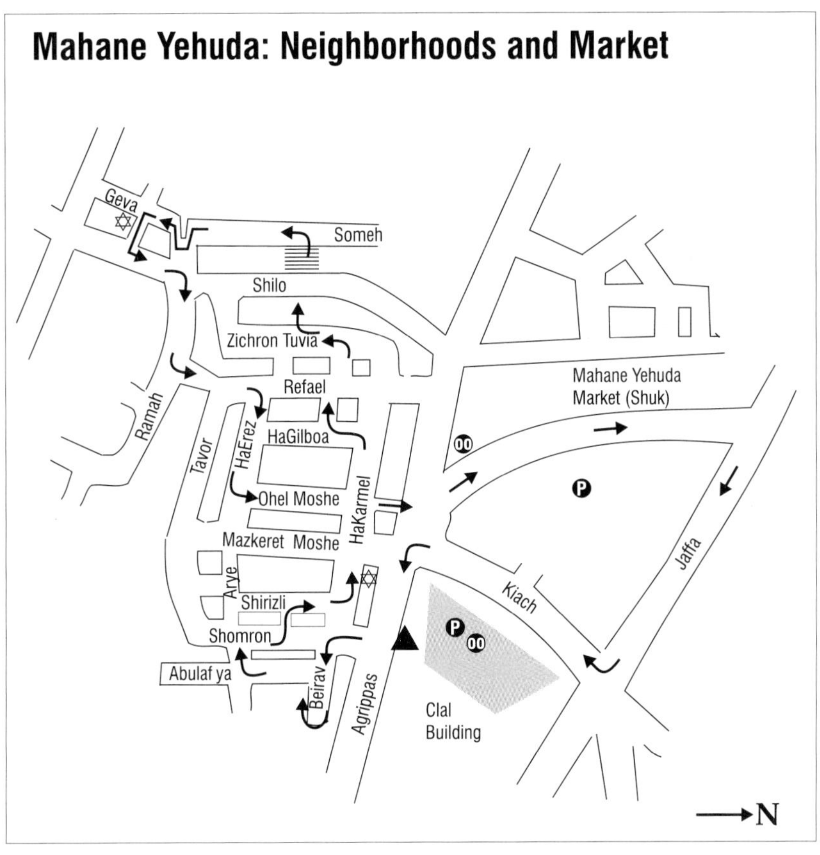

Mahane Yehuda: Neighborhoods and Market
Geva
Someh
Shilo
Zichron Tuvia
Refael
HaGilboa
Ramah
Tavor
HaErez
Ohel Moshe
HaKarmel
Mazkeret Moshe
Arye
Shirizli
Shomron
Abulaf ya
Beirav
Agrippas
Mahane Yehuda
Market (Shuk)
P
Kiach
Jaffa
P
Clal
Building
N

Mahane Yehuda: Neighborhoods and Market

- **Begin and end**: on Agrippas Street, at the Clal Center
- **Take bus**: 6, 13, 18, 20, 23 (alight on Jaffa Road)
- **Park your car**: in the market lot, or on a side street
- **Time frame**: 1-1^1/2 hours
- **Take note**: Weekdays it is hard to park, so come by bus; Saturdays you can leave your car on Agrippas Street or near Liberty Square (Kikar Herut).

Most people think of Mahane Yehuda as a bustling fruit and vegetable market, a Jerusalem landmark. But the market and the streets that surround it are far more than colorful places to shop: they are venues rich with atmosphere that exude an old-fashioned charm. As sites on which some of Jerusalem's earliest neighborhoods were established, they also abound with historic interest. Indeed, many people who played significant roles in Jewish history grew up in tiny communities near the market.

Mahane Yehuda Market — people, color and atmosphere.

A community clothesline in Mishkenot Yisrael — rare for these modern times!

Take a good look up and down Agrippas Street. One side of the road is crammed full of modern commercial centers; the other contains charming structures dating back to the late 1800's.

Now turn into Shomron Street, directly across from the Clal Center. Head left onto the first lane (Berav) and stop in the courtyard. This is the neighborhood called Mishkenot Yisrael (Dwelling Places of Israel) and was originally inhabited solely by religious Ashkenazic (East European) Jews. One of the first neighborhoods to be built outside the Old City walls, it was established in 1875 and named for the biblical passage *"How goodly are your tents O Jacob, your dwelling places, O Israel"* (Numbers 24:5).

Mishkenot Yisrael was one of many early neighborhoods established adjacent to Jaffa Road, the main axis linking the port city of Jaffa with Jerusalem. Surrounded by stone walls, the early neighborhoods looked like fortresses and had gates that could be tightly shut at night. This provided protection from highway robbers, and from the wolves and jackals that roamed the open fields outside the Old City walls.

Each enclosed neighborhood had its own central courtyard. It also had water cisterns whose cement openings protruded well above street level. The opening you see before you, like others in the neighborhood, has been sealed so that no one will fall inside.

In the beginning, when only one or two families resided in a new community, their water was brought to them from the Old City. Cisterns for collecting rainwater were built only after a few more families moved in. A cistern in the center of the courtyard meant that the neighborhood was there to stay!

These public reservoirs became neighborhood social centers much like the wells of our ancestors. Women met by the cistern each morning to talk and gossip; in the evening children would gather there for play.

In order to draw water from the cistern, you tied a rope to a pail and then lowered it down. The pail was then lifted out as carefully as possible, so that water wouldn't spill out of the bucket. Once clear of the cistern the precious liquid was poured into jars or tins. Afterwards it was strained through a cloth that was placed over a container.

Cisterns were cleaned out once a year, usually before winter. At that time workers descended into the cistern and removed stones, sand and other types of dirt that had accumulated inside. They then replastered the sides. During a drought, the residents had to haul the precious liquid from springs in Lifta and EIN KEREM.

Retrace a few steps, then turn down Abulafya Street to enjoy the special old-world ambiance of the little alleyways. On your left at the corner of Rabbi Arye Street and kiddy-corner to a house with purple shutters is an unprepossessing dwelling. This was once the home of a saintly rabbi. His name was Arye Levin, but those who knew him called him "Reb Arye."

Better known as the "prisoners' rabbi," Reb Arye ministered tirelessly to Jews incarcerated in the Jerusalem Central Prison during the British Mandate. Among the convicts were members of the Jewish underground resistance movements, as well as ordinary criminals.

Reb Arye's wife Hannah, considered as virtuous as her husband, sewed deep pockets in his overcoats so that the messages he carried to the prisoners wouldn't rustle as he walked. She prepared seams in his clothes for the dozens of missives the prisoners sent outside the walls with her husband, who would then walk all over the city until they were delivered.

One of my all-time favorite stories about Reb Arye concerns a charitable, righteous woman who was raising small children alone. One day, during weekly rounds at a Jerusalem hospital, the rabbi came upon the woman lying unconscious. She was suffering from a serious illness and had been surrounded by curtains — indicating that her case was hopeless. Too preoccupied to care whether or not he was making a spectacle of himself, Reb Arye spent the next hour alternately scolding the Almighty for his abandonment of the woman and sobbing a prayer that God would be merciful and compassionate. Then he left. Soon afterwards the woman awoke, asking for water and food. She recovered completely, for no apparent reason. Anyone who knew Reb Arye, however, had a ready explanation!

Turn right on Rabbi Arye Street (more of a lane, really), then take the next right back onto Shomron. Continue on Shomron a few dozen meters, and pass through an arch on your left. Arches like this one are typical of the early neighborhoods; the passageways were high and narrow and the gate could be closed each night.

You are now in a second neighborhood, Mazkeret Moshe, founded in 1882 and considered super-modern for the times. Well-known educator David Yellin lived in the neighborhood for a time and on one exciting day was able to relate that the Turks had put up a mailbox! **Go right at the next street, Shirizli.** The open area on your left, including the spot where a small community center is situated today, was originally a large central courtyard surrounded by houses.

At the end of Shirizli Street turn left. On your right is the Hessed VeRahamim Synagogue. Beautiful stained-glass windows are incorporated into the doors. In the period before the Day of Judgment (Yom Kippur) many of the residents here wake up in the wee hours of the morning, then gather in this and other neighborhood synagogues to chant prayers of forgiveness. If you wander the little lanes at about 2:00 a.m. you will join thousands of tourists, youth groups and school children who also throng the streets. They have come to see how an ancient tradition is still alive and well in Mahane Yehuda.

Cross the next street (Mazkeret Moshe). You have been walking on HaKarmel Street. This part of it is located within a third little neighborhood, Ohel Moshe, which was founded in 1883. Residents here were religious Sephardic Jews who spoke Ladino, a Spanish dialect with Hebrew elements. This is where former Israeli President Yitzhak Navon, an expert in ethnic folklore and a noted author, spent his childhood.

Walk atop the hump on HaKarmel Street, which covers several cisterns. Turn at the first lane on your right, walk to the end, and pass under an arch to exit at Agrippas Street. Then look up to see the name "Ohel Moshe" inscribed above the arch. You will also see a barely visible testimonial in English to Sir Moses Montefiore, whose Montefiore fund underwrote the neighborhood.

Return to HaKarmel and turn right. Walk to the end of the small courtyard, then turn left at the water cistern; a playground will be on your left, a row of houses on your right. This is HaGilboa Street. When you reach the fence at #16 turn right. You will then pass by a synagogue and walk beneath another arch.

The Ainee Building (above). Ohel Moshe is a typical Mahane Yehuda area lane (p. 82).

Cross Ezra Raphael Street. Then enter a little lane leading to Zichron Tuvia, new Jerusalem's very first commercial center. Look for an ugly commercial high rise in the background. It is called the Ainee Building. Jerusalemites can be exceedingly superstitious. During the 1970's a mystic named Mordechai Shar'abi is said to have cursed the Ainee Building. Some people believe that he hexed the Ainee because he was upset over plans — never realized — to add a movie theater to the structure. But most people say that Ainee cast a shadow on the balcony where Shar'abi liked to soak up the sun. Whatever the reason for the curse, it had quite an effect. Those few souls who thumbed their noses at the curse and rented shops in the high rise lost their money or even went bankrupt. Tenants tended to die before their time. Business only picked up after the Yemenite mystic went to his maker in the mid-1980's.

Yet things have never been really right at the Ainee building. And near the end of the 20th century, when the Jerusalem municipality began renovating the city's early neighborhoods, they found that residents of the area near Ainee wouldn't co-operate because they considered the building to be cursed. In 1997 the City Core Administration announced that it was going to hold a ceremony near Ainee and invited no less a personage than the former Chief Sephardic Rabbi Mordechai Eliahu to attend the ceremony and lift the curse! Judge for yourself it the ceremony worked: is Ainee now hopping with business?

Today the relatively wide street on which you are walking is lined with houses. However when it was built, in 1890, it was not residential. Considered a separate neighborhood, it was filled with little shops and alcoves where tailors, tinkers, locksmiths, shoemakers and blacksmiths carried on a thriving trade.

Another market operated parallel to this commercial center. This was a disorganized, open-air Arab *shuk*, or market which is Mahane Yehuda of to-day. As Mahane Yehuda gradually evolved into a permanent Jewish market, business in Zichron Tuvia slackened to a trickle. Eventually the tradesmen disappeared and families began moving into houses in the neighborhood.

Head left on Zichron Tuvia Street. Then turn right at an alley across from #21. Cross the next street, descend 10 steps, walk a few meters, then turn left onto Somech Street. Follow the little lane around to the left where it intersects with Ramah Street. Take a right onto Gevah, then *immediately* look up to see two second-story balconies. These not only face each other from opposite sides of the street, but are so close together that their inhabitants can pass sunflower seeds back and forth — a favorite Israeli pastime.

Immediately past #12 turn left. This is the Ades Great Synagogue, built by immigrants from the community of Aleppo. They brought with them the oldest known Bible in the world, dating to the 10th century. Today the original is

Enjoy the ambience as you walk through the market.

housed in the Israel Museum, but you can see a copy inside. This synagogue is larger and much more elegant than other neighborhood houses of worship.

Turn left again, (Shiloh Street), then go right across from #36 onto Ramah Street. This street boasts a house with a small gabled roof (#5) and a wild combination of building styles. **Head left across from #3, and you will be sauntering along Raphael Street. Turn right on HaErez, next to a modern-looking house, turn left under a bougainvillea-covered arch to come out facing another blocked cistern. If you walk to the right for a few short meters you will come to Ohel Moshe Street; turn left to view some very pretty houses**.

Pass a bench-lined park and a small playground, then walk through the arch at the far end of the street to reach the Mahane Yehuda Market. This is your chance to stroll through the market all the way to Jaffa Road. In the late 1980's a roof was built over the market, so you are protected from summer sun and winter rain.

When you reach the main street — Jaffa Road — turn right and stop across the historic structure at #92. This was Jerusalem's first skyscraper! The moving force behind this lofty building was American immigrant Rabbi Shmuel Levi, who constructed the three-story edifice at the beginning of the 20th century.

Over the years it grew from three to five stories and was known for its hospitality to indigent pilgrims. On the fourth floor was the Zoharei Hama, frequented by the venerated Rabbi Arye Levin.

What makes this building so famous is its huge sundial. Moshe Shapiro, a rabbi from Mea She'arim who taught himself astronomy, put it up in 1918. Before its construction Orthodox Jews would climb the Mount of Olives and the slopes of the Bayit VeGan neighborhood to determine the exact hours of sunrise and sunset. Following its appearance, however, they were able to set their pocket watches by the sundial on Jaffa Road.

The tower on the fourth floor tumbled down during an earthquake in the late 1920's. In 1940 a short circuit in the building caused a fire: the fifth story burnt down and the synagogue below was badly damaged. The facade was restored and the sundial reconstructed in 1980.

I happened to be walking across the street from the clock one Friday afternoon, when the Sabbath eve began. Suddenly, the air was pierced by a horrible shriek! That's how I learned that one of the sirens heard when the Sabbath begins in Jerusalem originates from somewhere in this historic structure.

Restrooms: The Clal Center

At the Mahane Yehuda Market the food is always fresh.

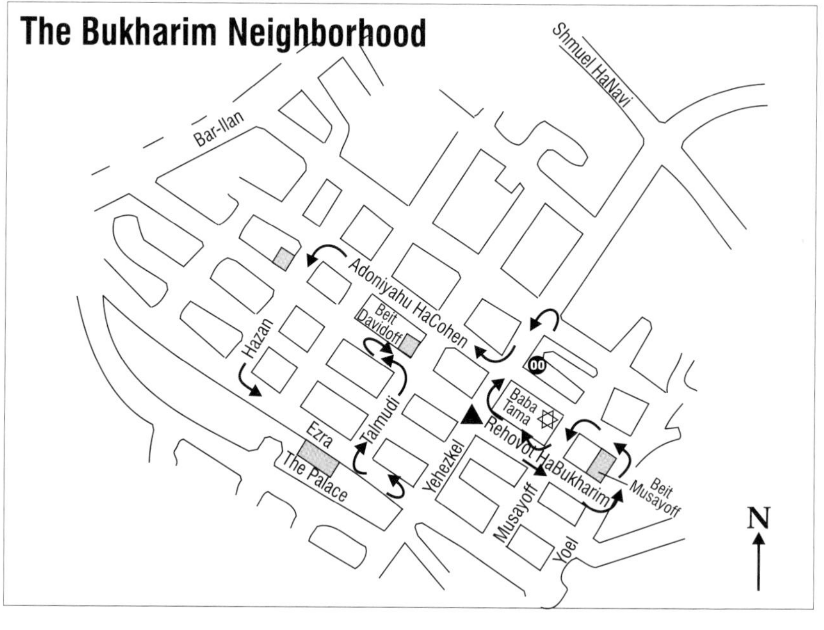
The Bukharim Neighborhood
Shmuel HaNavi
Bar-Ilan
Adoniyahu HaCohen
Beit Davidoff
Hazan
Talmudi
Ezra
The Palace
Yehezkel
Baba Tama
Rehovot HaBukharim
Musayoff
Beit Musayoff
Yoel
N

Bukharim Neighborhood

- **Begin and end**: at the corner of Bukharim Street and Yehezkel Street
- **Take bus**: 9, 27, 35, 36
- **Park your car**: on David Street — the continuation of Bukharim Street
- **Time frame**: 1 hour
- **Take note**: This is an ultra-orthodox neighborhood. Please dress appropriately.

Very little is left of Jerusalem's once elegant Bukharim neighborhood. While the community originally housed wealthy immigrants from the Central Asian Bukhara region of Uzbekistan and was known for its warmth and tolerance, today it is home to ultra-orthodox families and newly observant Jews. Indeed hardly any of the old buildings remain, the earliest residents are gone and the atmosphere has undergone a change.

Yet when it was first established, the Bukharim neighborhood boasted some of the grandest structures in the city. A few have been restored to something resembling their former glory, but most have either been torn down to make room for new developments or are crumbling and covered with rubble. In fact, the stories surrounding many of the houses are a lot more exciting than the dwellings themselves. Nevertheless, a walk through the streets of this neighborhood is still a fascinating experience.

This particular tour is made up of two rectangular routes which come together at the corner of Rehovot HaBukharim Street and Yehezkel Street. Saturday visitors with cars should park well outside the neighborhood.

Until the Russians conquered Bukhara in 1868, the Jewish community living in the province was almost totally cut off from its brethren around the world. Yet the Jews never wholly assimilated with their Moslem neighbors. And although their prayers included the Arabic phrase *"Allah hu Akbar"* (Allah is Great), children's lessons were often conducted in Hebrew.

When the Russians took over Bukhara they granted the Jewish population religious freedom as well as a monopoly in the silk and woven-goods trade. The more enterprising of them took excellent advantage of the opportunity and became wonderfully affluent. Indeed, when the first Bukharan immigrant reached Jerusalem in the early 1870s, he brought his wife, his children, *and a servant!* to the Holy Land.

By the 1890's about 200 Bukharan immigrants had reached Jerusalem and all of them lived inside the Old City. The community established an association to provide services to its members and in 1891 decided to found its own neighborhood outside the Old City walls.

The Bukharim neighborhood: a decorative Star of David.

The Bukharans were a traditional bunch. In the very beginning their neighborhood was called Rehovot (wide spaces) after a well dug by Isaac in the Valley of Gerar: "... *He named it Rehovot, saying 'Now the Lord has given us room and we will flourish in the land"* (Genesis 26:22). Unlike the other newly built Jewish neighborhoods, the Bukharan suburb was not adjacent to any existing communities. And its design was unusual for Jerusalem: the plan called for spacious homes on tree-lined boulevards with main roads a generous width of 10.5 meters and side streets five meters wide. Houses were to take up an entire block and to center around an elegant courtyard.

Try to ignore the street's contemporary lack of beauty and all the garbage on Rehovot HaBukharim Street as you follow it away from Yehezkel. Instead, look for some of the neighborhood's characteristic elements — like the Stars of David which often include a floral decoration of some kind.

When you get to the second corner take a very sharp left onto Yoel Street. The first opening on your left is now more of a junkyard than the courtyard paradise of fruit trees and flowing water described in a contemporary Hebrew book. The house, the first in the neighborhood, was put up in 1894 by one Shlomo Musayoff.

Typical of other houses that would be built in the Bukharan neighborhood, this first structure's courtyard included several stairways leading up to the homes of members of the extended family. And like the other dwellings that would be constructed here, the Musayoff complex included a synagogue for family prayers. Though many affluent Jews considered their Jerusalem residences summer homes or used them only on pilgrimages to the Holy City, the Musayoff family lived here all year 'round.

Continue along Yoel Street. Immediately to your right you will see a tiny bakery where you can pick up flat Oriental bread that Jerusalemites call *esh tanur* (oven fire). On your left is the entrance to the Musayoff synagogue complex.

When you reach Adoniyahu HaCohen Street, look back at the beginning of Yoel to get a feel for the dimensions of the Musayoff house. Now turn left to follow Adoniyahu HaCohen. The metal container you pass is not a garbage bin. Rather, it is a *geniza* where locals store worn-out holy books until they can be given a proper burial.

Push open the door at #4. Inside the courtyard you will see a citrus fruit tree and an arcade of arches and stained-glass windows. **Back outside, walk to the end of the street. Then look across the road to see the house at #13.**

The Tzufayoff House at #13 Musayoff Street — next page.

World War 1 was a terrible period for Jerusalem's Bukharan Jews. All connections between residents of the neighborhood and the wealthy relatives back in Bukhara were severed, and the Jews living here became absolutely destitute. By the end of the war all they had left were their Jerusalem homes. This house belonged to Shlomo Tsufayoff, a merchant who lost his entire fortune during the war.

Turn left and go up Musayoff Street and into #9, where a different kind of entrance leads to a block of "dedication homes" or *batei hekdesh.* The closely knit Bukharan community took excellent care of their poor and, in 1898, built 25 apartments to house people from their region who couldn't afford to put up their own homes.

Walk back out, then turn right and right again onto Rehovot HaBukharim Street. At the far corner (the intersection with Yehezkel) is the Baba Tama, the neighborhood's central synagogue. It was put up in 1894 and later was incorporated into the dedication homes. If the door is open take a look inside at the superb *bima* (raised platform), colorful benches and lovely chandeliers.

You have now completed one of the circles in your tour — it is time to begin another! Cross to the other side of Yehezkel Street, turn right, and walk down the hill. Across the road, below the Baba Tama and above a doorway, is a rusty Star of David. To make certain passersby could identify it, the words Magen David (Hebrew for Shield of David) are written in wrought-iron letters inside the star. On weekdays you will see the Bukharan market, set up and operating along the back wall of the dedication homes. Today's stands, while colorful, only vaguely resemble those from the large and bustling market of yesteryear.

Turkish Baths once occupied the building at **#36**, further down the road. On one of his trips to Europe Shlomo Musayoff visited the saunas of Paris and was so impressed that he decided to reproduce them here. The Baths were a Jerusalem institution well into the 20th century.

Retrace about 15 of your steps up the hill and you will almost run into a huge, aging eucalyptus tree, one of many planted by the Bukharan Jews to beautify their neighborhood. At one time reflective arrows were plastered onto the trunk so that cars wouldn't crash into the tree. Other neighborhood trees became firewood for the Turkish rulers of Palestine during World War I. Not far from the tree, at **#35**, you will see a Star of David with a lovely rosette in its center. **Turn right at Adoniyahu HaCohen Street.**

You are now walking in a mini-quarter within the Bukharan neighborhood, called Giv'at Shaul (to be distinguished from a suburb with the same name at the entrance to Jerusalem). Established by Jews from the Iranian city of Mashhad, Giv'at Shaul runs from here to **#28 Adoniyahu HaCohen**.

In 1839 the tyrannical ruler of Mashhad, a holy Moslem city in Iran, decided to do something about the Jews. Claiming that one of his Jewish subjects had insultingly named his dog "Moslem," he decreed death for all or, alternatively, conversion to Islam. The Jews converted and to outsiders seemed to have become good Moslems. In fact, however, they continued to practice Judaism in secret.

At the beginning of the 20th century Mashhad Jews were permitted to visit the holy city of Mecca in Saudi Arabia and there received the honored title of Haj. On their way back they passed through Jerusalem ... and decided to remain. They picked the Bukharan neighborhood as their new home because, they said, it reminded them of Mashhad.

Stroll into the courtyard at #16, the home of Haj Adoniyahu HaCohen. What you see is absolutely charming, especially a tree bursting with citrus fruit amid quiet early 20th-century surroundings.

The house at **#28** is unique, for its history is written on its exterior walls. Like the other Mashhad Jews who returned to Judaism, Haj Mohammed Ismaeli Hebraized his name and became Haj Yehezkel Ben Ya'akov HaLevy. You find it all in the Hebrew text under the windows, as well as the phrase in which HaLevy dedicates the house for public use "until the Redeemer comes."

Continue on Adoniyahu HaCohen Street to David Hazan Street and turn left. Until the 1990's there was an elongated house on the other side of the street. In fact, for years a rather amusing sign was posted in front that read "Danger, preservation and destruction."

That house, Beit Mash'hayoff, contained the biggest group of courtyards in the neighborhood and you could see the seams where they were stuck together. This complex would later be called House of the Officials, for when penniless Bukharan residents rented out rooms, Jerusalem's elite often moved in. Among its inhabitants were Yitzhak Ben-Zvi (later Israel's second president) and his wife, famous labor movement activist Rachel Yanait. In 1999 reckless contractors destroyed most of the house, but if you walk up Hazan street you should still be able to see the original lion. It is found under a large arch on the facade.

Way at the top, on Ezra Street, turn left. Beit Yehudayoff, at **#19**, is often called the "Palace." Incredibly grand, the building was built in 1905 and for decades remained the most spectacular of Jerusalem dwellings. According to legend, the house was meant to house the Messiah when he comes to Jerusalem and that's why it is also known as Beit HaMashiach (house of the Messiah). But family members have said that this is hogwash, and the name actually popped up after one of the babies was called Mashiach.

People who have toured Italy claim that the Palace's Renaissance design is reminiscent of Rome's Capitolina Museum. And, indeed, it is truly a splendid edifice. Beautiful pillars are topped with Corinthian capitals, and at least one of a row of stone goblets is still standing on the roof. Two arched doors, decorated with Stars of David, led onto a balcony that was supported not by steel girders but by stone. Behind the two balcony doors was a room covered with a glass roof. On Succoth, the Feast of the Tabernacles, the glass was taken away and replaced by thatch.

From 1948 to 1967 the neighborhood was situated on the Israeli-Jordanian border and the horrendously ugly cement wall in front of this grand building was used to shelter inhabitants from attack by Jordanian snipers. Perhaps, by now, the unsightly wall has disappeared.

After the British conquered Palestine during World War I, Jews stood along the roads to cheer the victorious troops. And when Jerusalemites needed just the right setting for a reception in honor of the general who commanded the British forces in the Middle East they picked the Palace. On May 22, 1918, dozens of important people lined the double winding staircase to receive the conquering hero — General Edmund Allenby.

Ironically, just over 20 years later the Palace became a center for Etzel, an underground Jewish military force organized to combat Arab terror and engage

Exotic courtyard in the Bukharim Neighborhood.

A remarkable restoration: Beit Davidoff.

in retaliatory attacks against the British Mandatory authorities. For years the Palace's exterior walls were defaced with graffiti: one slogan read "Down with English Imperialism."

Continue along the street to the end of the house to view the main entrance, where the reception took place. Then backtrack a few steps to the alley directly across from the Palace and walk down all the way to David Hefez Street (a section of Rehovot HaBukharim Street). The magnificent building at **#10** is Beit Davidoff. A remarkable restoration by the Jewish Agency has kept this jewel of a dwelling from the deterioration that cost the loss of so many others in the neighborhood. **Turn left on Rehovot HaBukharim Street until you can see Beit Davidoff's distinctive red-tiled double roof.**

Windows are lined by mini-columns and topped by beautifully carved gables. Look for floral patterns and an unusual gutter pipe, made of stone instead of tin. On occasion, the handicraft shop in the building is open offering some wonderful gifts.

Restrooms: For men only! On Rehovot HaBukharim Street; men and women on Yehezkel Street, opposite **#35.**

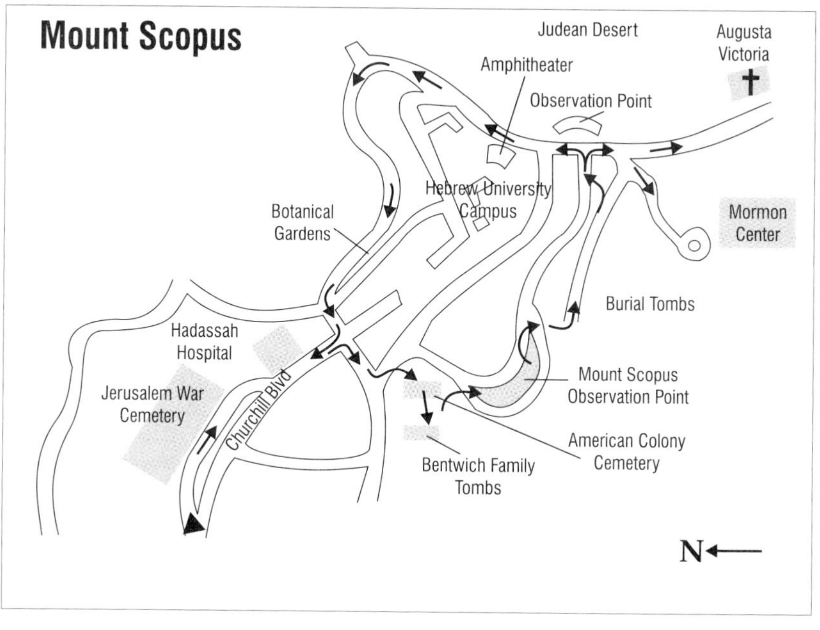

Mount Scopus
Judean Desert
Augusta Victoria
Amphitheater
Observation Point
Hebrew University Campus
Botanical Gardens
Mormon Center
Burial Tombs
Hadassah Hospital
Mount Scopus Observation Point
Jerusalem War Cemetery
Churchill Blvd
American Colony Cemetery
Bentwich Family Tombs
N

Mount Scopus

- **Begin and end**: at the Jerusalem War Cemetery, Mount Scopus
- **Take buses**: 4a, 9, 26, 28
- **Park your car**: on the street
- **Time Frame**: 2-3 hours

At 834 meters above sea level Mount Scopus is one of the loftiest peaks in Jerusalem. From one of its overlooks there is a superb view of the Judean desert and the Dead Sea just beyond; another offers a panorama of the picturesque Old City, East Jerusalem and the modern hotels which break the western horizon. Scopus is a Greek word, meaning "the place from which one observes"; in Hebrew the mount is called Har HaTzofim (Lookout Mountain).

Begin your walk at Britain's Jerusalem War Cemetery, located next to the Hadassah Hospital. Look through the stately entrance and you will see a large cross in the middle of the well-tended site. This, Israel's largest British burial ground, was established after World War I. At that time Britain's Lord Balfour announced that "His Majesty's Government views with favor the establishment of a national home in Palestine for the Jewish people." Euphoric over the Balfour Declaration and certain that the British were on their side, the Jews of Palestine presented them with the gift of land for a cemetery. A special British fund is responsible for its meticulous maintenance.

Most of the 2,500 soldiers buried within the peaceful cemetery fell in battles over Jerusalem. The troops belonged to Commonwealth forces and were from South Africa, Britain, India, Australia and New Zealand. A number of Jewish graves are located high on the slope, to the left and near the far wall: many of the soldiers who are buried there served together in the Royal Fusiliers.

A striking domed edifice was built here as a chapel for the soldiers' relatives. Guarding the entrance is a statue of St. George, a 2nd-century Roman soldier who is believed to have slain a dragon in order to save a princess. St. George was declared patron saint of England in the 13th century.

Stop under the shade of an enormous, flourishing strawberry tree (*ktalav* in Hebrew), one of the largest I've seen in Israel. Scattered throughout riverbeds in the Jerusalem hills and in the forests of the Galilee, strawberry trees have warm, reddish brown limbs and they bear a tasty red fruit. Because of their extraordinary beauty many people have tried to plant strawberry trees in their gardens; however they grow only in very special soil and these homegrown attempts are generally unsuccessful. This huge tree must be receiving tender, loving care.

Mount Scopus is such an integral part of Israel that we tend to take its presence for granted. Yet Mount Scopus wasn't always as readily accessible as it is today. Indeed, from the War of Independence in 1948 to the 1967 Six-Day War the mountain held a dubious special status as a demilitarized zone. During those 19 long years the mountain's ultra-modern Hadassah Hospital lay idle and desolate; its historic Hebrew University was neglected and bare.

Some of the most traumatic events in Jewish history were played out here nearly 2,000 years ago. At that time the Tenth Roman Legion camped on the mountain, and it was from here that General Titus commanded the conquest and destruction of Jerusalem.

Scopus' modern-day importance began in 1925 when it became the site of the prestigious Hebrew University. The university's opening ceremony was graced by the most illustrious personalities of the time: former British Foreign Secretary Lord Arthur James Balfour, Dr. Chaim Weizmann (later to become the first President of Israel), and General Allenby, who led the 1917 Allied conquest of Palestine. Thirteen years later the Hebrew University was joined by the Hadassah Hospital, without question the most up-to-date and well-equipped medical facility in the entire Middle East.

However, there was a serious drawback to their Mount Scopus locations. The road to both hospital and university was surrounded by hostile Arab neighborhoods through which any service vehicles had to pass.

It didn't take the Arabs long to realize how easy it would be to blockade the road and already in the early stages of the War of Independence they ambushed any Jew naive enough to try passing through. This despite the fact that the British had promised the Jews safe conduct to Mount Scopus.

On April 13, 1948 a large group of doctors, nurses, patients, teachers and students joined a supply convoy which was traveling to the hospital on Mount Scopus. The convoy was ambushed and its vehicles blown up as it made its way through the affluent Arab neighborhood of Sheikh Jarrah — only a few hundred meters from a British military outpost.

With the British looking on, bloodthirsty Arab attackers mercilessly slaughtered any personnel attempting to escape the inferno. Incredibly, having resisted Haganah attempts to rescue Jews caught in this death trap, it still took the British over six hours to intervene! Seventy-eight people were murdered in the attack, or burned to death after their ambulances and buses were set on fire. Among the victims was the director of the Hadassah organization in Palestine, Dr. Chaim Yassky. Fewer than 30 of the passengers survived.

As soon as the British pulled out of Palestine in mid-May of 1948, the Arabs managed to get complete control of the road to Mount Scopus. Hadassah and the Hebrew University were effectively cut off from the rest of the city, becoming a lonely enclave deep in enemy territory.

On July 7, 1948, Israel and Jordan signed an agreement in which Mount Scopus remained part of the Jewish State but was now located within an Israeli demilitarized zone. The only people permitted on the mountain were Israeli policemen and the only defenses they were allowed were light weapons. Needless to say, in the fortnightly

supply convoys that ascended Mount Scopus the "policemen" — actually Israeli soldiers — smuggled in as many arms and as much artillery as they could.

Although the soldiers donned made-to-order police uniforms prepared especially by tailors at an Israeli army camp, the Jordanians knew exactly what was going on. Often they would shout across at the new arrivals "are you from the Paratroopers, or Artillery?"

Between 1948 and 1967 Israel slowly fortified Mount Scopus. When the Six-Day War began this was Israel's strongest border position and it was ready to do battle. As it happened, however, the fiercest fighting took place on the roads leading to Mount Scopus, at the Police School and Ammunition Hill.

Stand on the long driveway that passes immediately in front of the cemetery entrance. This was part of the road on which convoys traveled to Mount Scopus when the mountain was cut off from the rest of Jewish Jerusalem.

Walk up the driveway to reach Hadassah Mount Scopus, the original Hadassah Hospital. During the 1950's, when this facility was out of reach, a whole new hospital and a new branch of the university — Givat Ram — opened in West Jerusalem. Immediately following the Six-Day War, however, renovation began on the two earlier Scopus institutions.

As you continue your gradual ascent you will begin seeing some of the hospital's early structures. The Judith Riklis building on the left housed the nursing school; the edifice across the street was an outpatient clinic.

An elegant older building becomes visible as you get close to the university. Originally the home of the National Library, today it houses the university's Law School. It is of relatively dark stone and capped by a dome.

When you reach the main gates turn right and then continue walking parallel to the university. At the intersection turn left in the direction of the Mount of Olives, still walking across the street from the university. Soon you reach sign leading to Parking Lot #2. Pass the sign, and then look down and to your right to see a stone wall. The wall surrounds a cemetery.

Descend, and enter through the gate. You are standing among the graves of the AMERICAN COLONY, whose members came to Jerusalem from Chicago in 1881. A deeply religious society that was completely immersed in good works, the Colony helped anyone in need regardless of religion or nationality. Among those who benefited from their largess was a group of Jews which immigrated from Yemin to the land of Israel after a long, arduous journey. Few of Jerusalem's more veteran Jews had the desire or the means to help the arrivals from Yemin, and the American Colony came to their rescue. The Colony fed and clothed the new immigrants, looking after them for many years to come.

Group leader Horatio Spafford is said to have introduced the eucalyptus tree to Israel. It is believed that he presented a Jewish friend with eucalyptus seeds that were planted at Israel's first agricultural school, Mikveh Yisrael. That eucalyptus was the forerunner of the trees that helped dry up northern swamps and today provide many spots of green in the desert.

Far newer graves are found in a family plot just below the American Colony cemetery. To get there, exit the gate and follow the stone wall to its end. Then descend a steep but short dirt path that takes you into University National Park. Turn right just below the American Colony graveyard.

In this burial ground members of the prestigious and influential Bentwich family lie at rest. Patriarch Herbert Bentwich was a diehard Zionist even before Theodore Herzl appeared on the international scene. Beginning his legal career as an attorney to Sir Moses Montefiore, Bentwich helped shape the famous 1917 Balfour Declaration proclaiming British support for the establishment of a national Jewish homeland in Palestine. The double tombs of Herbert Bentwich and his wife Susannah are located on a raised platform.

Son Norman, who served as Attorney General in the Mandate government and helped found the Hebrew University, is buried here as well. On the left is a very special tomb adorned with a carved harp and a line of musical notes.

This is the grave of Daniel Balfour Bentwich, a musical prodigy who took his own life at the age of 18.

Walk back up to the sidewalk and turn right to find that you are right next to the Mount Scopus Observation Point. This stunning overlook features burial caves from the Second Temple period and an unparalleled view that is especially romantic at sunset.

Landmarks to your left include the tall tower of the Russian Ascension Church, and the Augusta Victoria hospice built by German Emperor Wilhelm II and named for his wife. Between the two are the domes and arches of the Center for Near Eastern Studies on Mount Scopus (Mormon Center), one of the most sensational buildings in the city.

Look for the brilliant golden dome topping the Dome of the Rock directly across from you. It underwent major renovations whose cost was covered by the Kingdom of Jordan. Beyond it is the dark-gray dome of the El Aksa Mosque. Both are located on Mount Moriah, the site of the First and Second Temples. To your right is the Hyatt Regency Hotel, originally planned as a high rise. Today it fits snugly into the landscape and has literally hundreds of windows and balconies facing the view.

Descend the stone walkway to reach a number of Second Temple period tombs. From here continue on a path that is parallel to the University. You will be shaded by the trees in the garden, with a constant lovely vista of Jerusalem on your right. Upper intersecting paths lead back to the sidewalk; I prefer the middle and lower paths, where the landscaped slopes are so heavy with brush that the university is often blocked from view. Just keep the Dome of the Rock on your right at all times and you won't get lost.

The path ends abruptly with two cave-like overhangs and a dirt ascent. Follow the stone steps up to the Wall of Life, located on the sidewalk across from the university. Directly in front of you is the pink-tinted Truman Institute. This was the first university building constructed after the reunification of Jerusalem.

Turn right and walk to the corner. From here you have two possible side trips, described at the end of this chapter. When you are finished, or if you are skipping one or both of these tours, continue on your walk across from and parallel to the university.

On the other side of the road is the Gerald Halbert Park and Observation Plaza, another great observation point. Stand here to look toward the Dead Sea and the Judean Desert.

Walk on a few dozen meters. There is an amphitheater to your left. Built especially for the university's inauguration ceremony in 1925, the amphitheater

Overlooks and views: Mount Scopus . . .

was partially destroyed during the War of Independence and later restored. It was here that former Prime Minister Yitzhak Rabin, then Commander-in-Chief of the Israel Defense Forces, received an honorary doctorate immediately following the Six-Day War. Here, too, Leonard Bernstein conducted the Israel Philharmonic Orchestra in a concert celebrating the city's reunification.

Next on your route as you walk around the university is the Bezalel Academy of Arts and Design. Bezalel was the brainchild of Boris Dov Schatz, one of Jerusalem's most famous figures. A Bulgarian who was both an art professor and a court sculptor to the king, Schatz dreamed of creating a Jewish arts center in Jerusalem. He suggested the idea to Theodore Herzl in 1903 and it was accepted by the Zionist Congress of 1905.

The name "Bezalel" comes directly from the scriptures. *"Then the Lord said to Moses, 'See, I have chosen Bezalel son of Uri, the son of Hur, of the tribe of Judah, and I have filled him with the Spirit of God, with skill, ability and knowledge in all kinds of crafts to make artistic designs for work in gold, silver and bronze, to cut and set stones, to work in wood, and to engage in all kinds of craftsmanship'"* (Exodus

31:1-5). The biblical Bezalel also fashioned the brass altar on which King Solomon offered his sacrifices.

Schatz came to Israel in 1906 together with art teachers and a few pupils. He started putting his vision into action from rented premises on Ethiopia Street. A few years later he moved into an empty Arab estate on Shmuel HaNagid Street in the center of town. Called the Bezalel School of Arts and Crafts, its main building was stunning, designed in the form of an ancient city wall.

In the 1960's the charming school became the Bezalel Academy of Art and Design, and it was transferred to Mount Scopus thirty years later. As you can see, today's ultra-modern structure fits quite harmoniously into the Scopus complex.

Finally you reach Gate 6, the entrance to the Mount Scopus Botanical Gardens. Developed by the Jewish National Fund, the gardens include 2,000-year-old tombs, the graves of two leading Zionist figures and romantic, shady spots for contemplation. The gardens contain representative foliage from all over the country. You can stroll through them, although you may need a Latin-English dictionary to help you understand the signs!

. . . and from the Augusta Victoria tower (p. 101).

The strange stone structure you see in the Gardens is a *shomera,* meant to resemble the watchtowers which are described in the Bible and which were used by Judean farmers to store crops. It was put here as a memorial to a Canadian colonel and four Israeli soldiers who were killed on Mount Scopus in 1958.

Exit the gardens, continue around the university, and turn right at the intersection across from the main gate. You will have returned to the Judith Riklis Center and will soon be back at the British cemetery.

Side Trip One: Jerusalem Center for Near Eastern Studies

From the university junction near the Truman Institute, take a very sharp right and follow the road. One of half a dozen such institutions scattered all over the world, the Center for Near Eastern Studies on Mount Scopus is housed in one of the most exquisite structures in Jerusalem. Completed in 1988, it offers a semester-abroad program for students at Utah's Brigham Young University.

The Center is built of Jerusalem stone, Italian marble, imported teakwood and large quantities of glass. Known locally as the Mormon Center, this eye-catching eight-story edifice would be worth a visit even without the panoramic views it offers to students, faculty, and guests.

In order to not to offend Israel's religious establishment, the smiling guides who take you around the center will not answer any questions about religion. Instead, they focus on the stupendous building, its extraordinary architecture, the lovely interior decoration and the fragrant biblical garden.

Side Trip Two: Augusta Victoria

After you visit the Jerusalem Center, return to the main road. Turn right at the intersection and head for the Augusta Victoria Hospice. If you omitted the Center, and have reached the junction, turn right and walk only a few dozen meters. You have just moved from Mount Scopus onto the historic Mount of Olives! You will reach Augusta Victoria, today a medical facility and pleasing guest house, after only a few moments' stroll.

Your first glimpse of Augusta Victoria may make you think that you have traveled backward in time, for directly in front of you a medieval fortress guards the ridge of the mountain! Enveloped by stone walls, protected by a heavy gate, the compound consists of massive rectangular structures placed around an inner courtyard. The buildings are reputed to contain underground chambers, as well as secret tunnels that pass under the walls and wind up outside the complex.

Augusta Victoria is one of the most impressive German structures in the country. It was built by German Emperor Wilhelm II, who visited Jerusalem in 1898. Eager to have the German presence prominently visible in the Holy City, he initiated this monumental tribute to his wife, Auguste-Victoria.

The Augusta Victoria Hospice opened in 1910, on a spot about 80 meters higher than the Temple Mount and tall enough to be seen from almost every part of Jerusalem. Some of Augusta Victoria was meant as a hospice for people suffering from malaria; the rest consisted of comfortable lodgings for pilgrims to the Holy City.

Indeed, inside the enclosure there were many beautifully appointed rooms for the use of distinguished guests. The entire complex was so handsome that Sir Herbert Samuel, the very first British High Commissioner in Palestine, chose Augusta Victoria as his residence in 1920.

Situated inside the austere compound is a surprisingly ornate German Lutheran sanctuary called the Church of the Ascension — named for its proximity to the site from which Jesus traditionally rose to heaven. The church's ceiling and walls are decorated with magnificent mosaics and paintings. On view in the center of the ceiling is a picture of Jesus and the 12 disciples.

Dressed in medieval costume, Wilhelm and his Empress appear in one of the paintings next to German kings who took part in the Crusades. This drawing is situated above the church's century-old pneumatic organ, an instrument that was specially ordered from Frankfurt for the playing of German romantic music — among others, the works of Mendelssohn and Brahms.

Four huge bells donated by Wilhelm and his wife were transported with much difficulty from the port of Jaffa up the treacherously winding roads to the heights of the Mount of Olives and duly installed in the Augusta Victoria bell tower. Look for the names of the royal couple on two of the bells, all of which are rung six days a week without fail. On occasion, their chimes join in harmony with those of Wilhelm's two other churches — Dormition Abbey and the Church of the Redeemer.

From the top of the church's bell-tower, which is over 45 meters high, visitors have a tremendous view of Jerusalem and its surroundings. Go on up — by foot or by elevator — for a superb panorama.

Hours: **HEBREW UNIVERSITY BOTANICAL GARDENS**:
Sun.-Thurs., 10:00-17:00; Sat., 10:00-14:00; closed on Fri.

JERUSALEM CENTER [626-5666]: Tue.-Fri., 10:00-12; 14:00-16:00. Entrance only by free guided tour, offered on the hour and half-hour; *wheelchair accessible*. Call for free tickets to melodious Sunday night concerts at the Jerusalem Center.
AUGUSTA VICTORIA [628-7704]: **Bells ring**: Mon.-Fri., 12:00 noon; Sat., 18:00. **Church**: Mon.-Sat., 9:00-17:00; Sun. closed to the general public; **Small fee for climbing about 200 steps to the tower; slightly more for taking the elevator almost to the top**. The public is invited to wonderful concerts at the Church of the Ascension. Call for information.

Restrooms: Jerusalem Center and Augusta Victoria Church

Ammunition Hill has become a symbol of heroism under fire; young paratroopers are guided through the battle site.

Ammunition Hill

- **Begin and end**: at the Ammunition Hill Museum
- **Take bus**: 9, 22, 25, 28, 39, 45 — and buses 13 and 22 off Highway One
- **Park your car**: in the Ammunition Hill lot
- **Time frame**: 1-2 hours

I n 1997, 30 years after Israeli paratroopers conquered Ammunition Hill, Suleiman Salam El Salita returned to the site of the battle. During the Six-Day War El Salita had been stationed at Ammunition Hill as commanding officer of a company in the Jordanian El Hussein Battalion. His unit was made up of Bedouin soldiers, among the finest and fiercest of Jordanian troops.

Now a great-grandfather, the former officer and survivor of the Battle of Ammunition Hill looked thoughtfully to the west. After gazing at the homes that cover previously barren hills, he turned back to his Israeli hosts and reflected on the battle. "Every time we thought we finally had the upper hand, you would reappear and we would have to fight again," he told them. "We Arabs battled like lions, down to the last bullet. But *your* men — they fought like fedayun (suicide warriors)!"

So savage was the battle for Ammunition Hill, so heroic were the soldiers who fought there, that the site where it took place has become an Israeli symbol of heroism under fire. Each year on Jerusalem Day a memorial ceremony for all soldiers who fell in the Six-Day War takes place on Ammunition Hill.

Begin at the Ammunition Hill Museum. If the museum is open, you can view an audiovisual program that provides an exciting and comprehensive picture of the battle for Jerusalem in 1967. Notice as you walk through the museum that the walls are of concrete — symbolically reminiscent of a bunker. You will want to examine explanatory maps, the golden memorial wall, and dozens of poignant displays that include letters by and about fallen soldiers.

After you exit the museum, follow the road a few meters and turn right across from Yitzhak Feniger Road and in front of a stone wall. Stand above the open trench with your back to the water tower (square structure on stilts) and facing the amphitheater.

At the beginning of the Mandate Period the British rulers of Palestine established a school for policemen in northern Jerusalem. Natural and burial caves on the adjacent height were utilized for storing great stocks of ammunition. Inevitably, the site became known as Ammunition Hill.

When the British left Palestine in mid-May of 1948 they turned some of their positions over to the Jews and some to the Arabs. Ammunition Hill was given to the Jews but was conquered by the Jordanian Legion soon afterward. Following the division of the city it became the Jordanians' northernmost border post.

The Jordanians turned Ammunition Hill into a highly fortified military position. Their fortifications were awesome, including tremendously well-protected bunkers, intricate communications trenches, heavy machine guns, and the best of the Jordanian Legion — a highly trained Bedouin company.

Hoping to keep the Israelis from reaching MOUNT SCOPUS in the event of another war, the Jordanians pointed their biggest guns in the direction from which they expected enemy tanks to attack — today's Eshkol Boulevard. Now a wide avenue surrounded by apartments, parks and shops, at the time it was a wilderness of rocky fields.

Picture things as they were prior to the Six-Day War. From 1948-1967 Jerusalem was split in the middle, with Mount Scopus just to the northeast an isolated Jewish enclave surrounded by enemies. Ammunition Hill belonged to Jordan, and bordered the Israeli Jerusalem neighborhood of Shmuel HaNavi a few blocks to the south. A shaky cease-fire between Israel and Jordan was often broken, sometimes by Jordanian artillery fire but more frequently when Arab snipers took pot shots at Jewish neighborhoods.

Tension increased between Israel and the surrounding Arab countries with the passing of years. In 1967 Egyptian forces massed in Sinai, screamed war slogans into well-publicized microphones and ordered the United Nations peacekeeping forces out of Gaza and the Sinai Peninsula. Worst of all, in mid-May President Gamal Abdel Nasser closed the Straits of Tiran to Israeli shipping, blocking access to Israel's southern port of Eilat and effectively declaring war. Egypt and Syria escalated their warmongering at the end of May and international diplomatic efforts to prevent an inevitable confrontation came to naught.

Israel had two choices. If taken by surprise and invaded by the Arabs, the tiny new country would suffer unspeakable losses and perhaps indeed be pushed into the sea as Nasser repeatedly predicted. Or- Israel could strike first and hope for the best. Israel opted for the second alternative. Preemptive strikes aimed at neutralizing both Egyptian and Syrian air capabilities commenced at dawn on June 5th and within a matter of hours the Arabs' air forces had crumbled.

Time and again Israel urged Jordan to stay out of the war, but diplomatic missives and direct messages were all to no avail. Jordan entered the fray on the first day of the Six-Day War. Not relying solely on diplomacy, Israeli's already-mobilized defense force reserves had been ordered to report for active duty. Many of the soldiers were university students; some were married, a few had already become fathers.

In the early evening of June 5, 1967, several reserve paratrooper units that had been preparing for a parachute drop into the Sinai Desert were brought, instead, to Jerusalem — and some of them sent to Ammunition Hill. Their assignment: to attack the Police Training School and Ammunition Hill and to take them at all cost.

The trench behind which you are standing was part of a well-fortified defensive system. Imagine that Jordanians are inside, ready for action. In front of you, as you face the amphitheater, is a large cement bunker that contained a huge machine gun with its turret pointed straight ahead.

To your right, stretching from the amphitheater all the way up the hill, is the fortified position known as the western trench. Inside, crack Bedouin troops were ready for the Israeli assault. The well-fortified central trench was on your left, on the other side of the stone wall. Today a garden, at the time it continued around and down the hill, all the way to the amphitheater.

Israeli intelligence concerning the layout and fortifications at the Police school and Ammunition Hill was sketchy at best. What made things worse was the time of day scheduled for the attack: the assault began at 2:30 in the morning when the sky was dark and the paratroopers charged with taking Ammunition Hill could barely see where they were going. It would have been hard enough to attack the hill using a map, but without one, in the darkness and under heavy fire, it seemed an almost impossible mission!

The first company of paratroopers was instructed to cut through three rows of barbed wire. Yet instead of the three perimeter fences that they anticipated, there were four. While improvising to cut this final, unexpected fourth obstacle, several of the men were hit.

Another company was ordered to take the main building of the Police Training School, located somewhere between and beyond the two buildings behind the amphitheater. You can see it later on if you stand on the amphitheater's highest step — it flies a blue United Nations Flag. After capturing the principal building they were to secure four additional structures closer to Ammunition Hill.

More paratroopers gathered together in the area of the restored elongated building behind the amphitheater. Three platoons were to take each of the three trenches (central, eastern, and western) and they started in your direction. *But the confusion! The fire! Units tried to connect with one another, cover for one another. They moved into the exposed area before you, the Triangle of Death.* Caught in fire coming from the machine gun in front of you, from the western trench and from the central trench along the side, they sustained heavy casualties. The Jordanians, however, were in excellent shape: you can see how the bunkers were built each a little higher than the next, offering cover to the bunker below.

Now walk down and stand inside the trench. Every few meters, but not at regular intervals, there were fortified positions. Each was different, so the advancing troops never knew what to expect. As you can see, the trench is narrow and only with difficulty could they try to carry out the plans they had perfected during maneuvers: throw grenades or fire until you run out of ammunition, then move to the side so the next armed soldier can continue.

The men advanced single file, with the lead soldier continually firing into the trench in front of him in order to surprise the enemy. When he reached a junction or a fork in the trench he would shoot, take a quick peek, then move back and report what he had seen. A commander would give the order and he would prepare, then throw, a grenade. While doing so the lead soldier would be shooting beyond him at any Jordanians who were advancing toward the Israeli troops. If the lead soldier was killed or wounded the next in line stepped over him, or on him, and continued forward … *It was dark, it was frightening, but still the soldiers proceeded on … fire came from in front of you, from on top of you, it was mayhem and bedlam, the noise of shots and explosions, a yellow flash and your best army buddy shot to death in front of your eyes … But still you advanced.*

Begin walking through the trench, going as far as the first intersection. It is called "wounded junction," as the injured were concentrated together here for medical attention. Here medic Yigal Arad saved lives as fast as he could and whenever he could, in one case putting a large rock under the arm of an injured soldier to stop the bleeding. Soldiers who woke up in the hospital would open their eyes and their first words would be: "did Yigal make it through?" (He did, but was killed in the Yom Kippur War six years later.)

You continue to push forward through the trench, here and there passing a fortified position and going as far as a V-shaped junction. If you want to walk like the soldiers did, keep your head down, *crouch, BEND DOWN!* Expose yourself and the Jordanians on top of the hill will be on you like a flash! Jordanian soldiers are advancing toward you as you run in their direction, you see the burst of fire, you retreat, then continue on … The noise, the glare, the dust and smoke, the strong smell of cordite — it goes on and on, it never lets up …

Officer Nir Nitzan in the western trench asked one of his gunners to climb out of the tunnel and offer the troops covering fire. The soldier, Eitan Naveh, "didn't hesitate for a moment" according to the song which immortalizes the Battle for Ammunition Hill. Furiously firing his machine gun, he provided the soldiers inside with the opportunity to move on another 30 meters before he was shot and killed.

At the V-shaped junction, take the left fork and you will come to a partially open space — the site on which the Large Bunker once stood. Inside was an enormous machine gun facing today's Ramot Eshkol neighborhood. Above this trench there was a cement ceiling and a highly fortified wall.

The Israeli army is proud of its commanders, who shout, "follow me" and advance ahead of their men. As a result of this ingrained policy, however, many of the officers were quickly taken out of action at Ammunition Hill. Private Yaki Hetz suddenly found himself first in line. His commander, Yoram

Names — and more names — are inscribed on stone plaques.

Eliashiv, had led the platoon slowly and systematically along the length of the trench and had served as a great example for his men. But Yoram had been shot and killed. Yaki felt as if he were all alone on the hill. His call for help brought two more privates — Yehuda Kendal and David Shalom — into the trench. As they were being fired upon from all directions Kendal climbed up and out of the trench to the left bank, then threw a grenade into the bunker from the slit that opened onto today's Ramot Eshkol. Theoretically, there should have been no one left alive in the large bunker, and the men prepared to pass through it and then move on.

At the last minute Yaki has a strange feeling, he fires into the bunker and ducks. Jordanian fire shoots out from inside the bunker. There are now two small Israeli forces on each side of the large bunker but they can't get past the Jordanian position to connect. Ofer Feniger appears on one side with a bag of explosives. Each time that the Jordanians fire from within the bunker they take a break to reload. During that short pause Ofer and Yaki throw explosives to David on the other side of the entrance. When 20 kilograms have piled up David activates the fuse and all run for cover. A loud explosion is heard, the wall and part of the ceiling collapse, and the men inside are buried among the ruins. Finally the way is clear. The Israelis hadn't had any idea of this position's strength: the bunker, used to store ammunition, consisted of a series of well-reinforced fortified rooms that were completely impenetrable by grenade attack or even bazooka shells.

Above the trench, to the right, there is a monument. **At the first chance you get, climb out of the trench and make your way up there.** Names — names and more names — are inscribed on stone plaques.

The last stage of the battle was perhaps the worst — collecting the wounded and counting up the bodies of those comrades who had died. In one company of about 90 soldiers, only seven men made it through the battle unharmed. One of the troops buried over a dozen Jordanians in a mass grave and wrote on top of it "Here are buried 17 Jordanian soldiers"; another Israeli soldier inserted the word "brave" …

Three days later Commander Yossi Yaffe gathered together those men that remained from the 66th Paratroop Battalion and asked each soldier to take a stone and place it on the ground. These stones form the base of the Ammunition Hill memorial. On the stone slate are the names of 36 men from the 66th Paratroop Battalion who fell in the battles for Jerusalem — most of them in battles for the Police Training School and at Ammunition Hill. Added later were the names of paratroopers killed in the Yom Kippur War, then in the Peace for Galilee War and now, sadly, the sons of men from the battalion who have died in action more recently.

Pass the monument. On your right is a hut that was left standing after the battle. Across from it protrudes the curved roof of the Ammunition Hill Museum that, as you can see, follows the same architectural lines as the cabin. **Walk around the hut and through the olive grove to reach the museum entrance, where you began your Ammunition Hill trek.**

The grove consists of over 180 trees planted in 1972 by the families of the men who fell in the battle for Jerusalem in the Six-Day War. They are here both as a memorial and as a symbol for peace. And, indeed, hopes for peace were realized with a long-sought and universally hailed agreement between Israel and Jordan in 1994. It was as a direct result of that peace that Suleiman Salam El Salita and his Israeli hosts stood together on Ammunition Hill not as foes — but as friends.

Hours:	**MUSEUM** [582-8442]: Sun.-Thurs., 8:00-17:00; Fri., 9:00-13:00; *the museum is wheelchair accessible* Audiovisual program available in English; **Entrance fee** **Excellent library with books on Jerusalem**: Open all day Sun.-Thurs.
Picnic Area:	Open 24 hours a day
Note:	Ammunition Hill has been free for many years and — except for the museum — open on Saturday. If that is the day you plan to visit, call during the week to find out if there has been any change in policy.
Restrooms:	at the site, *wheelchair accessible*

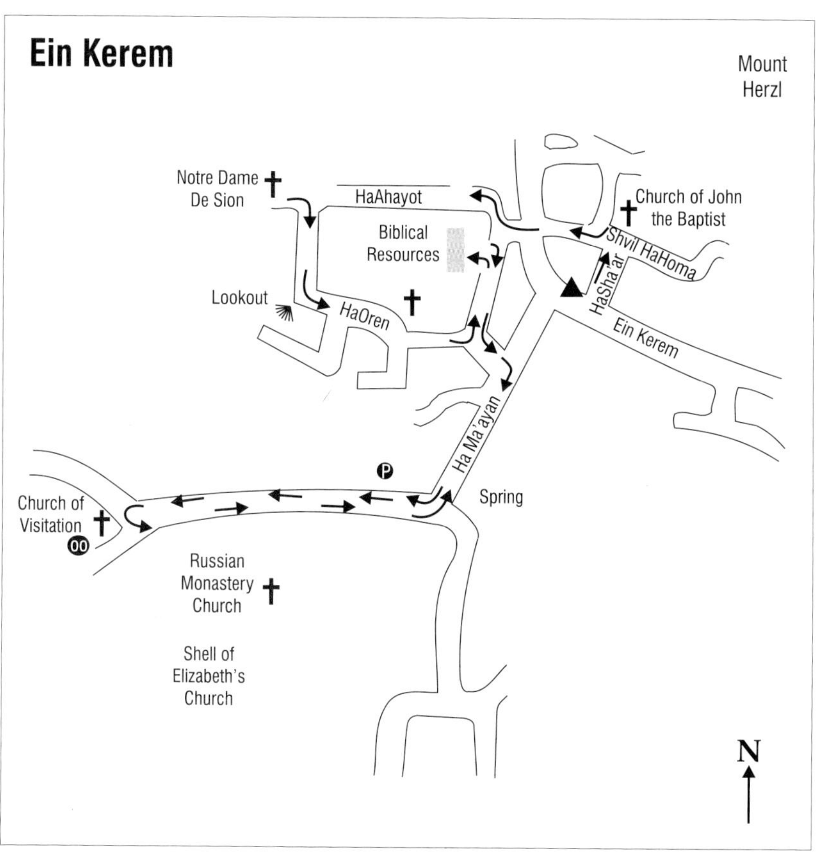

Ein Kerem
Mount Herzl
Notre Dame De Sion
HaAhayot
Church of John the Baptist
Biblical Resources
Shvil HaHoma
Lookout
HaOren
HaSha'ar
Ein Kerem
Ha Ma'ayan
Spring
Church of Visitation
Russian Monastery Church
Shell of Elizabeth's Church
N

Ein Kerem

- **Begin and end**: at the intersection of the following streets: HaMa'ayan, HaSha'ar and Ein Kerem
- **Take bus**: 17, 17A
- **Park your car**: along HaMa'ayan Street, Ein Kerem Street, or near the spring
- **Time frame**: 2 hours
- **Take note**: On Saturdays the neighborhood is jammed and the churches are closed to the public

As soon as the State of Israel was declared in May of 1948 a harried government began seeking housing for the multitude of immigrants pouring into the country. One December day at the end of that year, two trucks pulled into the deserted village of Ein Kerem on Jerusalem's southwestern border. Many of the passengers were men, women and children who had only recently moved to the brand-new State of Israel from Morocco and Iraq. The government had decided to settle these new arrivals in Ein Kerem.

But when they saw the sewage in the streets, realized that there was no water or electricity in the village, and got a look at the state of Ein Kerem's rundown houses, the immigrants balked — and with vigor. Loudly protesting the situation, they refused to descend from their vehicles.

Veteran settlers relate that the ensuing ruckus reached the ears of Elizabeth, a senior nun at the Russian convent located on a nearby slope. Dashing down to the corner where you are standing she is said to have shouted at the newcomers in Russian: "This is paradise, you ungrateful fools, you don't deserve this wonderful place. Get down! Get down! " *Someone* must have understood, because at least one of the trucks emptied its riders into the streets and families began moving into the unoccupied dwellings.

The other truck moved on, taking its passengers with it. And it's a safe bet that those who passed up the opportunity to live in Ein Kerem wish, today, that they hadn't! For Ein Kerem is quite definitely a paradise on earth. Blessed with wildflower-covered slopes, terraced agricultural land and captivating old-fashioned homes, it is an enchanting anachronism within a noisy, modern Jerusalem metropolis. Somehow, thank goodness, it has evaded the ravages of progress and continues to preserve a pastoral aura.

Guidebooks often identify Ein Kerem with the biblical village of Beit HaKerem. Although that view is disputed, Jews certainly lived in this ancient village during the Second Temple period. Indeed, according to Christian tradition, Ein Kerem is the Judean town in which John the Baptist was born.

The New Testament relates that a priest named Zechariah and his wife Elizabeth lived in the hill town of Judea. Well along in years, they were good and righteous people. But Elizabeth was barren, and they had no children.

One day, while Zechariah was burning incense in the inner sanctums of the Holy Temple, the angel Gabriel appeared. He told an astonished Zechariah that his wife would bear him a son whose name would be John. When Zechariah expressed doubts at this prophecy he was struck dumb by the angel.

A son was, indeed, born to Zechariah and Elizabeth. Relatives and neighbors joined the happy parents at the infant's circumcision and asked what the child's name would be. Zechariah's speech returned immediately after he wrote on a slate that the child would be called John. His ensuing words of praise eventually became incorporated into the famous prayer known as the *Benedictus*.

Young John wore camel-hair coats with leather belts and roved through forests and deserts with only animals for company. He subsisted on wild honey, locusts and flowing spring water. People who were drawn to John and to his ideas would often accompany him to the Jordan River, where they confessed their sins and immersed themselves in the waters to experience a physical and

Symbols cover the arched entrance to the church (p. 112).

spiritual cleansing. John's most famous baptism was, of course, the immersion of his cousin Jesus of Nazareth.

Your first stop is at the Church of St. John the Baptist. Ascend the steep alley called HaSha'ar to see a sign that reads "St. John Ba Harim" (St. John in the Mountains — the name by which the village was known in the Middle Ages). As you walk up, note that the decorative arched gateway holds two distinct symbols. On your right is the distinctive Jerusalem Cross, which was adopted by the Crusaders in the Middle Ages. On your left is the Franciscan symbol, dominated by two intertwined arms. The bare arm is that of Jesus, and the robed one belongs to St. Francis of Assisi.

In the middle of the 14th century, Franciscans began returning to the holy sites that the Crusaders had abandoned after losing Jerusalem to the Moslems. It was at that time that the Franciscans who lived in the Holy Land began to include the Jerusalem Cross as part of their symbol. You will find the complete emblem on each of four altars inside the church.

Pass through the gate and walk into the courtyard. Twenty-three tile plaques cover one of the walls (the 24th plaque is located around the corner). Each of them displays the *Benedictus,* recited daily during morning prayers.

A splendid wooden door opens into the church. Originally a Crusader sanctuary built above Byzantine ruins, the church was reconstructed by Franciscan monks in the 16th century. Restoration continued in 1674 with the aid of the Spanish royal family, whose royal coat-of-arms can be seen inside the church above the entrance.

The most revered site in the church is the grotto. Believed to be part of the home in which John the Baptist was born to Zechariah and Elizabeth and perhaps even the site of his birth, it was incorporated into the church's left apse. **You reach the crypt by walking through an elaborately adorned green and gold gate and descending a few marble steps.**

John the Baptist met with a terrible end. Herod Antipas, ruler of the Galilee after the death of his father Herod the Great, had married his half-brother's divorced wife Herodias. John roundly condemned the marriage as both illegal and immoral, so Herod Antipas arrested him and put him in prison.

On Herod Antipas' birthday his talented stepdaughter Salome danced at the festive celebrations. In return, and apparently after consulting with her mother Herodias, Salome asked for John's head on a platter. Although reportedly distressed, Antipas ordered his prisoner beheaded.

Walk around the church, then exit the complex and turn right into the first alley you see (called Shvil HaHoma). Cross the main road and continue to the end of the alley. When you see a blue sign telling you that you have

Ein Kerem homes are enchanting.

reached HaAhayot Road, turn right. Then follow the road around to the left. As you stroll along watch for fruit trees — including prickly pears (*sabras*, in Hebrew). You will also see Washingtonian palms and cypress trees.

The road leads you to Notre Dame de Sion, a convent run by an international community of Catholic nuns. Visitors are welcome to wander through the fabulous gardens and enjoy a breathtaking set of views. Marie Alphonse Ratisbonne, the apostate Jew who founded the convent, is buried here in the cemetery below the gardens.

Fondly called Father Mary by the nuns, Ratisbonne was born in France in 1814 into a wealthy and respected Jewish family. When he was a teenager, his older brother Theodore converted to the Catholic faith and became a priest. Relations between the two were strained.

Almost two decades later, engaged to be married and scheduled to head the family banking business, Ratisbonne took a trip to Italy. While visiting the Church of St. Andrea Delle Fratte in Rome he experienced a miraculous vision of Mary. This event was to change his life completely: he was baptized a Christian less than two weeks later. Taking on the additional first name of Marie, he became Marie Alphonse Ratisbonne. And, like his brother, he became a priest.

In 1850 Theodore founded an order called the Sisters of Zion (Notre Dame de Sion). A few years later Marie Alphonse traveled to Jerusalem, where he established a branch of the new order in the Old City. Then he bought land along the Via Dolorosa on which he erected a convent and an orphanage.

Next Ratisbonne opened a new convent in the Arab village of Ein Kerem. The nuns there took in orphaned girls whose parents had been massacred during inter-communal wars that raged in the Lebanese mountains. Later they built a school for young Arab women and taught them basic homemaking skills. The orphanage and school operated until the onset of Israel's War of Independence.

When the War of Independence broke out Ein Kerem's Arab inhabitants feared that Israeli troops would take over the village. Thus in July of 1948, soon after the army conquered nearby Mount Herzl, the vast majority of Ein Kerem's Arab residents abandoned their homes. The village remained empty until new immigrants arrived five months later.

Left with vacant dormitories, the Sisters of Zion began taking in lodgers of all religions. Many of them were new immigrants and students at the Hebrew University. Decades later the first guests continue to return, bringing their children and grandchildren to the convent rest house to bask in its serenity, peace, and beauty. The nuns will tell you that their aim — and what they believe to have been Father Mary's true intention — is to bring Christian and Jew closer together.

Take an enchanting walk to the cemetery. You will pass "Mary's House" — the humble dwelling in which Marie Alphonse Ratisbonne lived until his death in 1884. Stop in at the church, whose walls are decorated with pilasters. Then stroll through the gardens to savor a delightful mix of herbs, flowers and sculpted trees. The view from the gardens is marvelous, and there are plenty of tranquil corners for contemplation. Only the occasional lilt of a singing bird breaks the quiet.

Turn right when you exit the convent. You are on HaOren Street, which you follow to the end of the stone wall on your right. This is a good place to stop for a fantastic view of Ein Kerem. Below you is the Ein Kerem Valley, whose slopes are covered with the terraces typical of biblical agriculture.

But growing crops in the mountains is difficult, for when it rains the water flows along the surface to the valley below and takes with it a shallow layer of arable topsoil. Israelite farmers solved this problem by building man-made terraces along the slopes to create plots in which their crops would thrive.

On the slopes to your right stands the distinctive Hadassah Hospital, built in the 1950's to replace the modern medical facility on MOUNT SCOPUS. The earlier hospital was choked off by an Arab blockade during the War of Independence and was unreachable when Jerusalem was divided. Today there are two Hadassah Hospitals in Jerusalem: one in Ein Kerem, and the original hospital on Mount Scopus.

Look for the steeple topping the Church of the Visitation directly across from where you are standing. To the left of the church is the Gorny Convent, where the indomitable nun Elizabeth lived from 1913 until her death in 1978.

High up the mountain, above but inside the Gorny Convent, stands a large, unfinished building. A second Elizabeth, Russian Grand Duchess Elizabeth Fyodorovna, is believed to have initiated this uncompleted sanctuary. Wife of the Czar's brother Sergei and sister to the Czar's wife Alexandra, this Elizabeth was English and the granddaughter of Queen Victoria. Yet she adopted the Russian Orthodox religion when she married grand Duke Sergei. Thereafter most of her life was devoted to the Church and to charitable pursuits.

One of her projects was the Jerusalem Church of St. Mary Magdalene on the Mount of Olives. Although it was launched by her brother-in-law the Czar, this church became very much her own creation. It was Elizabeth who supervised the artwork, emphasizing a style from the 16th and 17th centuries.

The Ein Kerem church, however, was never finished. Construction was halted when World War I broke out in 1914 and it never resumed because the saintly Elizabeth was put to death. She was killed together with the last of the ruling Russian Romanovs after the Bolshevik revolution of 1917.

Bolsheviks executed the immediate royal family — and its servants — on the night of July 16, 1918. On the following day Elizabeth and others were thrust live down the shaft of an abandoned coal mine. Grenades were thrown down the shaft in a further attempt to finish off the aristocracy, but Elizabeth stayed alive long enough to rip off her clothing and bandage the wounds of her companions. It may have been her voice, singing hymns to comfort the others, which eventually led a passerby to the deserted mine. By the time he returned with help, however, everyone inside was dead. Two unexploded hand grenades were found next to Elizabeth's lifeless form.

Elizabeth's corpse was taken secretly to China and later transferred to the Mount of Olives. Elizabeth was buried in the Church of St. Mary Magdalene in 1921 and canonized in 1982.

Look for the red rafters of the Rosary Orphanage, located below and to the left of the Russian complex. You will pass it on your way to the Church of the Visitation. Above the orphanage and far to the left is the St. Vincent de Paul Hospice, where nuns provide tender, loving care for dozens of severely disabled children. You can easily identify it by the palm trees in its courtyard.

Now descend the continuation of HaOren Street. It winds along for a bit, past a Greek Orthodox church, then runs into HaAhayot Road. *You will be returning to this small junction.* **Turn left to visit Biblical Resources, an establishment that hosts an innovative illustration of terms mentioned in the Scriptures.**

Return to the junction of HaOren and HaAhayot, and continue your descent on HaOren. This takes you directly to the middle of HaMa'ayan Street. Turn right and walk to the end of the street. You will have reached a stone-encased spring topped by a minaret. Identified with a historic journey that Jesus' mother Mary made to Ein Kerem, this spot has long been known as the Virgin's Fountain or Mary's Spring. At one time the water here was considered the finest in the region. It is now heavily polluted and I strongly recommend against taking even the tiniest sip!

The New Testament tells us that Jesus' mother Mary and John's mother Elizabeth were cousins. One day Mary traveled from Nazareth to visit the pregnant Elizabeth. When they met *"Elizabeth was filled with the Holy Spirit … she exclaimed: 'Blessed are you among women, and blessed is the child you will bear!' …. And Mary said, "My soul glorifies the Lord …"* (Luke 1:39-46).

Ein Kerem retains a pastoral aura; the shell of Elizabeth's church stands in the foreground.

Mary stayed in Ein Kerem for several months and she and Elizabeth would undoubtedly have come here to draw water. Imagine the scene — two women of the Second Temple period, chatting as they fill their jugs and carry them away on their heads …

With the spring directly behind you, follow an asphalt path in the direction of a black iron gate. It belongs to the Rosary Sisters' Orphanage. Founded in 1880 by a Christian Arab from Ein Kerem, the Sisters of the Rosary is an order named for the circular string of beads with which Catholics recite a prayer called the Hail Mary (Ave Maria). Arab youngsters, some of them groups of siblings who have lost their parents under tragic circumstances and others from broken homes, grow up under the care of these Russian nuns. Washingtonian palms and brilliant bougainvilleas line your path as you walk below the orphanage.

From the path you have an excellent opportunity to observe the charming old houses of Ein Kerem. **Stop to do so, then continue up the steps (and ramp) that lead to the Visitation Church.**

The New Testament relates that in or around the year 4 B.C.E. Herod the Great was told that a new king of the Jews had been born in Bethlehem. Fully aware that the populace hated him with a passion, Herod decided to take quick steps to prevent a rival from ascending his throne. Like the biblical Pharaoh, and in what some have called the "massacre of the innocents," Herod is believed to have ordered the immediate death of all male babies aged two and under that lived near Bethlehem.

Ein Kerem is only a few kilometers from Bethlehem, and John the Baptist was just a toddler when Herod's soldiers came looking for infant boys. His mother Elizabeth heard the Roman soldiers approach. Grabbing John by the hand she ran with him to the woods. Legend has it that an angel suddenly appeared, opened a rock, and helped John's mother slip him quickly inside. John was allowed out only after all of the soldiers had left the area.

Small bronze statues of Elizabeth and Zechariah, John's mother and father, top the wrought-iron gate that leads to the Church of the Visitation. Elizabeth and Zechariah actually lived in the heart of Ein Kerem where the present Church of St. John the Baptist is located. But during the Crusader period the meeting between Mary and Elizabeth — the "Visitation" — was commemorated on a slope not far from their home that eventually became known as the couple's summer dwelling.

Early Christians had already built a shrine on this spot to commemorate the event in which John, as a toddler, had been safely hidden from Roman soldiers. A large piece of the rock that saved him is found within. It was carried here from the fields many centuries ago in order to save it from destruction: pilgrims kept hacking off little pieces to keep as sacred mementos. The Crusaders built a two-story church here and dedicated it to the Visitation.

This unusual contemporary church, consisting of both a lower and upper sanctuary, was designed by famous Italian architect Antonio Barluzzi. A genius who created several of Jerusalem's most inspiring houses of worship, he also built the city's magnificent Italian Hospital.

One side of the courtyard in front of the lower church offers visitors a small contemplative garden. The opposite wall is covered with diverse plaques, each trimmed with colored ceramic reliefs. Containing writings in over 40 different languages, the words are those with which Mary responded to Elizabeth's cry of joy. In some translations they begin "My soul doth magnify the Lord"; the hymn, chanted often during worship, is called the *Magnificat*.

In order to give pilgrims the feeling of having entered into a small summer lodge, Barluzzi paved the mosaic floor of the lower church in a woven, mat-like design and covered the ceiling with depictions of grapevines.

Since the upper church is closed to individual visitors, simply wait until you can join a group as it climbs up to the second-story sanctuary. Barluzzi was fond of China alabaster, visible on the windows you see as you ascend the steps to the church. On the left, outer wall of the church are remnants from the original Crusader structure.

A talented Italian artist named Vagharini painted most of the frescos in this sanctuary. Facing you as you enter the church is a picture of Mary and her young son Jesus attending a wedding in the Galilee village of Cana. This was the setting of Jesus' first miracle — the transformation of water into wine. To its left is a fresco of the Council at Ephesus in 431, at which it was decreed that Mary was the mother of God. Notice how everyone is bowing or kneeling in Mary's direction except for one man. Tour guides call this "Vagharini's joke," for the man is meant to be Barluzzi, complete with suit and bow tie and looking straight at you.

Leave the church and return to the junction where you first began your Ein Kerem journey. As you reach the intersection note the blocked-up wall of the house on the corner to your right. Before leaving Ein Kerem a few of the Arabs apparently buried gold inside the houses. When this road was widened in 1949, the house here was knocked down and two containers filled with gold were discovered — never to be seen again!

Hours: **NOTRE DAME DE SION CONVENT** [641-5738/643-0887]: Mon.-Thurs., 13:00-17:00; Fri., 9:00-17:00; Sat., 9:00-13:00; closed Sun.
VISITATION CHURCH [641-7291]: Sun.-Fri., 8:00-11:45; 14:30-17:00; closed Sat.
ST. JOHN'S CHURCH [641-3639]: Mon.-Fri., 8:00-12:00; 14:30-17:00; Sun., 9:00-12:00; 14:30-17:00; closed Sat.
BIBLICAL RESOURCES [643-0196]: Mon.-Sat., 8:30-17:30

Restrooms: At the Church of the Visitation

Jewish Quarter Synagogues and Historical Sites

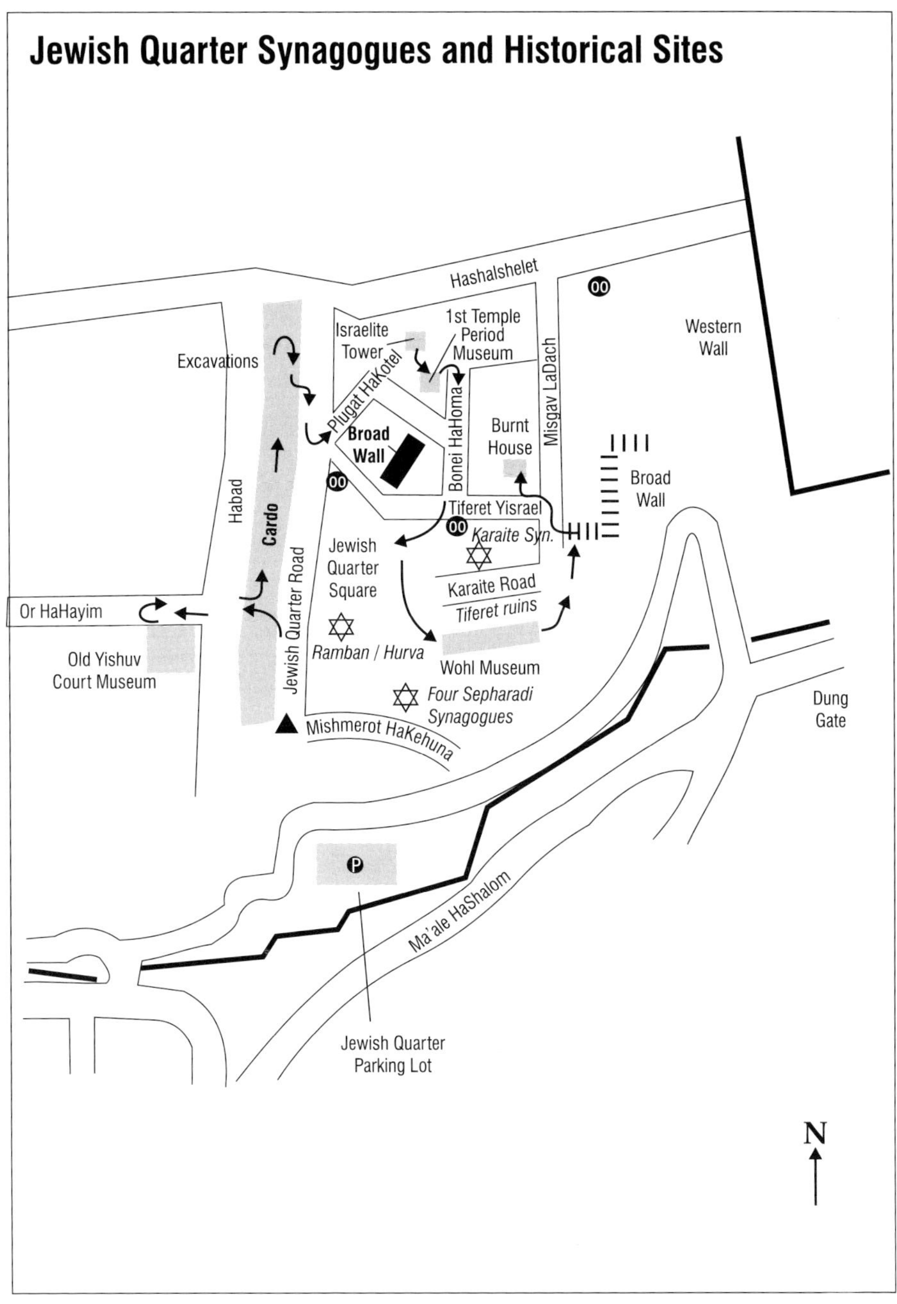

Jewish Quarter Synagogue Tour

- **Begin and end**: at the Four Sephardi (Sephardic) Synagogues near the Jewish Quarter parking lot
- **Take bus**: 38
- **Park your car**: in either the Jewish Quarter lot or in the Zion Gate lot
- **Time frame**: 1 hour
- **Take note**: Synagogues are closed to visitors on Fri. afternoon and Sat.

Rabbi Yochanan Ben-Zakkai was a renowned sage and a member of the Sanhedrin (the highest Jewish court and council in ancient times). Tradition holds that when Jerusalem was under Roman siege in the year 69, the rabbi's pupils hid him in a coffin and spirited him out of the Holy City. He then climbed out of the casket and walked — or was taken — into the tent of Roman commander Vespasian.

The two conducted an audience in which Rabbi Ben-Zakkai predicted that Vespasian would one day become emperor of Rome. And the rabbi made one small request: he asked that when his prediction came to pass Vespasian spare the small town of Yavne (Jabne) and its sages from destruction.

The prophecy came true within a few months, when Vespasian was indeed crowned emperor. One year later Jerusalem was conquered and totally destroyed amid scenes of wholesale slaughter but Ben-Zakkai was permitted to lead a group of his followers to Yavne southwest of Jerusalem. There he revived the Sanhedrin, built a Talmudic academy and turned Yavne into the new Jewish spiritual center.

Visit the sanctuary named after Rabbi Yochanan Ben-Zakkai on a fascinating walking tour of Jewish Quarter synagogues. Start your tour with a group of Sephardic synagogues adjacent to the Jewish Quarter parking lot at the beginning of Mishmerot HaKehuna Street. It is here that the Chief Rabbi of the Sephardic community has been anointed since 1893, and these sanctuaries have served as the spiritual, educational and financial center for Sephardic Jews for several hundred years.

The entire Sephardic complex you are going to visit was constructed below street level, as Moslem authorities didn't permit Jewish houses of worship to be higher than their own. **Look for a sign on the wall in big black letters that reads: Four Sephardi Synagogues — and walk in.**

While the first of the sanctuaries you are going to see was established in the 16th century, more were added in later years. By the 18th century there were four different houses of prayer here, permitting Jews of differing origin and slightly dissimilar shades of liturgy to pray in the same building.

In earlier times the synagogue complex contained small nooks used for *geniza* — the storing of flawed scrolls and prayer books. It is said that once a year nearly three dozen men would march in a festive procession to the Mount of Olives and bury these sacred texts.

Inside the Ben-Zakkai Synagogue.

Walk into the complex. The largest and fanciest of the four chambers you will be seeing is the **Yochanan Ben-Zakkai Synagogue** on which site, according to tradition, the revered rabbi taught Bible. Look up: near the very high ceiling there is a shelf containing a jug of oil and a shofar. Some believe that these are reserved for the sole use of the prophet Elijah: he will blow the shofar to announce the coming of the Messiah and light the oil lamps of the *Menorah* in a newly rebuilt Temple.

Go through to the Elijah Synagogue via the door at the back of the sanctuary. Named for the famous biblical prophet, this innermost room is also the oldest.

Of all the stories describing how this synagogue got its name, my favorite is the one about the sad day when only nine Jews showed up for prayers (services can't start without ten). Suddenly a stranger appeared and the worshippers happily began to pray. Immediately after the service the stranger vanished. It was obvious to the others that the tenth addition had been Elijah the Prophet — who saves the day on all kinds of different occasions.

Descend a few steps to a candle-lit cave and look for a large chair named for Elijah. This is where eight-day-old infants have traditionally sat on their godfathers' laps while being circumcised. The current chair is a replica; the original was stolen around the time of the War of Independence.

The door to the right of the ark will take you through to the Middle Synagogue or Kahal Zion, the third and smallest place of worship. On the wall are framed computer-produced memorials. These take the place of the stone memorials that are typically found on synagogue walls and which were destroyed by the Jordanians during and after the War of Independence. Some of the broken memorials can be found in an intriguing museum below the sanctuary.

Kahal Zion's wooden ark was originally situated at the Torat Chaim Synagogue in the Moslem Quarter. During Arab riots in 1920 the ark was heavily damaged and the Ten Commandments on its facade were smashed. Look for what remains of the stone tablets behind two glass walls. Aryeh Grayewsky, who had been cantor at Torat Chaim, brought the ark and tablets to the Middle Synagogue.

If you see anything strange about the crown atop the ark, that is because there has never been another one like it! This crown was fashioned by an Arab craftsman in the Negev, who found a cannon shell and tried to shape it into a flower. Displeased with the result, he sold it to a shop and Grayewsky bought it and placed it here.

You will find the tiny museum of great interest, as it displays photographs taken during the turbulent years at the beginning and middle of the 20th century. Eric Matsson, a member of Jerusalem's picturesque AMERICAN COLONY, shot the photos rimmed in black.

Built by immigrant Jews from Istanbul and today used by Jews from Kurdistan as well, the fourth chamber is called the **Istambuli Synagogue**. This 18th-century sanctuary boasts an extraordinary pulpit with exquisite ornamentation; its gold-plated wooden ark has been lovingly restored.

Because the local authorities refused to allow reconstruction or even repairs on the synagogue over the years, all of the rooms were in disastrous physical condition by the beginning of the 19th century. In the mid 1830's, however, benevolent Egyptian ruler Muhammad Ali granted permission for a complete overhaul. Not only were the roofs repaired but the Middle Synagogue — until that time only an open yard — was completely covered.

In 1948 this place of worship was a last refuge for the Jews of the Old City, who were forced to surrender when the soldiers of the Arab Legion closed in on them. Nineteen years later, when Jewish soldiers re-entered the synagogue complex, they found that the Jordanians had turned the historic house of worship into a stable! Since that time the synagogue has been completely restored. The chambers are open to the public both for viewing and for prayers.

Exit the complex and follow Mishmerot HaKehuna Street until you pass through a short arched passage. Directly in front of you are remains of the Hurva Synagogue as well as one beautifully reconstructed arch from that once lofty, proud sanctuary.

Climb the steps for a better look, and peer down into the courtyard below. The original synagogue that stood on this site was built in 1705 by followers of Rabbi Yehuda HaHasid. Five years earlier, the rabbi and his disciples had come to Jerusalem from eastern Europe to hasten the coming of the Messiah. They bought land for an Ashkenazic sanctuary and began its construction.

Rabbi Yehuda HaHasid died soon after immigrating to the Holy Land. Money was scarce and the Jews borrowed heavily from the local populace. The Jewish community was unable to return their debts and, 20 years later, Moslem rioters demolished the synagogue.

In 1836 a small place of Ashkenazic worship called Menachem Zion was built at the site and a house of study, Sha'arei Zion was added in 1856. But the very large center for Ashkenazic Jews that would stand here eventually was completed only in 1864, with the help of the prosperous and philanthropic Rothschild family. The synagogue was called Beit Ya'akov, after the Baron James (Ya'akov in Hebrew) de Rothschild. It had another name as well: the Hurva (or "Ruin") of Rabbi Yehuda HaHasid.

The highest structure in the Jewish Quarter, Beit Ya'akov was a magnificent edifice with lovely interior wall decorations and a beautiful Holy Ark from Russia. When the Jewish Quarter fell in 1948 the Jordanians blew up this splendid house of worship and ironically, like its namesake, it was reduced to a pile of rubble. The famous arch you see above you has become a symbol of the Jewish Quarter's former glory.

Middle Synagogue (above) and reconstructed Hurva arch.

Retrace your steps and descend the stairs. Your next stop is the Ramban Synagogue, located directly below the lookout platform on which you were standing. Established in 1267, this was the very first synagogue to be built in the Jewish Quarter. Its founder was a well-known Spanish biblical commentator, Rabbi Moshe Ben-Nahman (1194-1270). His name is abbreviated in Hebrew as the famous acronym: the Ramban.

Rabbi Moshe Ben-Nahman immigrated to the land of Israel after participating in a debate on religion with the royalty of Spain. Having won the debate, he was then forced to leave the country!

Spain's loss was Israel's gain. Rabbi Ben-Nahman wasted no time in building a synagogue, utilizing marble pillars and a lovely dome from an abandoned edifice in its construction. Since the synagogue was a religious center for all of the Jewish groups in the city, the Jewish Quarter developed around it.

In the 15th century a house next to the synagogue became Moslem property and a mosque was built at the site. You can see the mosque today, rising above Jewish Quarter Square. Late in the next century Jews were forbidden to worship in the synagogue; Moslems took over the building and used it as a storeroom for the neighboring mosque.

The beautiful interior of the synagogue, reconstructed after the reunification of Jerusalem and returned to use after almost four centuries of neglect, contains one of its former columns. The pillar bears the Hebrew inscription "Avraham, Yitzhak, Ya'akov" (Abraham, Isaac and Jacob).

Two more houses of prayer, Tiferet Israel and the Karaite Synagogue are located on Karaim Road past the Jewish Quarter Square. Completed in 1872, Tiferet Yisrael was three stories high and its dome was one of the tallest spots in the Old City.

Tiferet Yisrael was built by followers of a religious movement founded in the 18th century. At that time Judaism was sometimes considered the sole

Before the War of Independence Tiferet Yisrael boasted one of the tallest domes in the Old City.

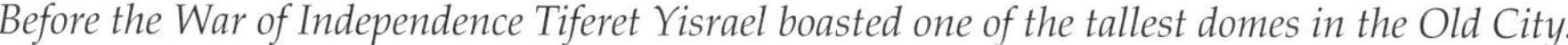

domain of the learned Jew, of scholars and community leaders who looked down at poverty-stricken common folk. The new movement, called Hasidism, gave simple Jews hope and dignity by making Judaism accessible and attractive to all. It taught that even an ignorant person could find grace in the eyes of God if he had a pure heart and prayed with devotion. And it introduced the concept of serving the Lord with joy and enthusiasm.

The synagogue was apparently named in honor of the father of the Hasidic movement, Rabbi Yisrael Baal Shem Tov. But it is commonly known as the Nissan Bek Synagogue because the famous Jerusalem sage Rabbi Nissan Bek was instrumental in its construction.

In 1948 Tiferet Yisrael became an important military position and lookout point for Jewish defenders, and the battle over the building led to its destruction. Already badly damaged by heavy shelling, Tiferet Yisrael was completely demolished by Jordanian sappers in the days following the capitulation of the Jewish Quarter. Dome and walls collapsed and covered the building's foundations. When the rubble was cleared away after the Six-Day War, a lower floor containing a *mikvah* (ritual bath) and an ornate upper entrance were uncovered.

Across the street from the Tiferet Yisrael ruins stands a house of worship built nearly a thousand years ago by Karaite Jews- the oldest synagogue in Jerusalem. While it appears to be located underground, it was actually built at street level — the height of which has changed drastically over the centuries.

Like other Hebrews the Karaites made the exodus with Moses, wandered in the desert for 40 years and received the Torah at Sinai. But in the 8th century the Karaites felt that, unlike other Jews, they could no longer accept post-scriptural interpretations of the Bible that changed the message of God's law. It was at this time that their mentor, Anan Ben-David, bestowed upon them the name of "Kara'im." The name stems from the Hebrew word for Scriptures and emphasizes the sect's firm belief in the written law.

Karaites take the Bible quite literally. Thus, in Karaite doctrine, Jewish holidays are celebrated on their true dates as set forth in the Good Book and not according to later decisions which made the timing more convenient. Jewish dietary laws are strictly observed, but interpreted differently and more literally than in other Jewish sects; so are strictures concerning female impurity, which follow the biblical commands.

Karaite customs — and even their synagogues — differ from those to which we have become accustomed after millennia of rabbinical interpretation. Thus rugs cover the floors of a Karaite synagogue, permitting worshippers to kneel and bow to the Lord as commanded in the Bible.

Worshippers remove their shoes, which are impure, before entering the synagogue. Karaite literature notes that this custom was traditional in Jewish communities in many parts of the world: India, for instance, Yemen, and Iran.

Although the Karaites prospered and multiplied until the Crusader era, today they number only in the tens of thousands. Most Karaites live in Israel, and the majority of these reside in Ramle, Ashdod and Beer Sheva. In Jerusalem there are several dozen Karaite families.

The Jerusalem sanctuary was slightly damaged during the War of Independence in 1948. It was completely renovated by Israel's Karaite community in 1977 and re-opened for prayer in 1981. If you ring the bell, you will be given a key to the interesting museum through which you view the synagogue.

By now you might feel the need for some refreshment. Walk back along Karaim Street and stop along Jewish Quarter Square for a cold drink. Opposite the Hurva arch, follow Mishmerot HaKehuna Street back to the parking lot.

Hours: **FOUR SEPHARDI (SEPHARDIC) SYNAGOGUES** [628-0592]: Sun., Mon., Wed., Thurs., 9:30-16:00; Tue., Fri., 9:30-12:30; **Entrance fee**
KARAITE SYNAGOGUE: daily except Sat. and religious holidays

Restrooms: Plugat HaKotel Road, near the Broad Wall; opposite the Burnt House near the top of the Rabbi Yehuda HaLevi Ascent

Jewish Quarter Historical Sites

- **Begin and end**: at the Cardo on Jewish Quarter Road
- **Take bus**: 38
- **Park your car**: in the Jewish Quarter parking lot
- **Time frame**: 4-5 hours
- **Take note**: All of the museums are closed Friday afternoon and Saturday

---

Busily preparing a chapter on the Jewish Quarter one mild winter's day, I paused for a moment to watch grownups and youngsters milling about in its central square. Although familiar with the Jewish Quarter's turbulent history, I found it hard to reconcile its former devastation with the tranquility of the moment. Incredible as it seems, the Jews have persevered, multiplied and prospered.

Begin your walk on Jewish Quarter Road overlooking the open section of the Cardo. Ascend the steps to your right and continue up HaHayim Road until you reach the Old Yishuv Court Museum on your left — your first stop.

With the passage of time, fewer and fewer people remember the Jewish Quarter as it was before the War of Independence. Old Yishuv Court is the house in which a Jewish family lived from 1812 until the Jewish Quarter surrendered to Jordanian soldiers in 1948. Although much of the building was destroyed by the Jordanians, the site has been restored and should help keep

Jewish Quarter Square.

The Cardo was built nearly 2,000 years ago.

memories alive. It gives visitors some idea of what life was like here during the 19th and early 20th centuries.

Now return to the Cardo, and gaze down onto the ancient street. You are going back almost two millennia — to the Roman-Byzantine period.

In the year 132, 62 years after the Great Revolt against the Romans and the destruction of the Second Temple, the flames of Jewish rebellion were fanned once again as Emperor Hadrian banned circumcision and reneged on a promise to let the Jews rebuild their sacred Temple. His decision to dedicate a shrine to Jupiter and to remake Jerusalem into a heathen Roman city only worsened a situation already seething with resentment.

That's when a powerful and charismatic figure appeared on the scene — Simeon Ben-Kosiba (or Kosba). You may know him as the legendary Shimon Bar-Kochba, Son of the Star, a name bestowed upon him by the great sage Rabbi Akiva. The appellation originated in the prophecy "*… a star will come out of Jacob …*" (Numbers 24:17). The revered rabbi, believing Bar-Kochba to be the Messiah, offered the fearless warrior spiritual support when he led the Jewish people into combat against the mighty Roman armies.

Wild tales and fantastic legends sprang up about the heroic, impetuous and autocratic messianic warrior. It was said that Bar-Kochba breathed fire, could throw catapult stones back at his aggressors and would test his volunteers' mettle by having them chop off one of their fingers. And, in the beginning, his relatively small group of warriors soundly trounced the mighty Roman army.

Emperor Hadrian finally became alarmed enough by Jewish success to bring seasoned commander General Julius Severus back from Britain and send him to the land of Israel. Severus decided to refrain from frontal battle and to slowly crumble Jewish resistance by gradually wearing the Jews down.

His strategy worked and the Romans began to get the upper hand — retaking villages, cities and forts. Jews took shelter in underground tunnels that they had prepared at the beginning of the war. The entrances were so narrow that Roman soldiers wearing unwieldy armor and bearing clumsy weapons had quite a struggle negotiating the narrow and winding labyrinths.

However after the Romans discovered the caves they stuffed brushwood into ventilation shafts, piled on green leaves and then set it all on fire. Once the men, women and children living in the caves had been smoked out they were systematically massacred by the Romans.

In the year 135 the Romans placed the fortified city of Betar under siege. Traitors may have revealed Betar's secret passages to the enemy for Roman legions managed to infiltrate into the city. Betar is believed to have fallen on the ninth of the Jewish month of Av, traditionally the same day on which the First and Second Temples were destroyed. The defeat followed a bloody battle in which Bar-Kochba perished along with his men. Finally the war was over, but the three-year revolt had taken a devastating toll. Fifty fortified towns and almost a thousand villages had been leveled to the ground; over half a million Jewish lives were lost and the Jews were banished from Jerusalem.

Following his victory Hadrian began to build a pagan town atop the ruins of the Holy City of Jerusalem. He regally bestowed upon it his very own middle name — Aelius. Thus for the next 200 years, until Constantine established Christianity as the official religion of the Roman Empire and changed the name back, Jerusalem was called Aelia Capitolina. Israel became known as Palaestina.

At the heart of many Roman cities was a bustling avenue lined with pillars known as the Cardo. Jerusalem's Cardo was 22 meters wide with columns on both sides. It stretched from Damascus Gate all the way south to Mount Zion. The Roman Cardo was improved upon and extended during the Byzantine period, a time during which Christian pilgrims swarmed into the city.

Walk down to the partially reconstructed Cardo and along the ancient street into the first covered area. On the wall is a copy of a detailed mosaic map of Jerusalem as it looked in the Byzantine era. Discovered in 1884, the original decorated the floor of a church in the Jordanian city of Madeba and for this reason is known worldwide as the Madeba Map. Not only does it depict the churches of Jerusalem and the Cardo, but it also shows a pillar at Damascus gate. Indeed, excavations have confirmed that a pillar stood at the gate, which at the time served as a main entrance to the city. When the Moslems conquered Jerusalem in the 7th century, they called Damascus Gate Bab El Amud, or Gate of the Pillar.

Continue on through the Cardo, lined with beautiful Jewish shops. As you near its end, before the entrance to the Arab market, look left to see excavations. They include parts of Hasmonean (Maccabee) walls which preceded the Roman conquest, as well as even older Israelite remains of a wall from the First Temple period. Note how they relate to the level of the Cardo.

Now backtrack a bit, to take the nearest exit out of the Cardo to the left. You are now on Jewish Quarter Road. Turn right and then left onto Plugat HaKotel Road.

You should now be standing opposite an enormous ancient wall. After the Six-Day War, when Israeli authorities decided to restore the Jewish Quarter, bulldozers were constantly turning up incredible archeological finds and the decision was made to leave almost everything *in situ*. Some of these finds — like the Broad Wall — were left uncovered; others were incorporated into the basements of structures in the Jewish Quarter and are generally accessible to the public for a fee.

King Hezekiah ordered construction of the wall you are facing at the end of the 8th century B.C.E., at a time when Jerusalem was in danger of being overrun by the Assyrians. *"Then he worked hard repairing all the broken sections of the wall and building towers on it. He built another wall outside that one and reinforced the supporting terraces of the City of David. He also made large numbers of weapons and shields"* (2 Chronicles 32:5).

Although the Assyrians destroyed most of the kingdom of Judah, they were defeated in Jerusalem. The Bible tells us that the Lord *"sent an angel, who annihilated all the fighting men and the leaders and officers in the camp of the Assyrian king. So he withdrew to his own land in disgrace. And when he went into the temple of his god, some of his sons cut him down with the sword"* (2 Chronicles 32:21).

About 200 years later, King Zedekiah added towers to the city's defenses. One of them is called the Israelite Tower, and is on view nearby. To see it, you will descend 13 meters, to what was the deepest dig in the Jewish Quarter. **Walk left and follow signs to the "Israelite Tower" to examine this ancient fortification.**

After leaving the tower, cross the street to visit the First Temple Period Museum where a topographical model of Jerusalem offers an illuminating glimpse of what the Holy City was like nearly 3,000 years ago. A 30-minute audio-visual presentation, which includes the use of 3-dimensional glasses, utilizes the model and its movable parts to make that ancient era come to life.

In addition to the presentation, visitors can enjoy the delightful permanent exhibits. These include the jewelry of a woman of the times — who was probably Jewish. What does it say about jewelry in the Bible? *"The Lord says, 'The women of Zion are haughty, walking along with outstretched necks, flirting with their eyes, tripping along with mincing steps, with ornaments jingling on their ankles. Therefore the Lord will bring sores on the heads of the women of Zion; the Lord will make their scalps bald'"* (Isaiah 3:16-17).

And if your daughter has rings in her nose, it may make you feel better to learn that her ancestors wore them in the same manner. Isaiah continues: *"In that day the Lord will snatch away their finery: the bangles and headbands … the earrings and bracelets … the headdresses and ankle chains … the perfume bottles and charms, And the signet rings and nose rings"* (Isaiah 3:18-21).

The Broad Wall was constructed by King Hezekiah just before the Assyrian invasion.

Among other features of the museum are two models: a hands-on First Temple Period house that illustrates beautifully how people lived during that era, and a model of a burial cave. Look for an especially absorbing exhibit that demonstrates the development of the Hebrew alphabet. If you make arrangements in advance museum staff will provide your offspring with educational activities to help them understand how the Hebrew language came about.

During the 8th century B.C.E., Assyrian King Sennacherib lay siege to Jerusalem in an attempt to conquer the Judean capital. Fortunately, however, King Hezekiah had anticipated this move and Sennacherib failed to conquer the city. Another exhibition offers a fascinating look at this significant period in Jewish history, and lets you explore King Hezekiah's well-thought-out preparations for the Assyrian siege. Special feature: a dry walk through "Hezekiah's Tunnel." (For the wet version see p. 152 in DAVID'S CITY.)

Next stop is the Wohl Museum — also known as the Herodian Quarter or Herodian Mansions. This startling museum offers an in-depth look at daily life during the period before the destruction of the Second Temple. Exhibiting archeological remains mainly from that era, Wohl contains the ruins of six houses that were part of a larger neighborhood. All of them are elegant but the one called "the Mansion" is unusually elaborate.

To get there, exit the First Temple Period Museum and turn right. When you come to a wall (Bonei HaHoma Road) turn right again. This leads you to the main Jewish Quarter Square. On one of the buildings on the left-hand side of the square you will see a sign pointing to the Wohl Archeological Museum. When you pay your entrance fee, make sure you get a combination ticket that includes the Burnt House as well (the last stop on this tour).

This fabulous museum displays colored mosaic floors decorated with geometric shapes, original ritual baths in their entirety, pottery, tools and wall frescoes. Remains of burning beams that fell to the ground provide concrete evidence of the fire that destroyed these homes. Everything on display looks either exactly as it did when discovered, or has been reconstructed consistent with remains found on the site.

Note the columns with intricate capitals, parts of a frieze and a replica of a drawing by a long-ago artist who may actually have seen the original *Menorah* when it stood in the Temple. These were most probably the houses of Jewish priests belonging to the sect known as the Sadducees, who were characterized by their strict observance of laws concerning ritual purity. This may be why there is such a profusion of ritual baths. The Sadducees belonged to the affluent upper class, which explains the houses' lavish interior design and decor. The largest mansion may even have belonged to the High Priest himself!

Exit the Herodian Mansions and ascend to the top of the stairs. Then continue a few dozen meters further, walking under a series of arches to reach the Burnt House (on your right.) You have reached a second private residence that has been turned into a famous museum.

In this house dwelled a family by the name of Kathros. Apparently they were less than righteous, for it says in the Talmud *"Woe is me because of the house of Kathros ... for they are the high priests, their sons are the Temple treasurers, their sons-in-law hold powerful positions, and their servants hit people with their sticks"* (Talmud, Pesachim 57a). At the time there were two major opposing religious groups in Jerusalem, the learned Pharisees and the rich and aristocratic Sadducees. This was a Sadducee house and perhaps even was the home described in the Talmud. It may have contained an incense factory whose products were used in the Temple. Among the other treasures recovered from the Burnt House were a mold for making coins, some nails, and a drainage canal.

But the most dramatic finds may send a shiver up your spine. Discovered among the ashes were bones from the hand of a 17-year-old girl who died when the Romans set her house on fire. No other physical remains from the Jerusalem population have ever been discovered from this period and they are a somber reminder of the travails of Jerusalem's Jews.

Emerging from the museum turn right and go back up through the Jewish Quarter to the Cardo. If you crave sustenance, stop at one of a number of little cafes. You can watch as people in the streets fulfill the biblical prophecy: *"This is what the Lord Almighty says: 'Once again men and women of ripe old age will sit in the streets of Jerusalem, each with cane in hand because of his age. The city streets will be filled with boys and girls playing there'"* (Zechariah 8:4-5).

Hours:	**OLD YISHUV COURT** [628-4636]: Sun.-Thurs., 9:00-14:00; closed Friday; **Entrance fee** **ISRAELITE TOWER** [628-2005]: Sun.-Thurs., 9:00-17:00; Fri. 9:00-13:00; **Entrance fee** **FIRST TEMPLE PERIOD MUSEUM** [628-6288]: Sun.-Thurs., 9:00-16:00, Fri., 9:00-13:00; You need to call in advance to let the museum know what time you will want to see an English-language program; **Entrance fee** **WOHL ARCHEOLOGICAL MUSEUM (HERODIAN MANSIONS)** [628-3448]: Sun.-Thurs., 9:00-16:30; Fri., 9:00-12:30; **Entrance fee** **BURNT HOUSE** [628-7211]: Sun.-Thurs., 9:00-16:30; Fri., 9:00-12:30; **Entrance fee** (buy ticket at the Herodian Mansions)
Restrooms:	Plugat HaKotel Road near the Broad Wall; and just off Misgav LaDach Street, opposite the top of Ma'alot Yehuda HaLevi

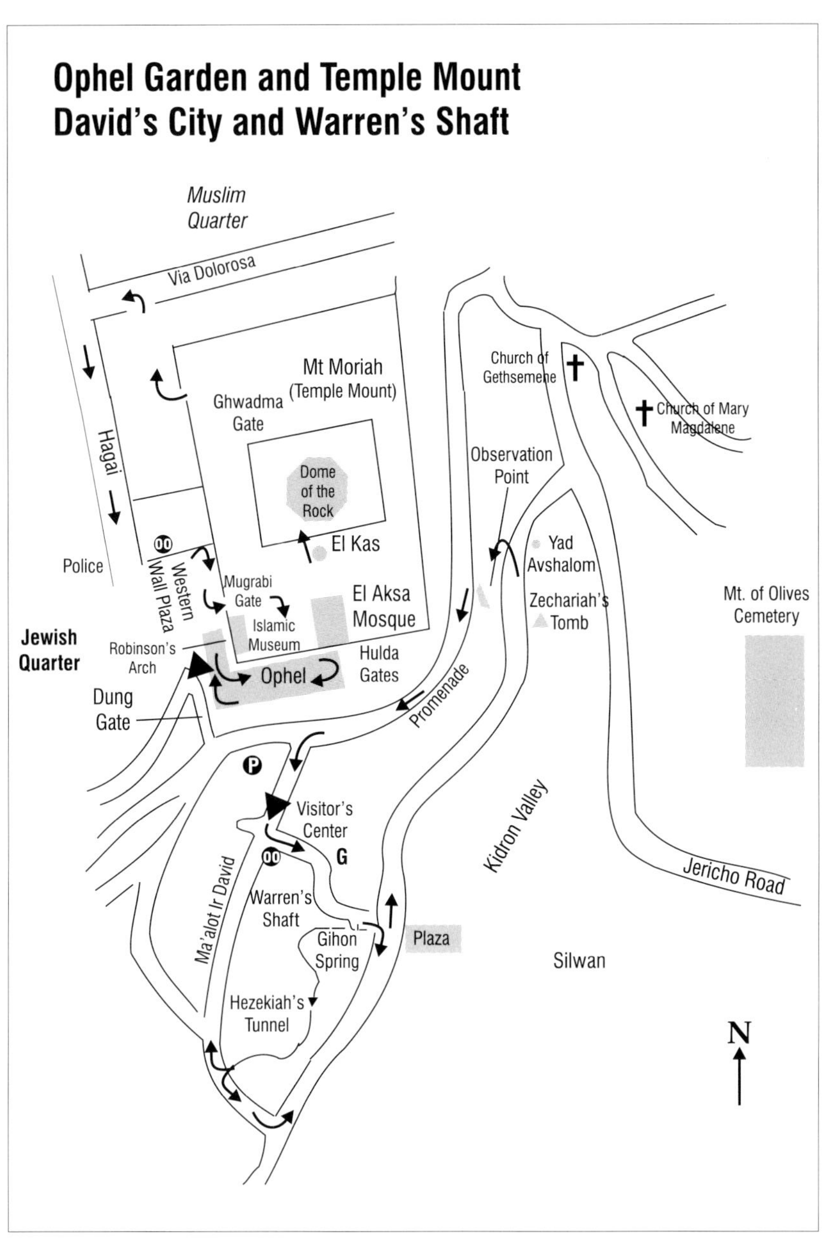

Ophel Garden and Temple Mount
David's City and Warren's Shaft
Muslim
Quarter
Via Dolorosa
Mt Moriah
(Temple Mount)
Ghwadma
Gate
Hagai
Dome
of the
Rock
El Kas
Police
Western
Wall Plaza
Mugrabi
Gate
Islamic
Museum
El Aksa
Mosque
Jewish
Quarter
Robinson's
Arch
Ophel
Hulda
Gates
Dung
Gate
Promenade
Church of
Gethsemene
Church of Mary
Magdalene
Observation
Point
Yad
Avshalom
Zechariah's
Tomb
Mt. of Olives
Cemetery
Kidron Valley
Jericho Road
P
Visitor's
Center
G
Ma'alot Ir David
Warren's
Shaft
Gihon
Spring
Plaza
Silwan
Hezekiah's
Tunnel
N

Ophel Gardens and Temple Mount

- **Begin and end**: next to Dung Gate, at the Ophel Gardens
- **Take bus**: 1, 2
- **Park your car**: on the street or in the Givati parking lot
- **Time frame**: 3-4 hours
- **Take note**: It may help you to visualize the ancient Temple Mount if you visit the SECOND TEMPLE MODEL in western Jerusalem before you take this walk.

"Three times a year all your men must appear before the Lord your God at the place he will choose: at the Feast of Unleavened Bread, the Feast of Weeks and the Feast of Tabernacles. No man should appear before the Lord empty-handed: Each of you must bring a gift in proportion to the way the Lord your God has blessed you" (Deuteronomy 16:16-17).

In ancient times a Jewish pilgrim carrying out this biblical command would set out from his village by foot or by donkey, by horse or by camel, each according to his means. At every new town or city other travelers would join the procession, eventually converging into large convoys which often journeyed for weeks on end. Despite the hardships of the long expedition and the dangers that they faced, these pilgrims were joyously united in a common purpose and fairly bursting with anticipation. Soon — very soon — they would reach the Holy Temple in Jerusalem!

During its 3,000-year history Jerusalem has been home to two magnificent Jewish Temples. Erected by Solomon in the 10th century B.C.E., the First Temple was destroyed by Babylonian King Nebuchadnezzar in the year 586 B.C.E. A few decades later some of the Jews who had been exiled to Babylon were permitted to return to the Holy City, where they built a modest Second Temple.

Around 20 B.C.E. King Herod began what would become the most memorable of his colossal building projects: the renovation, expansion and glorification of the Temple. When construction was complete the Temple Mount contained spacious courtyards, a fabulous royal portico and lovely colonnaded walkways. At the center of the complex, crowning the Mount, sat the magnificent Temple.

To fully understand the grandeur that was Jerusalem you can begin at the Ophel Gardens excavations. Mentioned by name several times in the Bible, Ophel refers to the area between the Temple Mount and the CITY OF DAVID across the road to the south.

Toppled stones — mute testimony to the Jewish tragedy (p. 138).

Enter the Ophel complex. Then descend to the base of the huge wall in front of you, so that you are standing next to the corner of the western and southern walls which surround the Temple Mount. You may want to sit on the ledge located a few meters across from the wall so you can examine it at your leisure. The bottom half of the wall dates back to King Herod, who constructed it to support his expansion of the Temple complex. A whopping 485 meters in length, it includes a small section commonly known as the Western or Wailing Wall which attracts worshippers and tourists from all over the world.

Two thousand years ago the stones at your feet were part of a busy street. Here stood the lower Jerusalem market, in which jostling crowds bargained furiously with the merchants who offered their wares. To the newcomers the air seemed charged with excitement and was full of exotic fragrances.

Shops were located on both sides of the lower market road. If you were a pilgrim you could buy anything you needed right here: souvenirs, silver amulets, animals for the sacrifice and provisions to take with you when you retired to your tent for the night. Did you bring the wrong kind of money? Not to worry: you could have found plenty of moneychangers happy to convert your currency into the coin of the land.

Examine the stones that make up the retaining wall. The laborers who put these immense blocks in place utilized engineering know-how perhaps even superior to that we have today. The smallest stone weighs a couple of tons, about the average weight of an elephant. And the heaviest — which you will see when you walk through the Western Wall Tunnels — has been calculated at the mind-boggling weight of 570 tons!

It is easy to identify Herodian masonry, for on each chiseled stone there is a distinctive recessed margin. The heavy blocks were so precisely carved that no mortar was necessary in construction and there is, indeed, none visible between the stones. Herodian workmanship was meant to last. In contrast, those layers of stones that were added in later centuries and which are located higher up the wall are already starting to crack.

Lift your gaze to find several tiers of rock protruding midway up the wall. You are looking at Robinson's Arch, named for famous American biblical scholar Professor Edward Robinson. At one time it was thought that Robinson's Arch was a Second Temple era bridge which stretched from the Temple Mount over to Jerusalem's Upper City, and that it rested on the roofs of housetops in the valley. However now it seems quite certain that the arch was actually part of a gigantic staircase leading to and from the enormous Royal Portico that occupied the entire southern area of the Mount.

Considering the high quality of construction at that time, the street is awfully uneven. That's because, when the Romans destroyed the Second Temple in the year 70, the arch crashed into the pavement and ruined its symmetry. Remains from the arch are piled up to your left — mute testimony of the tragedy that befell the Jewish people.

Discovered at the base of the wall, one extremely large rock has been partially reconstructed. Look for it across from the wall's southwestern corner. It contains a replica of an ancient inscription, the original of which is on view at the Israel Museum. The inscription reads: "To the house of the trumpeting to procl …" Biblical scholars are quite certain that the sentence ended with "to proclaim the Sabbath."

Picture the trumpeter standing directly above the hawkers, stridently warning them to conclude their wheeling and dealing and go home to prepare for the Sabbath. In much the same way, perhaps, ultra-orthodox Jews patrol the Mahane Yehuda market on Friday afternoons and remind contemporary merchants to close their stalls.

You can get a better idea of how the arch looked in ancient times by walking up the staircase and turning back to gaze at the street. Try to imagine the bustling crowds that swarmed below, then make your way to the shaded

plaza located to the right of the southern wall. As you cross the plaza note the pottery shards that have been incorporated into the floor.

Look left to see a wall built during the early Moslem period at the same time as the gray-domed El Aksa Mosque that juts out above it. Remains in this area are mostly from the 7th-8th century Omayyad era, when Moslem royalty built luxurious palaces adjacent to the Temple Mount.

Walk through Excavation Gate on the other side of the plaza. Directly across from you are a few steps leading down to a *mikvah*, or ritual bath. Dozens of ritual baths have been uncovered in this area.

The low walls next to the mikvah were once part of a large building. That structure may have contained dressing rooms used by people planning to immerse themselves in the ritual bath before ascending the steps to the Temple. Next to the mikvah is a tiny pool in which pilgrims could rinse the dust off their dirty feet before descending to the bath.

Now climb steps that lead to the Hulda Gates. Some of the stairs look just as they did 2,000 years ago while others have been reconstructed. You will be amazed at their size and irregularity. This may have forced the crowds to walk slowly, and perhaps to meditate on the sanctity of the site they were about to visit. They may have also kept people — especially children — from racing down the steps on the way out.

During the Second Temple period pilgrims entered and left the Mount through two main sets of gates. With a few exceptions they walked in through the triple gate on your right and departed the Temple complex through the double gates on your left.

Some scholars believe that the gates were named for the prophetess Hulda, who lived during the First Temple period. Hulda declared that God had called for the destruction of Jerusalem because its inhabitants had turned to idolatry. Her prophecy induced King Josiah to undertake reforms so comprehensive that the Lord deferred this disaster until a later time.

But it is also possible that the name "Hulda" is from the Hebrew word for mole (*holed*). Once pilgrims had walked through the gates they found themselves in long, wide covered tunnels; when they finally emerged from these "burrows," they were blinded by the sun as it reflected off the walls of the resplendent gold-and-white Temple.

Perhaps while you are gazing at the gates a modern-day group of pilgrims will be ascending the ancient steps. They do so with reverence, chanting quiet hymns of praise. Does this help you imagine what the Jewish pilgrims must have felt as they climbed the stairs to the Temple Mount? Perhaps they sang a verse from Psalms 126: "*A song of ascents. When the Lord brought back the captives to Zion, we were like dreamers."* How they must have hushed their rowdy youngsters and gazed in awe as they walked through the gates to the Temple!

Roam around this area to discover an intricate water system. *Watch your head as you walk through its tunnels!* **On your return to the Excavation Gate search the ground for the many ancient mosaics which remain in the area.**

Now cross the plaza in the other direction, and exit the Ophel Gardens. If you have made arrangements in advance to tour the Western Wall Tunnels you can now visit an incredible Hasmonean aqueduct and the full extent of the Herodian wall. On occasion, you can just buy a ticket and join a group that has already formed. Tickets are available opposite the Western Wall, at the ticket booth just inside the Police Station.

Your next stop is the Kotel Ma'aravi — the Western Wall, where Jews can be found in worship 24 hours a day. Although this is only a small section of the retaining wall and was not part of the Temple itself, its proximity to the Sanctuary has bestowed upon it a hallowed status.

Walk over to the plaza and face the Western Wall. Over the centuries, when they had access to the Holy City, Jews would stand in front of this sole remnant

Ancient stairs, columns and an intricate water system next to the blocked-up Hulda Gates.

The Western Wall — all that remains of the Second Temple compound.

of the Temple and mourn its loss. Sages maintained that a Divine Presence lingers at the site of the demolished Temple and this has given it extra sanctification.

During the 16th century Ottoman ruler Suleiman the Magnificent set aside a very small portion of the Western Wall for Jewish worship. Over the next few hundred years, and until Jerusalem was divided in 1948, the Western Wall served as the focus of Jewish hope, longing and fervent prayer.

With the division of Jerusalem in 1948, even the tiny area allotted to them by Suleiman was denied to the Jews. And this despite a specific provision in the Israeli-Jordanian Armistice agreement which permitted Israelis to visit the Western Wall.

On June 7th, 1967, East and West Jerusalem were reunited. When the Israeli flag was proudly raised above the Western Wall, some of the battle-weary paratroopers who had fought to regain the Old City from Jordanian control were overcome with emotion — and burst into tears. Army Chief Chaplain Shlomo Goren blew the shofar as in the days of old. He recited hymns of praise and thanksgiving, and prayed, in a whisper, for those who had died to make this historic day possible.

The plaza on which you are standing was constructed after the war, when the prayer area was deepened and expanded and additional layers of stone were revealed. Jewish worship is continuous at the Western Wall, which hosts military and religious ceremonies as well as festive processions.

Jews and non-Jews alike often leave requests stuffed into cracks between the stones. **Before you ascend to the Temple Mount, your next stop, you may want to do so as well. Then climb the ramp to the right of the Western Wall and enter the Temple Mount through the green Mugrabi Gate.**

With only a short hiatus during the Crusader era, there has been a Moslem presence on the Temple Mount since the 7th century. Indeed Moslems venerate the complex, which they call Haram Esh-Sherif (Sacred Compound), as the third holiest Moslem site after Mecca and Medina.

Moslems follow Islam, a faith that originated with a Mecca-born camel driver named Mohammed. In 610, at the age of 40, Mohammed experienced the first of a series of visions in which he was charged by the Angel Gabriel to become the messenger of God. He was instructed to preach that there is but one true God (Allah, in Arabic) to whom Moslems must totally commit themselves. This and later revelations were incorporated into Islam's holy book, the Koran.

To your right after you enter the complex you will see the Islamic Museum. El Aksa Mosque is located directly across from the museum, while the world-famous Dome of the Rock rests on a platform to your far left. Tickets for the museum, El Aksa Mosque and the Dome of the Rock are available in a booth right near the door through which you entered the complex.

Mount Moriah, the height on which you are standing, is first mentioned in Genesis 22:2: *Then God said, 'Take your son, your only son, Isaac, whom you love, and go to the region of Moriah. Sacrifice him there as a burnt offering on one of the mountains I will tell you about.'*

Hundreds of years later, when King David decided to build a temple to the Lord, he acquired the heights of Mount Moriah from Jebusite farmer Araunah. But God didn't want a man of war to build the sanctuary, which was to be dedicated to peace. As a result it was David's son Solomon who was allocated the task: *Then Solomon began to build the temple of the Lord in Jerusalem on Mount Moriah, where the Lord had appeared to his father David. It was on the threshing floor of Araunah the Jebusite, the place provided by David* (2 Chronicles 3:1).

One after the other over the next millennia the sacred First and Second Temples were destroyed. Mount Moriah became a refuse-covered garbage dump and remained so until Moslem Arabs conquered Jerusalem in 638.

At the time of the city's fall, the Caliph Omar ruled the Moslem world. Like other Moslems, Omar revered many of the Old Testament's most significant personalities. He also honored the holy sites — including the peak on which Solomon had erected his magnificent Temple. Upon ascending to Mount Moriah Omar was enraged to find the esplanade overflowing with trash. He ordered the rubbish removed (some sources say he cleared it with his own hands), and erected a simple wooden mosque on the southern edge of the Temple Mount plaza.

Begin this part of your tour by visiting the Islamic Museum, whose collections include huge, handwritten samples of the Koran and glazed tiles hundreds of years old. Look for ancient stained-glass windows and decorative doors that were removed during the restoration of El Aksa and the Dome of the Rock and that are now on display here.

When you leave the museum walk over to the El Aksa Mosque. This lovely and harmonious structure was erected around 710 by the Moslem caliph El Walid. If you think that the seven arched doorways you see today are majestic, imagine what the mosque must have looked like 1,300 years ago: El Walid's mosque was double the size of the contemporary one!

Moslems believe that one dark night, accompanied by the angel Gabriel, Mohammed flew on a winged horse to a place far from Mecca. Upon reaching his destination he ascended to paradise and received the Koran. Although Mohammed is not known to have visited Jerusalem, an Islamic tradition developed in which the "far place" was considered to be the Temple Mount. Aksa in Arabic means "the furthest."

You must remove your shoes before your enter, keeping earthly dirt from finding its way inside. Cameras, cellular phones and even water bottles (!) have to be left outside the door as well, so someone will have to watch your belongings.

There is a good reason for these unusually stringent security measures. In 1951, liberal Jordanian King Abdullah was assassinated at the entrance to the mosque before the horrified eyes of his grandson, the late King Hussein. And in 1969 Christian Australian Michael Rohan simply walked in and set the mosque on fire. Among other irreplaceable items destroyed in that conflagration was a priceless ebony pulpit made in Syria hundreds of years earlier. In a painstaking process culminating at the very end of the 20th century, the pulpit was reconstructed and plans were made to install it in the Jerusalem mosque. Look around you — it may already be standing in place!

El Aksa was built over enormous arches that helped support King Herod's temple complex and thus was not constructed on solid ground. As a result the mosque has been severely damaged by earthquakes time and time again. The present house of worship was restored following 20th-century earthquakes and again repaired after Rohan torched the site.

View of the Temple Mount.

Once inside, you will be struck by El Aksa's bright interior. White walls and columns are artistically set off by gorgeous, authentic Persian rugs — another good reason for taking off your shoes before coming inside. To your right are a few limestone pillars from an earlier period, but the marble columns and the ceiling's gorgeous mosaics are new additions. Notice that there are no stools, benches or chairs in this or any other mosque. Moslems either kneel, prostrate themselves, or stand up when praying.

Look for the gray, red and white striped prayer niche called a *mihrab* at the far end of the mosque. If you walk all the way up to the rope that keeps you from getting too close you will be able to view the decorative underside of the dome. Some scholars believe that the wall and the *mihrab* beyond the rope remain from Walid's construction. As you look around you, feast your eyes on superb stained-glass windows scattered throughout the mosque.

Quakes, arson and murder are not the only earth-shattering events to have taken place in this mosque. In 1977 the first modern Arab leader to offer the Israelis peace visited Jerusalem, spoke in the Parliament and prayed at El Aksa. He was Egyptian President Anwar Sadat, later assassinated in his own country by militant Moslem fundamentalists.

Pick up your belongings and cross the courtyard in the direction of the Dome of the Rock. Moslems use El Kas, the goblet-shaped fountain you see here, for ritual ablutions. Pink marble chairs are strategically located next to little faucets all around the fountain's circular stone base. Worshippers can sit next to a tap and comfortably wash their hands, face and feet before prayer.

Now advance to the Dome of the Rock, a structure that dominates the Temple Mount and holds a prominent place in every photograph and picture of the Old City. Often favorably compared to India's Taj Mahal, Jerusalem's golden-topped, octagon-shaped Dome of the Rock was erected on the Mount in 691. Its shiny dome tops what is indisputably one of the most historic rocks in the world and the edifice itself is the world's oldest intact Islamic structure.

When King David bought Mount Moriah from Araunah, he acquired a rock that had been used as the Jebusite's threshing floor — thought to be the same rock on which Isaac had lain for sacrifice. Some people believe that this rock is the foundation stone of the universe and the Bible says that David raised an altar here in penance and prayer to the Lord. Solomon, who built the First Temple on this mount, may have set the Holy Ark on a fairly level rectangular portion of the stone. Imagine — this rock is the sole remnant from that sacred house of worship!

The rock is of extreme importance to Islam as well, for on his famous night journey Mohammed is said to have stepped onto the rock before his ascent. Legend has it that the rock tried to follow Mohammed as he and Gabriel rose up to heaven. Tales differ. According to one version, Gabriel pushed the rock back into place. In another, Mohammed stopped it with his hand and his movement created the grotto below.

The Dome of the Rock is often mistakenly referred to as the Mosque of Omar. However Omar, the ruling caliph at the time that the Moslems conquered Jerusalem, had nothing to do with the structure's construction. And its real founder, Abed El Malik, erected it not as a mosque but as a monument that would provide a suitable shrine for Mohammed's historic rock.

El Malik may also have built this masterpiece hoping that its splendor would dazzle Moslem tourists to Jerusalem, for they tended to become awestruck when viewing the Church of the Holy Sepulchre. Perhaps, too, he wanted to divert Moslems from Mecca, where a rival for his throne was holding court. Nevertheless, mosque or not, you will undoubtedly find worshippers inside. This is possible because a Moslem may pray anywhere he likes as long as he faces Mecca.

Start walking towards the steps that lead up to the Dome of the Rock. An arcade tops the stairway: note the sundial in its center. When built by the Mamelukes in the 14th century the eight arcades heading each stairway were probably meant as decorations. Later on, however, tradition named them *mawazin*, or scales. Indeed, many Moslems believe that on Judgment Day their good and bad deeds will be weighed on these scales … **Look to your left when you reach the top of the stairs to see a splendid marble platform called the Summer Pulpit.**

Now feast your eyes on the Dome of the Rock, faced with white marble and glazed ceramic tiles first brought here from Turkey by Suleiman the Magnifi-

Dome of the Rock — in the background the golden domes of the Church of St. Mary Magdalene.

cent. This architectural gem contains gorgeous mosaics from the 7th century, stunning marble pillars and shiny golden capitals. But what catches your eye as your approach is the gigantic, glimmering dome. In the 1950's King Hussein of Jordan replaced the dome's heavy lead with a special light aluminum; about 40 years later he exchanged the aluminum for the gold plate that you see sparkling in the sun.

The 7th-century structure east of the shrine consists of a dome and 17 small pillars. Although at first glance it seems to be the model on which the Dome of the Rock was based, there are many differences between the two and no one knows for certain why it was constructed.

Enter the Dome of the Rock and begin circling the interior. You may feel like you are treading on air: Jordan's King Hussein donated the thick, plush carpets beneath your feet only a few years before he died of cancer in 1999.

Look up into the dome to view embellished inscriptions, and fabulous painted golden mosaics and stucco that are dominated by green, gold and red. Glorious stained glass windows adorn the upper portion of the drum. Some of the windows have tiny holes in them, providing air for visitors and worshippers.

Climb a few steps to the center of the shrine so that you are standing next to a tower-shaped wooden cabinet. Legend has it that after visiting a site Mohammed plucked a few hairs from his beard (or, perhaps, from his head) and left them behind. Inside this decorative reliquary are two hairs that are displayed to the faithful once every year.

From here you can view the celebrated rock. When the Crusaders ruled Jerusalem they sometimes cut off pieces of the stone and sold them as souvenirs. Afraid the rock would eventually disappear, Arab leaders preserved what was left by surrounding the rock with exquisite wooden balustrades. **You can also descend to the cave below the rock; some think that this was the silo in which Araunah stored his grain.**

Exit the Dome of the Rock and walk all the way to the northwestern corner of the esplanade. Climb down the stairs, leave the Temple Mount and turn right. You will be standing in front of the Via Dolorosa's second station. To return to the Ophel Gardens and the Western Wall turn left, walk to the bottom of Via Dolorosa Street, turn left again and walk straight ahead for 5-10 minutes. Enjoy the sights (and delectable smells) from the Arab bakeries and restaurants that you pass as you complete your circular journey.

Hours: **OPHEL GARDENS** [625-4403]: Sun.-Thurs., 9:00-16:00; Fri. 9:00-14:00; closed Sat.; **Entrance fee**; Partially *wheelchair accessible*
TEMPLE MOUNT: Sat.-Thurs., 7:30-11:00. Sometimes open in the afternoon. Closed to non-worshippers on Friday. **Entrance fee to El Aksa, the Dome of the Rock and the museum;** *only Israeli currency accepted*
WESTERN WALL TUNNELS TOURS [627-1333]: Office hours: Sun.-Thurs., 8:30-15:30; Fri., 9:00-12:00; You must reserve in advance. If you are confined to a wheelchair, please inform the office when you reserve and arrangements will be made for your visit; **Entrance fee**

Restrooms: Near the Police Station, by the Western Wall
wheelchair accessible

David's City and Warren's Shaft

- **Begin and end**: at the Visitors' Center by the Givati parking lot at Dung Gate
- **Take bus**: 1, 2
- **Park your car**: on the street, or in one of the lots
- **Time frame**: 2-4 hours
- **Take note**: This walk involves steep inclines and over a hundred stairs. If you plan to go into Hezekiah's Tunnel prepare to get wet at least up to your knees. Bring along shoes for walking in water, and a flashlight or candles.

"A song of ascents. I lift up my eyes to the hills —
where does my help come from? My help comes from the Lord,
the Maker of heaven and earth" (Psalms 121:1-2).

When King David wrote these incomparably lovely lines, he didn't have far to look for inspiration. That's because his palace was located below the historic Temple Mount and was surrounded by the majestic Judean hills.

On your journey to David's City you can "lift your eyes" to these very same hills. In store for you as well are unique remains from the First Temple period and from the centuries that preceded it. While you are here watch the tour guides who bring groups to this spot. Inevitably, they bring along a Bible and read passages aloud to their flock. And no wonder: sites and individuals connected with David's City are mentioned in over half the books that make up the Bible!

Climb onto the observation deck just past the Visitors' Center. This site also had the advantage of some excellent natural fortifications. Between David's City where you are standing, and the Arab village of Silwan directly across from you, lies the deep Kidron Valley. Another valley, since filled in and now used as a road, was located behind you on the western side of this ridge. The two met in the south, creating a third, deep wadi. Add to these deep valleys a huge defensive wall that was reinforced on its vulnerable northern side, and the city they protected would be almost impossible to conquer.

Indeed, the Jebusites who resided here until David came along felt perfectly secure. In fact they felt so safe that, in a tone dripping with sarcasm, they told David that they needed only the lame and the blind to defend their walls. Despite the Jebusites' certainty, *"David captured the fortress of Zion, the City of David"* (2 Samuel 5:7).

Silwan, in Hebrew, is Shiloah — another biblical name for the Gihon Spring. The slope on which the village of Silwan was built is riddled with dozens of

Jewish burial caves, many of them dating back to the First Temple period. As Jewish law holds that the dead are to be buried immediately outside of the city, this strongly indicates that there was an Israelite city in this vicinity — and that Silwan was just outside its borders.

By studying the manner in which the houses of Silwan descend down the ridge you can imagine what the City of David must have looked like during the monarch's lifetime. Notice how from the balcony of one house you can look down onto the roof below. Just so may David first have gazed at Bathsheba *"One evening David got up from his bed and walked around on the roof of the palace. From the roof he saw a woman bathing. The woman was very beautiful and David sent someone to find out about her. The man said, 'Isn't this Bathsheba, the daughter of Eliam and the wife of Uriah the Hittite?'"* (2 Samuel 11:2-3).

Now walk down the steps and stand opposite the excavations in Area G, located directly below the observation deck. One of the country's most noteworthy finds was discovered in a cache below the level on which you are standing. On display at the ISRAEL MUSEUM, this treasure house yielded 51 lumps of clay used to seal official documents. Although the documents themselves were lost in the conflagration that also destroyed the First Temple, the clay seals — called bullae — were well baked by the fire and thus preserved.

Not only is this the largest group of bullae ever found in a single site in Israel, but these bullae are particularly important because they bear the names of high court officials. Experts think they may have stumbled onto the site of a royal archive, especially since the name on one seal is Gemariah Ben Shaphan:

"In the fourth year of Jehoiakim son of Josiah king of Judah, this word came to Jeremiah from the Lord: 'Take a scroll and write on it all the words I have spoken to you concerning Israel, Judah and all the other nations ... So Jeremiah called Baruch son of Neriah, and while Jeremiah dictated all the words the Lord had spoken to him, Baruch wrote them on the scroll ...' From the room of Gemariah son of Shaphan, the secretary, which was in the upper courtyard at the entrance of the New Gate of the temple, Baruch read to all the people at the Lord's temple the words of Jeremiah from the scroll" (Jeremiah 36:1-10).

That two-storied structure you see has been partially reconstructed in order to give you an idea of what it would have looked like thousands of years ago. Archeologists named it the House of Ahiel, based on an inscription found inside. In the ruins to the right of Ahiel's House there is a rock with a hole in the middle. This was probably a primitive privy that was connected to a sewage pipe.

Your next stop in David's City is a visit to Warren's Shaft. Return to the staircase and descend until you see the sign pointing you to the entrance on

your right. As you walk search the millennia-old walls for golden henbane, a yellow flower with sticky green leaves and a dark center. The poisonous and hallucinogenic henbane contains strong chemicals like scopolamine, said to be good for making spies "sing."

Charles Warren was a young British officer who was hired by the Palestine Exploration Fund in 1867 to lead its second survey of Palestine. He followed Captain Charles Wilson who had, a few years earlier, dug 20-30 meters into the earth near the Temple Mount, discovered an arch near the Western Wall, and prepared topographical maps to be used by the Jerusalem Water Relief Society.

For the current survey Warren was charged with exploring the Temple Mount even further. The captain was a good choice, for although he was only 27 years old he had experience in construction, cartography and defense.

Before the money for his expedition ran out and he left Jerusalem, Warren discovered pottery, cisterns, Herodian stones and an astonishing water system that appeared to date back to the 11th century B.C.E. This excellent water system would have enabled inhabitants to reach the Gihon spring without ever having to leave the city's protective walls. Blocked from the outside, the spring — and the city — would be safe from enemy hands.

The ancient City of David may have resembled the village of Silwan — goat and all!

Area G — Excavations in the City of David.

Biblical archeologists were most amazed, however, by what a 13-meter-deep shaft revealed during Warren's excavations. The shaft seemed to solve a biblical riddle that had been puzzling scholars for centuries: the question of how David's army managed to penetrate the Jebusites' highly fortified defenses. In 2 Samuel 5:8, King David declares that whoever conquers the Jebusites will have to use the *"tzinor"* (generally translated as "gutter"). After the shaft was discovered, some new editions of the Bible interpreted the word "tzinor" as "water shaft" instead. That's because many biblical researchers believed that they now understood how Joab, David's bravest soldier, had gained entrance to the city. All he had to do was climb up the shaft and enter the Jebusite water system!

Because Jerusalem is built over so many significant layers of settlement, it is standard procedure for experts to be called in to examine work sites before construction begins. In 1997 the archeologists who were asked to inspect a building project in the City of David chanced on discoveries that were to result in entirely new thinking about the water system here.

This is a good time to descend dozens of steep stairs to a spot from which you can view the shaft named after Charles Warren. Information gathered during these later excavations seems to indicate that the upper portion of the tunnel through which you just walked was hewn out by the Jebusites — or perhaps by the Canaanites who preceded them in David's City — and led to the spring house that you will view later on. If this is true, then the ground tread by the Jebusites was above your heads and nowhere near the shaft. Quite possibly, Warren's shaft was a natural crack still covered by hard rock during the period in which David's army neared the city. Essentially this means that even if Joab had managed to climb up the shaft, all he would have gotten was a headache!

During the 8th century B.C.E., while deepening the tunnel to the level on which you are standing, King Hezekiah's engineers may have stumbled upon the shaft and possibly widened it a bit. But in a complete reversal of the opinion held until 1997, many experts now believe that the shaft was never used for drawing water.

If the continuation of the tunnel is open, walk through it to the spring house. Alternately, climb back up to the entrance, return to the outside staircase, and descend all the way down to the plaza. Walk into the spring house, which contains the foundation of a Jebusite watchtower and the pool into which the Shiloah waters were channeled.

Now for the next stage of your visit: a fabulous water walk through Hezekiah's Tunnel. (Should you decide not to trudge through water you can skip this part of the tour and take the fascinating SIDE TRIP described later on.)

One of the marvels of modern engineering is the famous English "Chunnel," the twin-tubed rail tunnel that was bored beneath the English Channel. In order to complete that fantastic feat one team set out from the English coast and a second from the French side with the two planning to meet in the middle. Even the slightest deviation would have resulted in a horrendous engineering failure. Incredibly, and without the benefit of modern tools and technology, King Hezekiah embarked on an even more mind-boggling endeavor in 701 B.C.E. In preparation for a potentially disastrous siege by Assyrian King Sennacherib, he decided to convey the Shiloah waters to a large reservoir well inside the city. Water would then be easily accessible to Jerusalemites and, once and for all, completely out of the enemy's reach.

Carved out of the mountain's rock, Hezekiah's amazing S-shaped tunnel is over half a kilometer long. We know exactly how the King's men accomplished this seemingly impossible feat because they inscribed a description of the process on a rock inside the tunnel. Discovered in 1880, the "Shiloah Inscription" is on view at the Museum of the Ancient Orient in Istanbul.

According to the inscription, two groups of workmen began chiseling at opposite ends of the rock and were guided toward each other by the sounds they made while hewing at the stone. Their final meeting was made possible because they kept calling to each other until they managed to connect.

Put on waterproof shoes, roll up the legs of your trousers (or hike up your skirts), then walk down the steps and enter the dark tunnel. Even if the water is chilly don't get discouraged: this is an experience not to be missed! Light your candles or turn on your flashlights and begin your journey. It is impossible to get lost, so follow the glow of your lamp for about 40 minutes of adventure. Eventually you will see the light at the end of the tunnel …

When you leave Hezekiah's Tunnel turn right and then right again to ascend back up to the Visitors' Center. Watch out for cars! Better still, continue on to the Kidron Valley Side Trip.

Side Trip: Tombs in the Kidron Valley

After you exit the tunnel turn left and descend to a T-junction. Turn left again to find yourself on a road that leads you back to the plaza from which you entered Hezekiah's Tunnel. Continue walking straight and the road becomes a path that runs along the Kidron Valley. You will be visiting three monumental Jewish tombs and a burial cave before you walk up to a modern promenade. This will lead you back to the Visitors' Center.

The Kidron Valley is mentioned by name 11 times in the Old and New Testaments. It is also identified with the biblical King's Valley and sometimes called the Valley of Jehoshaphat as well. Jewish and Christian traditions intermingle in this wadi, where Israelite kings, princes, priests and prophets are believed to be buried, and where Jesus was wont to walk.

One biblical verse tells us that Asa, King of Judah, burned an image of the Canaanite goddess Asherah in the valley: *"He even deposed his grandmother Maacah from her position as queen mother, because she had made a repulsive Asherah pole. Asa cut the pole down and burned it in the Kidron Valley"* (1 Kings 15:13).

And according to the Gospels, Jesus crossed the Kidron on his way to Gethsemane: *"When he had finished praying, Jesus left with his disciples and crossed the Kidron Valley. On the other side there was an olive grove, and he and his disciples went into it"* (John 18:1).

Your first stop is at Zechariah's Tomb, the only pyramid-topped structure in the valley. Carved out of the slope's hard rock, and completely detached from the mountainside, it is over 10 meters high and dates back to the end of the Second Temple period. Pillars are cut into the stone all around the sides of the cube.

A great wrong was done to Zechariah, who predicted the downfall of Jerusalem and was executed by the King of Judah for his efforts. *"Then the*

Ancient Jewish tombs in the Kidron Valley.

Spirit of God came upon Zechariah son of Jehoiada the priest. He stood before the people and said, "This is what God says: 'Why do you disobey the Lord's commands? You will not prosper. Because you have forsaken the Lord, he has forsaken you.'" But they plotted against him, and by order of the king they stoned him to death in the courtyard of the Lord's temple" (2 Chronicles 24: 20-21).

Jews so revered Zechariah that over the centuries they asked to be buried as close as possible to his grave. If you climb above the tomb you will find the graves of pioneers who resided in the late 19th-century Bukharim Neighborhood and who desired to be buried near the great Zechariah. At one time the Jews of Jerusalem offered eulogies here and would come to Zechariah's tomb to mourn the destruction of the Temple on the ninth day of the Hebrew month of Av.

One year Jerusalem suffered from a terrible drought. Legend has it that the city's Arabs prayed to Allah, but rain didn't fall. They then sent a delegation to Jerusalem's Jewish inhabitants, warning them that if they couldn't make it rain they would be in deep, deep trouble!

According to this oft-repeated story, the Jews immediately declared a fast and on its third day made a pilgrimage to the tomb of Zechariah. Throwing themselves upon the ground next to the tomb they prayed, then walked around it seven times while singing psalms. By evening the sky was black. Heavy rain, accompanied by thunder and lightening, fell on the Holy City. The Jews were saved, the city's cisterns filled with water, and the sanctity of Zechariah's tomb was reaffirmed.

Right next to the tomb stairs lead into a famous burial complex. Examine the walls to see the chisel (and perhaps hatchet) marks indicating that this is not a natural cave.

When you walk inside you will find first one chamber, then within that another and yet another. Be careful when you step out onto the balcony in front of the columned entrance, as there aren't any rails to keep you from falling! Then look up to where you can barely make out an ancient Hebrew inscription. It tells you that the six sons of the Hezir family are buried within.

The Hezirs were a distinguished priestly family noted twice in the Bible, first mentioned when King David gives the priests their sacred duties and again at the end of the Babylonian exile. At that time Nehemiah places the Hezirs on the list of families who sign a declaration of faith and take an oath to follow God's Law.

The Church of St. Mary Magdalene on the Mount of Olives stands behind and above the Kidron Valley (p.157).

Tradition places King Uzziah at this site as well, but during his lifetime. It is believed that he lived here in what the Bible calls a "separate house."

Uzziah was a teenager of 16 when he became King and he reigned over Judah for 52 years. A great builder, he constructed towers, strengthened Jerusalem's defenses, and put together a great army. *"But after Uzziah became powerful, his pride led to his downfall. He was unfaithful to the Lord his God, and entered the temple of the Lord to burn incense ... Azariah the priest with eighty other courageous priests of the Lord followed him in. They confronted him and said, 'It is not right for you, Uzziah, to burn incense to the Lord. That is for the priests, the descendants of Aaron, who have been consecrated to burn incense. Leave the sanctuary, for you have been unfaithful; and you will not be honored by the Lord God.'*

Uzziah, who had a censer in his hand ready to burn incense, became angry. While he was raging at the priests in their presence before the incense altar in the Lord's temple, leprosy broke out on his forehead. When Azariah the chief priest and all the other priests looked at him, they saw that he had leprosy on his forehead, so they hurried him out. Indeed, he himself was eager to leave, because God had afflicted him. King Uzziah had leprosy until the day he died. He lived in a separate house — leprous, and excluded from the temple of the Lord ..." (2 Chronicles 26:16-21).

Christians call this the tomb of St. James for the man who was Jesus' cousin and the first bishop of Jerusalem. Tradition holds that after Jesus was crucified, James hid from the Romans in the Hezir family tomb. Later on James was martyred here: thrown over a wall of the Jerusalem Temple, stoned by the populace, and then clubbed to death in the Valley of Kidron.

Now walk over to the most magnificent structure in the Kidron Valley — Absalom's Tomb. A lofty 22 meters in height, it was hewn out of the rock and is completely separate from the slope behind it. Columns and capitals decorate the massive lower part of the monument, which is distinguished by a round top ending in a long, thin point. The shrine dates back to the 1st century B.C.E — nearly a millennium after Absalom rebelled against his father and was run through with a javelin by the King's captain.

It was a custom in ancient times to erect a monument in memory of your departed parents. If you had no offspring, however, you might have to put one up for yourself. While the Bible notes that Absalom fathered three sons and a daughter, they must have passed away while still young. For it says in the Bible: *"During his lifetime Absalom had taken a pillar and erected it in the King's Valley as a monument to himself, for he thought, 'I have no son to carry on the memory of my name.' He named the pillar after himself, and it is called Absalom's Monument to this day"* (2 Samuel 18:18). Tradition places that monument here, identifying the Kidron Valley with the King's Valley.

In earlier centuries passersby of all religions would throw stones at Absalom's mammoth structure. Indeed Moslems, who revere King David, almost covered it with rocks. It is said that Jewish parents would bring disobedient offspring to the almost hidden monument, point out the stones, and warn them that "this is what happens to children who behave badly to their fathers!"

A tomb believed to be that of King Jehoshaphat is situated behind and to the left of Absalom's monument. Uncovered in 1924, it contains several chambers and a beautifully decorated lintel. The Bible says that "… *Jehoshaphat rested with his fathers and was buried with them in the city of David his father. And Jehoram his son succeeded him*" (1 Kings 22:50). Discovery of the tomb helped strengthen an identification of the Kidron Valley with the Valley of Jehoshaphat. For it is written: "*I will gather all nations and bring them down to the Valley of Jehoshaphat. There I will enter into judgment against them concerning my inheritance, my people Israel, for they scattered my people among the nations and divided up my land*" (Joel 3:2).

Cross the valley and walk up a stairway and ramp to a beautiful, modern promenade just across the road from the Old City walls. Before following the promenade back to the Visitors' Center stop at the Observation Deck, built in 1999. From here you have a panoramic view of at the monuments you visited in the valley below. On the other side of the valley, facing you, is the Mount of Olives.

Some of the most important events in Jesus' life occurred on these slopes, which are studded with magnificent churches. From here look left to see the glistening facade on the Church of All Nations (Gethsemane), built by Catholics from all over the world. Adjacent to the church is the olive grove where Jesus spent the night after the Passover meal, only to be betrayed by Judas.

Further up the hill and to the right stands the Russian Orthodox Church of St. Mary Magdalene. Built by Alexander III of Russia, the Church of St. Mary Magdalene is probably the most conspicuous house of worship in Jerusalem. It owes its prominence to the presence of seven golden, onion-shaped domes jutting out from a monumental Muscovite-style structure regilded in 1999.

The unique tear-shaped sanctuary across from you and even higher up the slope is the Church of Dominus Flevit. The words Dominus Flevit mean, in Latin, "the Lord wept." Christians believe that on this site Jesus was overcome by the realization of the tragic fate in store for Jerusalem.

Now shift your gaze to the tombstones directly across from you on the mountainside. You are looking at a large and very ancient Jewish cemetery.

There are about 70,000 Jewish graves here, some of them dating all the way back to the First Temple period. Many believe that the prophets Zechariah, Malachi and Haggai are buried on the Mount of Olives, in a cave towards the top of the slope.

Unlike many other heads of the Jewish State, who were laid to rest at a special site on MOUNT HERZL, former Prime Minister Menachem Begin is buried on the Mount of Olives. So are defenders of the Old City's Jewish Quarter who fell during the War of Independence.

Just before the Jewish Quarter surrendered to the Jordanian Legion in 1948 and its residents were led away from their

Jews have been buried on the Mount of Olives for thousands of years.

homes, fallen Israeli defenders were hastily buried together in a mass grave. When the city was reunited 19 years later the defenders' remains were re-interred on the Mount of Olives in a full military ceremony. Their burial site is near a special memorial wall. Look for it below the multi-arched hotel on the top of the mountain: it is decorated with a *menorah* and the Star of David.

According to Jewish tradition, the Messiah will descend to Jerusalem from the Mount of Olives and enter the city through the Gates of Mercy. Since he will pass through the cemetery, located so close to the Temple Mount, those buried on the Mount of Olives will logically be the first to be resurrected.

Hours: **CITY OF DAVID AND HEZEKIAH'S TUNNEL** [626-2341]: Sun.-Thurs., 9:00-16:00; Fri. mornings. If you plan to visit on Sat., call during the week to find out if the site is open; **Entrance fee**

Note: Don't take anything unnecessary into Hezekiah's Tunnel and remember: parts of you will be wet when you come out!

Restrooms: Near the Visitors' Center at David's City

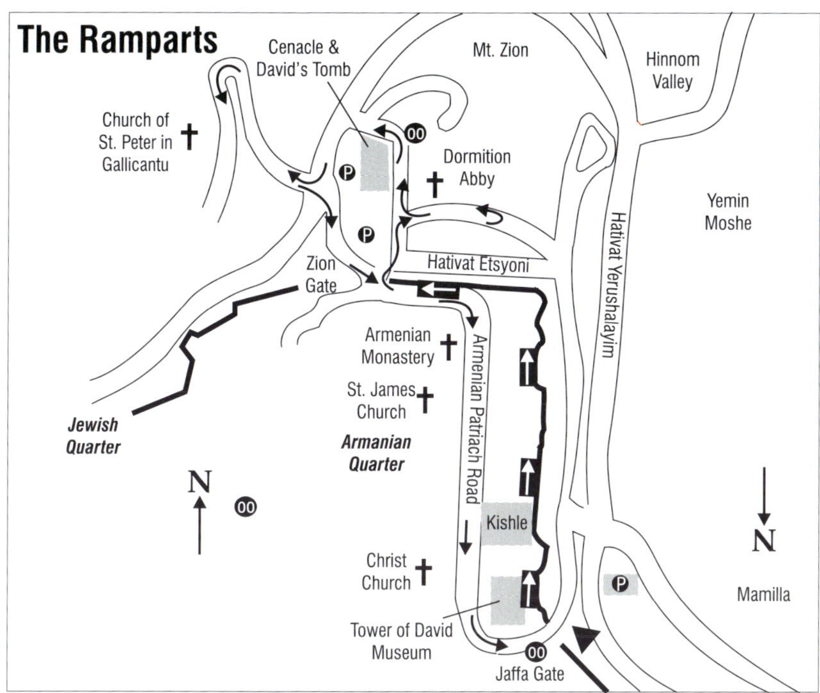

The Old City ramparts are an awesome sight at night.

On the Ramparts —
and Around Mount Zion

- **Begin and end**: at Jaffa Gate
- **Take bus**: 3, 6, 19, 20, 30, 38
- **Park your car**: in the Mamilla Street parking lot or next to the sidewalk
- **Time frame**: 2 hours
- **Take note**: If the dozens of steps involved in this walk present you with a problem or if you are afraid of heights, you may want to skip the first part of the tour and enjoy the Mount Zion portion instead.

Jerusalem has been surrounded by walls for over 3,000 years. Over the millennia as the city developed, new walls were built, old walls were strengthened and Jerusalem's fortifications were adapted as circumstances required. Many of the city's rulers, from Jebusite to Turk, built citadels for a local garrison. Soldiers stationed on the ramparts (fortified walkways) would patrol the city walls.

Since the reunification of Jerusalem in 1967, however, the ramparts are no longer the province of the military. In fact, today tourists and native Jerusalemites stroll atop the Old City walls for sheer fun. From the top of the ramparts visitors get a first-hand view of both Old and New Jerusalem. Inevitably, they also gain a feeling for the complexity of this unique and exciting city.

This tour takes you along the ramparts from JAFFA GATE to Zion Gate, then through the sites on Mount Zion and after that back to where you started.

As you approach Jaffa Gate to begin your ramparts tour, look up at the small parapet above the entrance. Its floor contains an opening called a machicolation, from which soldiers could dump boiling oil or hot tar on any enemy attempting to mount an attack on the city through the gate.

Begin your tour at the Jaffa Gate Road where it enters the Old City. Next to the corner of the impressive citadel which houses the Tower of David Museum there is a sign leading to the Ramparts Walk. ***Please note**: there is another route leading from Jaffa Gate northward to Damascus Gate. However this tour goes in the other direction, to Zion Gate.*

Follow the sign next to the citadel, so that you are walking between two walls and on a stone path. Turn left at the corner and soon you will reach the entrance to the Ramparts Walk. Pay your fee, then start the ascent.

The staircase leads you onto the ramparts, built in 1538 during restoration of the ancient walls. Continue walking until you reach the first opening to the left. Pass through it to reach a rooftop overlook.

You are facing the *kishle*, from the Turkish word for "barracks." It stands just inside the walls, on the site that is thought to have housed King Herod's magnificent palace 2,000 years ago. During the Ottoman period it was a jail; today it is a police station. If you are lucky you may see Jerusalem's mounted police exercising their handsome steeds in the *kishle's* paddock.

Since the 4th century there has been a continuous Armenian presence in Jerusalem and all of the buildings beyond the *kishle* and to the immediate right are part of the Old City's Armenian Quarter. Armenia was the first nation in the world to officially accept Christianity (in the year 301). Do you see a blue-gray dome with a cross? It tops the Armenian Cathedral of St. James.

Continually subject to persecution and oppression, the Armenian nation was devastated in the years between 1894 and 1922 when over a million people were slaughtered by the Turks. Although the Armenian Quarter originally housed mainly monks and nuns, it opened its gates to thousands of refugees who fled to Jerusalem after being expelled from their homes in 1915.

Life in the Armenian Quarter revolves around church institutions and residents here live behind locked gates. This not only separates the Armenians from all their neighbors, but also keeps them safe at night. Within the complex there are about 2,000 people, perhaps the only monastery compound in the world with a grocery store, nursery school, and entertainment!

Turn and look in the other direction, to view the New City — outside of the walls. Facing you and to the west of Jaffa Gate you will see the renovated neighborhood of MAMILLA. In its heyday Mamilla was Jerusalem's main business district, and during the roaring twenties bordellos and casinos stood shoulder to shoulder with the neighborhood's exclusive shops.

But because Mamilla was so very close to the Old City it was particularly vulnerable to attacks by hostile Arabs. On November 29, 1947, the night that Jews celebrated the United Nations decision to partition Palestine, Arab rioters and looters engulfed Mamilla. The British police made no effort to intervene, but fortunately for Mamilla the mobs dispersed when several Haganah squads came to the rescue.

From 1948 to 1967, the 19 years during which the city was divided, Jordanian soldiers sniped at Jewish neighborhoods from high atop these very ramparts. The once-prosperous Mamilla, already partially destroyed in the riots, quickly turned into a slum.

When the Israelis began preparing for the Six-Day War, they realized they lacked information about Jordanian positions on the ramparts. But how to lure the soldiers out of hiding so the army could see where they were stationed?

View from one of the towers placed strategically along the ramparts.

Officers came up with the perfect solution: they arranged for a shapely Israeli girl to stand on a balcony in Mamilla across from the Old City walls, and to slowly and provocatively remove her clothing. And as Jordanian soldiers exposed themselves in a rush to get a good view, Israeli forces successfully photographed their positions.

One guide, under the assumption that this was but one of thousands of Israeli legends, told the story during a tour he was leading at AMMUNITION HILL. To his astonishment, a woman who was with the group announced that every word of the story was true. She should know, she said, because she had been that young girl whose job it was to lure the soldiers out of hiding!

At the end of the 20th century Mamilla underwent a massive overhaul. It won't be long before it returns to its former glory as both a flourishing commercial center and fashionable residential area.

Return to the ramparts. As you walk on you will find that at regular intervals of 80-100 meters, more or less the range of an arrow, there is a set of stairs to climb. A few meters further on you will descend to your original height. Each ascent leads to the top of a small, fortified tower, of which there are several dozen along the ramparts.

Don't miss the changes that take place in the colors of the buildings below and around you. Late in the day, when the sun is low in the west, New Jerusalem's buildings begin to turn a pinkish-red color. In striking contrast, a white Dormition Abbey stands out against the background of a blue-gray sky.

German Emperor Wilhelm II visited Israel in 1898, and the Turkish Sultan presented him with a plot of land on Mount Zion. You can't miss the clock tower he built, part of the impressive Dormition Abbey. Imagine you are looking at the face of a Prussian soldier complete with helmet, eyes and nose. It is said that if you happen to view it at just the right angle at night, the clock tower looks exactly like the Emperor himself!

When you reach the southwestern tower, look to your right (west). Below you is the Hinnom Valley, which served as a natural border between the tribes of Benjamin and of Judah. As it says in the Scriptures: *"The boundary went down to the foot of the hill facing the Valley of Ben Hinnom, north of the Valley of Rephaim. It continued down the Hinnom Valley along the southern slope of the Jebusite city and so to En Rogel"* (Joshua 18:16).

Dormition Abbey and its clock tower are adjacent to the Catholic cemetery.

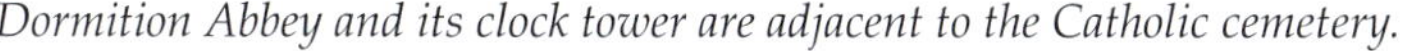

On the other side of the valley are the red-roofed houses of YEMIN MOSHE. To their left stand the windmill and the long buildings of the first Jewish neighborhood to be built outside the walls of the Old City — MISHKENOT SHA'ANANIM.

Several Christian cemeteries can be viewed on the southern side of the ramparts. That closest to the tower is the Catholic cemetery, and buried within is Irishman Christopher Costigan. In 1835 Costigan sailed from the Sea of Galilee to the Dead Sea. He contracted malaria while he was researching holy sites near the Dead Sea and was brought to the Franciscan Convent on Mount Zion. A tongue of land which protrudes into the southern portion of the Dead Sea is called Cape Costigan, after the young explorer who died of his illness at the age of 25.

Continue walking. This may be your only chance to get a glimpse of daily life within the Armenian Quarter, as it is not open to casual visitors. Soon you will see, on your left, a beautiful monastery.

Climb up and down the little tower on top of Zion Gate and across from the basketball court adjacent to the monastery. Descend to a courtyard, from which you walk even further down to the main road. At the moment you are inside the Old City walls: exit through Zion Gate to move onto Mount Zion.

A plaque inside the gate and numerous bullet holes on its exterior bear witness to a successful Israeli attempt to reach the besieged and beleaguered Jewish residents of the Old City on May 18, 1948.

Unfortunately, however most of the soldiers were withdrawn. And the handful of Jewish defenders that was left could not hold out against the might of the Jordanian army. On May 28, 1948, the Jewish Quarter was forced to capitulate to the Arab Legion.

Follow the signs to Dormition Abbey until you come to a fork in the road. The left fork leads to the Coenaculum and David's Tomb. You turn right, to reach Dormition Abbey.

During the Byzantine period many Christian traditions arose, among them the belief that Mary wasn't dead but lay deep in eternal sleep. Mary's crypt was said to be here and Dormition Abbey was built over the Byzantine church which housed it.

The name is an abbreviation for the longer phrase in Latin: *Dormitio Beatae Mariae Virginis* — the slumber of the Saint Virgin Mary. In 1906 members of the German Benedictine Order built a church and monastery on the ruins of a 14th-century Franciscan chapel. Completed in 1910, the abbey's massive towers give it the look of a medieval fortress.

Beautiful mosaics decorate the church's upper hall, while brilliant blue stained-glass windows add a stunning color to the interior of the church. In the basement crypt you will find a life-size statue of Mary lying in eternal rest. Made of cherry tree wood and ivory, the impressive figure is bathed in the glow of burning wax candles.

Your next stop is the Cenacle, or Coenaculum in its Latin form. Although the word itself means "dining room," it is often translated as "upper chamber." That's because, according to the New Testament, Jesus instructed the disciples to prepare the Passover in a "large upper room."

To get there, exit Dormition Abbey, return to the fork in the road, and turn right. Walk through the first opening on your left (there may not be a sign). Ascend the steps and enter.

With its vaulted ceilings and columns crowned with intricately decorated capitals, the Cenacle looks very much like a Crusader hall. And no wonder: it was almost certainly part of a Crusader church taken under the wing of the Franciscans and renovated in the 14th century.

Events of enormous importance to Christians occurred in the room where Jesus and his disciples shared the Last Supper. It was here that Jesus offered his own bread and wine to his followers: *"While they were eating, Jesus took bread, gave thanks and broke it, and gave it to his disciples, saying, "Take and eat; this is my body." Then he took the cup, gave thanks and offered it to them, saying, "Drink from it, all of you. This is my blood of the covenant, which is poured out for many for the forgiveness of sins"* (Matthew 26:26-28).

The Cenacle is believed to have hosted another landmark occurrence almost two months after the Last Supper. It happened on the Pentecost — exactly seven weeks after the Passover Seder and the day on which the Jewish Feast of Weeks (Shavuot) begins. Jesus' followers had gathered together in the dining hall when ... *"Suddenly a sound like the blowing of a violent wind came from heaven and filled the whole house where they were sitting. They saw what seemed to be tongues of fire that separated and came to rest on each of them. All of them were filled with the Holy Spirit and began to speak in other tongues as the Spirit enabled them"* (Acts 2:2-4).

When Moslem rulers expelled the Franciscans from the site in 1552, the Cenacle was converted into a mosque called Nebi Daoud (the prophet David) and a Moslem prayer niche, or *mihrab*, was introduced into the southern wall — facing the holy Moslem city of Mecca. During the regime of the enlightened ruler Muhammad Ali in the middle of the 19th century, Franciscans were permitted two visits a year — on Good Friday and on the Pentecost. However they were allowed to read only from the New Testament. And they were under no circumstances entitled to kneel!

Exit the Cenacle, then walk up the steps to the rooftop above it. Next to you is the dome which tops the mosque and on the other side is the closed door of what is called, in Hebrew, the President's Room.

From 1948 to 1967 Jews were not permitted in the Old City and Mount Zion was the closest place in Jerusalem from which they could view the TEMPLE MOUNT. Many a Jew would climb up to this rooftop to pray, as did Yitzhak Ben-Zvi, Israel's second president. He kept this special room on the rooftop for that purpose.

To reach King David's tomb, you must descend the stairs *all the way to the bottom*. Turn right and immediately right again to reach an arched outer courtyard. As early as the 12th century noted traveler Rabbi Benjamin of Tudela wrote that Mount Zion had become established as the site of King David's tomb. Later, like the Cenacle, King David's tomb was incorporated into a large 14th-century Franciscan cloister.

Legend has it that during the Middle Ages, when the Moslems ruled Jerusalem, a Jewish woman with a desperately ill child visited the tomb of King David. Jews were not allowed into the site and a Moslem guard barred their way. After the woman offered him a bribe the guard, hoping for a reward, ran straight to the city's ruler to report what had happened.

In the meantime the woman and her son had stepped inside the chamber that houses David's tomb. Suddenly, they heard footsteps approach. At that moment a door opened up from within the room and the two moved quickly inside. Here, they encountered a white-clothed old man with a beard (most likely Elijah the prophet, who appears often when needed). The stranger led the woman and her son through a tunnel which ended at the Yochanan Ben-Zakkai Synagogue in the Jewish Quarter.

Don't be surprised to find yourself face to face with a group of Moslem worshippers reverently removing their shoes before they enter the chamber. Remember: they, too, venerate King David.

Your next stop is the Church of St. Peter in Gallicantu, one of the most magnificent sanctuaries in Jerusalem. **To get there walk through the parking lot outside of Zion Gate and down to the main road. Cross the street and walk into the driveway that leads to the church, which is located on the eastern slopes of Mount Zion.**

You will find that a lot of writing in the church is in French. That's because St. Peter's belongs to the Assumptionist Fathers, a 19th-century French order named for Mary's assumption to heaven.

Peter was a disciple who thrice denied knowing Jesus and who subsequently regretted his awful deed. The shrine erected by the Byzantines and dedicated to Peter's remorse was later destroyed by the Moslems. When it was rebuilt by the Crusaders it was given a new name: St. Peter in Gallicantu. Gallicantu means "cockcrow" in Latin, and today a golden rooster protrudes prominently from the sanctuary roof.

The upper sanctuary in the contemporary church is an amazing blend of modern lines, primitive art, and antiquity. All have been brilliantly fused together to create a superbly designed masterpiece which makes it far more than an ordinary house of worship. Culminating in a giant, multi-colored interior, most of the joyous and lively shades fade into a progression of new and different hues. The most striking feature of this unusual church is its ceiling, which is dominated by a huge cross-shaped window shining with a radiant variety of colors.

St. Peter's Church is one of the city's most splendid sanctuaries.

Beneath the upper church is an unusually light and airy glass-enclosed chapel whose walls incorporate some of the mountain's natural bedrock. Three stunning icons decorate the walls of the chapel, all three relating to Peter. The New Testament relates that Peter emphatically insisted that he loved Jesus. Nevertheless, Jesus told him that *"before the rooster crows twice you yourself will disown me three times."* And Peter protests that even if the others disown Jesus, he certainly will not (Mark 14:30-31). The powerful image on the left depicts the full sentiment of that prophecy: in the icon, Jesus turns around and looks Peter straight in the eye.

In the center icon Peter weeps bitterly with remorse. And the right hand picture illustrates a passage from the gospel according to John in which Jesus asks Peter three times whether or not he loves him. When Peter replies that he does, Jesus tells him to feed his flock. (John 21:17).

On an even lower level there is easy access to a succession of caves from the Second Temple period. According to Catholic tradition, Caiaphas' palace was situated here and it logically follows that Jesus may have been held in one of these underground dungeons.

From here you exit into an excavated yard that includes a stone trail probably dating back to that same era. Many Christians believe that Jesus followed this path twice on the night before he was crucified. After the Last Supper he would have walked down the path, crossed the Kidron Valley and continued on to Gethsemane. And he may have been brought up this path again very early the next morning after being arrested by Roman soldiers.

Before you leave the church premises, walk out onto a balcony overlook for an unforgettable view of Jerusalem. Many of the hills surrounding Jerusalem are visible from this balcony: Mount Moriah, Mount Scopus, the Mount of Olives, the Mount of Evil Counsel and Mount Zion. Look for Potter's Field, as well: *"When Judas, who had betrayed him, saw that Jesus was condemned, he was seized with remorse and returned the thirty silver coins to the chief priests and the elders … then he went away and hanged himself. The chief priests … decided to use the money to buy the potter's field as a burial place for foreigners. That is why it has been called the Field of Blood to this day"* (Matthew 27:3-8).

Later renamed Akeldama — or "Field of Blood" in Aramaic — Potter's Field is located just above the Hinnom Valley. A wall-enclosed Greek Orthodox monastery is situated in Potter's Field on the slope across from where you stand. The monastery is named for St. Onuphrius — a 4th-century Egyptian hermit who kept away from other humans for several decades (some say as long as 60 years!). Also called the Naked Saint, Onuphrius supposedly wore nothing but a long white beard.   The patron saint of weavers, St. Onuphrius is believed to offer protection from sudden death.

During the late Second Temple period wealthy Jews entombed their dead in burial caves at Potter's field, and some amazing finds have been discovered at the site. Among them were two rare, hinged doors, and ossuaries (decorated containers for bones) whose Hebrew inscriptions relate to people mentioned in Jewish works of the Byzantine period. One Jewish ossuary was decorated with an oxhead, very unusual as there is a Biblical injunction against the use of graven images.

Now walk back up to Zion Gate. Pass through the gate into the Old City and turn left. Follow the road next to the Armenian compound all the way back to Jaffa Gate. Armenians are well known for their commercial and artistic skills and are justifiably famous for a particular kind of pottery sold in the inviting shops which line this road.

At one point you pass the main entrance to the Armenian Quarter. If the Cathedral is open, be sure to pay it a visit. St. James Cathedral is one of Jerusalem's most beautiful houses of worship. The cathedral entrance is symbolic, for its arch comes sharply to a point and greatly resembles the priestly Armenian hat. Both are said to represent Mt. Ararat, often identified as located in Armenia and believed to be the site on which Noah's ark came to rest during the Flood.

Bursting with rich ornamentation, the interior of the cathedral is bathed in the scent of eastern incense. Yet while the cathedral is distinctly Armenian, it reflects Crusader elements. Indeed, Crusader artists probably created many of the columns bearing animal sculptures typical of that era.

Just outside the main entrance to the cathedral is a pair of clappers. A 14th-century Moslem edict forbade churches to call their worshipers to prayer with the sound of bells. These gongs — actually a wooden and an iron board called *nakus* in Arabic — were substituted for the bells. Today church bells ring when it is time for prayer. However in memory of those centuries during which bell ringing was banned, an Armenian monk still emerges from within and hammers on the *nakus*.

Hours:	**RAMPART WALKS** [625-4403]: Sun.-Thurs., Sat., 9:00-16:00; Fri. 9:00-14:00; **Entrance fee** **CENACLE (COENACULUM)** [671-3597]: Sun.-Thurs., Sat., 8:00-17:00; Fri. 8:00-13:00 **DAVID'S TOMB**: Variable hours, approximately 8:00-18:00; Sun.-Thurs.; Fri. 8:00-13:00; Sat. closed **CATHEDRAL OF ST. JAMES** [628-2331]: During worship Mon.-Fri., 6:00-7:00; 15:00-15:30; Sat., Sun., 6:00-9:30 **CHURCH OF ST. PETER** [673-1739]: Mon.-Sat., 8:30-12:00; 14:00-17:00; Sun. closed; **Entrance fee.** *Much of the church is wheelchair accessible* **DORMITION ABBEY** [671-9927]: Open 8:00-12:00; 12:30-18:00; Sun. opens at 9:30
Restrooms:	Jaffa Gate, near David's Tomb, and at the shop of St. Peter's Church. At the church the facilities are *wheelchair accessible*

Inside Jaffa Gate

- **Begin and end**: at Jaffa Gate
- **Take bus**: 3, 6, 19, 20, 30, 38
- **Park your car**: at the Mamilla lots or along the street
- **Time frame**: 45 minutes without the museum

One fateful night — or so it is said — the Turkish Sultan Suleiman the Magnificent awoke covered in a cold sweat. He had dreamed that while he was walking in an open field a pair of hungry lions had pounced upon and greedily devoured him.

What could the dream possibly mean? When asked for his opinion Suleiman's advisor suggested that the Sultan should quickly perform a good deed — perhaps even replace the ruins around the Holy City of Jerusalem with a new wall. And so it happened that in the year 1538 Suleiman began putting up the wall which today surrounds Jerusalem's Old City.

Stand outside of Jaffa Gate. The thoroughfare next to this gate once led along Jaffa Road, to and from the all-important port city of Jaffa. The 16th-century Arabic inscription over the entrance gives Suleiman's name, the year of construction and the following words: "There is no God but Allah and Abraham is his friend."

There are presently seven open gates in the walls surrounding the Old City. Like most of the other entrances, Jaffa Gate's narrow opening is designed in the shape of the letter L. As a result, following the initial entry, enemy cavalry charging into Jerusalem would be forced to slow its pace.

Legend has it that Jerusalem will one day be conquered by a king riding a white stallion through a city gate. In 1898 Emperor Wilhelm II of Germany rode a white horse into Jerusalem, but not through Jaffa Gate. Before his arrival the Ottoman rulers of Jerusalem breached a gap in the wall that connected Jaffa Gate with the citadel, plugged up the adjacent moat and created a   second and wider point of entry suitable for the Emperor and his extensive entourage. Today this entrance provides cars with wheeled access into the city.

The doors, once made of wood but later covered with metal to prevent fires, were closed in the evening and reopened only after sunrise the next day. Look for a little opening in the right hand door: this is a "pishpash" in local jargon, a postern used for emergency exits and entrances.

A large *mezuzah* is fastened to the right hand side of the gate. A *mezuzah* is an encased scroll of parchment containing the words of the most important of

The bustle outside Jaffa Gate … and the bustle just inside.

Hebrew prayers. The custom of attaching it to the entrance of a Jewish home originates in the passage from the Bible that is encased within:

"Fix these words of mine in your hearts and minds ... Write them on the door-frames of your houses and on your gates, so that your days and the days of your children may be many in the land that the Lord swore to give your forefathers, as many as the days that the heavens are above the earth" (Deuteronomy 11:18-21).

If you stand next to the gate for even a few short minutes you will undoubtedly see Jews touch the *mezuzah* before they enter, and then press their fingers to their lips.

Stroll through the gate. Then pass a large shop and peer to your left to see an iron fence. Beyond it are two tombs intriguingly decorated with stone turbans. Although there are no names on the tombs they apparently contain the earthly remains of the two architects who planned the city walls. Local tradition maintains that an enraged Suleiman had them executed when he learned that, despite his orders, they had left David's Tomb and Mount Zion outside of the enclosed city. According to another legend, Suleiman ordered them beheaded so that the glorious walls of Jerusalem would never be reproduced. And some say that the two were assassinated because they knew the city's secrets. Once dead, of course, they wouldn't be able to report its weaknesses to any dastardly enemies.

Turn right before you reach the steps that descend to the market. Then walk to the large and handsome edifice housing the Christian Information Center on your left. It was built in 1858, 11 years after the Austrian monarchy opened a consulate in Jerusalem to accommodate the Imperial Austrian Post Office. Widely renowned for its efficient and reliable service, the Austrian Post Office was utilized by Jerusalem residents who wanted to make absolutely certain that letters reached their foreign destinations. Those writing to relatives in America suggested that return mail be routed through Trieste, the port from which Austrian ships bound for the Holy Land would depart.

During World War I the post office was closed down, later to reopen as a branch of the Bank of Rome. Following World War II it saw use as lodgings, a storehouse and as a commercial center. Franciscan monks purchased the lovely building in 1965 and began restoration a few years later.

The post office's colorful original sign is on view inside the Information Center. Austrian Post Office officials at the Vienna main branch presented it to the Franciscans in 1981.

To reach another historic site, walk through the gate and up the driveway across from the entrance to the Tower of David Museum. The 19th-century complex you have entered includes a guest house and the imposing Christ Church, the first Protestant sanctuary in the Middle East. Not a single cross decorates its exterior walls. Indeed, the church looks more like a European synagogue of the era than a Christian house of worship.

In the mid-1840's Protestants began actively trying to convert Jerusalem's Jews to Christianity. Simple proselytizing — and the promise of financial gain — had resulted in very few Jewish conversions, if any; the Protestant Bishopric in Jerusalem hoped that an attractive, accessible church might make it easier to draw Jews into the Christian fold.

At first, since the Moslems did not permit Christian use of a bell to call parishioners to worship, the church didn't even have a belfry. However after the Crimean War (1853-1856) had placed the Turks in debt to the English, the Anglicans added a modest bell tower and dared to ring the bell. Christ Church rang the first bell — and the Church of the Holy Sepulchre followed suit. Soon after that bells could be heard all over Jerusalem. Look for the bell tower to your left as you face the church.

While it reflects a typically Protestant lack of embellishment, Christ Church is a beautiful sanctuary. The design embodies a touch of traditional English beauty (rich, dark, wooden ceilings and tables) along with Middle Eastern stone walls and medieval vaulted arches.

Now cross the road to the steps that lead to the Tower of David Museum. In 1917 General Edmund Allenby, Commander of the British Forces in Palestine, stood on these steps and declared Jerusalem to be under British rule.

The foundations for Jerusalem's citadel were first laid by the Hasmonean rulers of Israel over 2,000 years ago. They erected a defensive tower and a city wall; remains of the wall were discovered during excavations.

Herod constructed a palace next to the Hasmonean city wall and added three towers, one of which still stands. Later, during the Great Revolt of 66, Jewish defenders holed up here when put to the rout by the Romans. After the fall of Jerusalem in 70, this is where soldiers of the Tenth Roman Legion were stationed.

It is highly improbable that King David ever set foot on this site. Nevertheless, in Byzantine times the citadel was called the Tower of David by Christian pilgrims who believed that the great Jewish monarch had been responsible for its construction.

The Mamelukes built the contemporary fortress in the 14th century. At that time, they erected a mosque so that the troops could worship without leaving

Historic buildings within the walls.

the area unguarded. The famous minaret, so distinctive above the walls, appeared only several hundred years later. Travelers in the 19th century erroneously referred to the minaret as the Tower of David and the name caught on. Thus to this day, despite a rather strange incongruity, some people think of this minaret when they imagine a tower dating back to the time of King David!

During the War of Independence the Old City fell into Jordanian hands. Jaffa Gate was blocked and the fortress became a Jordanian army post.

Today the citadel houses an unforgettable enterprise: the Tower of David Museum of the History of Jerusalem. Suitably located at the gateway to the Old City, this is the only museum in the world that deals exclusively with the history of Jerusalem.

The Tower of David Museum spans the colorful millennia of the city's history with a light, instructive and unusual touch. Not only do lively and exciting displays utilize holograms, laser projections, animation, models and dioramas, but the museum buildings and grounds are also historical sites just waiting to be explored.

My favorite of three suggested tours leads you chronologically through Jerusalem's history. It begins with the Canaanite period and moves through the First and Second Temple eras and ends with the Six-Day War. I find especially moving a multi-media presentation which closes with the establishment of the State of Israel.

A second tour sends you from one breathtaking observation point to another for panoramic views of the city. If you take the third route you visit an archeological garden whose remains span from the Hasmonean period to the Turkish era.

As if the museum and its fantastic exhibits weren't enough for Jerusalem's visitors, the museum also presents an educational evening production called "Mystery in the Citadel." Complete with costumes and historical clues, the production offers a diverting picture of Herod's era. Other citadel attractions include a nighttime sound and light show.

Hours: **CHRIST CHURCH** [628-4457]: all day every day
TOWER OF DAVID MUSEUM [626-5310]: Spring to fall:
Sun.-Thurs., 9:00-17:00; Fri.-Sat., 9:00-14:00; Winter: Sun.-
Thurs., 10:00-16:00; Fri.-Sat., 10:00-14:00; **Entrance fee**
Restrooms: Christ Church and the Tower of David Museum

Domes top the Church of the Holy Sepulcre (p. 185).

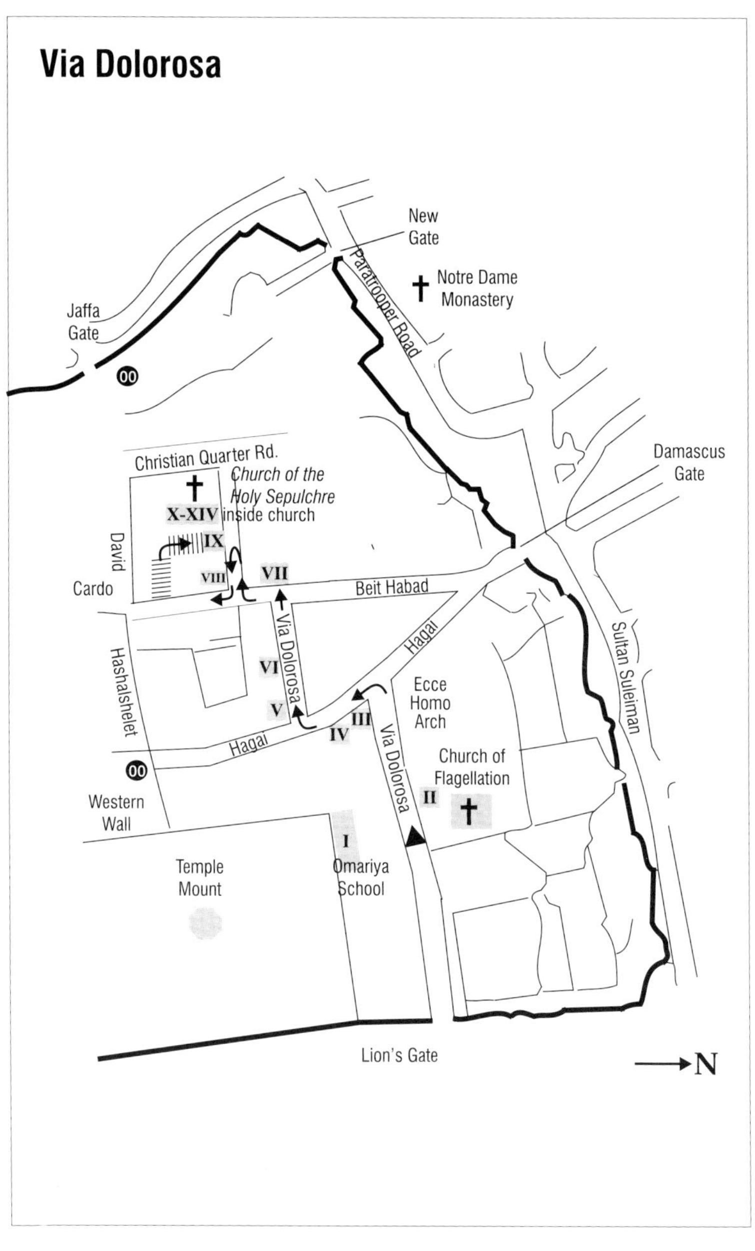

Via Dolorosa
Jaffa Gate
New Gate
Notre Dame Monastery
Paratrooper Road
Damascus Gate
Christian Quarter Rd.
Church of the Holy Sepulchre
inside church
X-XIV
IX
VIII
VII
David
Cardo
Beit Habad
Hagai
Via Dolorosa
VI
V
Hashalshelet
Hagai
Ecce Homo Arch
III
IV
Via Dolorosa
Church of Flagellation
II
Sultan Suleiman
Western Wall
Temple Mount
I
Omariya School
Lion's Gate
N

Via Dolorosa

- **Begin**: at the Omariyah School, about five minutes' walk inside Lions' Gate
- **End**: at the Church of the Holy Sepulchre
- **Take bus**: 3, 6, 19, 20, 30, 38 to Jaffa Gate
- **Park your car**: in MUSRARA (enter by way of Damascus Gate) or the Mamilla lots (enter through JAFFA GATE)
- **Time frame**: 1-2 hours
- **Take note**: On Friday mornings the Old City can be very crowded

---

Every Friday afternoon pilgrims to the Holy City follow brown-robed Franciscan priests along the Via Dolorosa. For many devout Christians this slow amble in the footsteps of Jesus is the highlight of their trip to Israel. Walking quietly behind a group leader who may be bent over under the weight of a large wooden cross, they pause at each of 14 different stations along the route. In somber contemplation they listen as the Franciscans read from the Bible. Then all recite a solemn prayer.

Franciscan priests begin the procession along the Via Dolorosa.

Sometimes called the Way of the Cross or the Way of Sorrow, the Via Dolorosa represents the route that Jesus followed from condemnation to crucifixion. It begins where the Antonia Fortress stood 2,000 years ago. Today that ancient site is occupied by the Omariyah School of Islamic Studies.

Starting the Via Dolorosa at Antonia Fortress is a 13th-century modification of several more ancient routes. But although the Byzantines commenced from Gethsemane (at the foot of the Mount of Olives) and medieval pilgrims began on MOUNT ZION, the final section of the Via Dolorosa has remained unchanged. It is the world-famous Church of the Holy Sepulchre — almost universally accepted as the site at which Jesus was crucified, buried, and subsequently resurrected.

Nothing remains of the large fortress that King Herod named Antonia after his friend Mark Anthony, for it was demolished at the same time that the Second Temple was destroyed. In its heyday the fortress was splendid and complex, with two main sections. It contained elegant lodgings for the Roman governor and big courtyards whose flagstone paving was called *lithostratos*.

A Roman infantry unit was garrisoned at the fort, encamped in the courtyard. At festivals the troops were placed on alert and told to watch for signs of Jewish rebellion — especially on the Temple Mount. In the absence of trouble the Roman soldiers stationed at Antonia would while away their time by playing games that they carved into the flagstone pavement.

Part of the walk along the Via Dolorosa is based on traditions, legacies from the past that have become accepted by the Christian world. However most of the stations along the route commemorate events specifically mentioned in the New Testament. Over the years chapels and oratories were built at some of the stations, a few of which are open only during the Friday afternoon procession. Each station is marked by Roman numerals.

Limited by their Holy Land timetable, not all pilgrims make it to the Friday procession. Thus groups can be seen walking the Via Dolorosa all week long from early morning until the late afternoon. Carrying their Bibles they tread the route so similar to that which Jesus would have followed, stopping outside each of the various stations to voice an earnest prayer.

Station 1: Jesus is condemned — Jesus was apparently condemned at the paved *lithostratos*, which may have been a public square of sorts. The New Testament states that the Roman governor *"brought Jesus out and sat down on the judge's seat at a place known as the Stone Pavement…"* (John 19:13). However prayers at the first station of the Via Dolorosa are spoken on the site where the Palace once stood, also called the Praetorium (today the courtyard of the

Omariyah School). Your only opportunity to enter this interesting courtyard is on Fridays before the procession begins.

A barred window on one side of the courtyard offers a truly incredible view of the Temple Mount. You will find that the Dome of the Rock and the people strolling between the mosques appear almost close enough to touch. Like you, the Roman governor would have been able to observe nearly everything that was happening near the Temple.

To reach the next station leave the school by descending a ramp and stand on the narrow road outside a Franciscan friary. Look for the phrase "II Statio" on the compound's exterior wall.

Station 2: Jesus is given the cross to bear — The New Testament relates that Pontius Pilate handed Jesus over to the Roman soldiers. Two striking sanctuaries inside the Franciscan compound commemorate the events that occurred next: Jesus was laughed at, mockingly called the King of the Jews, crowned with thorns and tortured. Then, *"carrying his own cross, he went out to the place of the Skull (which in Aramaic is called Golgotha)"* (John 19:16-17).

The Chapel of the Condemnation and Imposition of the Cross is located to your left after you walk through the entrance. Originally a Byzantine church of great beauty, it was transformed into a mosque during a later era. In 1904 the chapel was renovated and returned to its former Byzantine splendor.

Five shiny white domes top today's lovely sanctuary, each of them resting on a stained-glass window-enveloped drum. An interesting feature of this church is the Roman-period floor found next to its western wall. Typical of floors of that era, it is made of very large, striated stones.

The Church of the Flagellation is on the other side of the courtyard. In Roman times, those prisoners who were sentenced to die were first scourged with leather whips called flagella. This horrid instrument ended in leather thongs with bone or metal slivers that would rip the skin and draw blood — an especially cruel punishment for those condemned to death.

Jesus' crown of thorns makes up the basic motif of this powerful chapel. An extraordinary mosaic crown of thorns interwoven with light-colored flowers covers the inner dome of the sanctuary. Several of the geometric designs on the floor also resemble the spiky laurel, and an abstract half-circular thorn design dominates the entrance. There are even prickles within the cross that tops the chapel.

We don't know for sure exactly what Jesus was forced to carry, for some researchers believe that the vertical portion of the cross was a permanent fixture on Golgotha. What is certain, however, is that condemned persons normally toted either an entire cross or its horizontal beam through the crowded, noisy, narrow streets of the city.

To reach the next station begin descending Via Dolorosa Street. As you walk you will pass under an arch. From the 16th to the 20th centuries it was believed to be the arch from which Pontius Pilate displayed Jesus to the populace with the words *"Behold the man,"* or *"Here is the man" (Ecce Homo)* (John 19:5).

In the late 1850's Father Marie Alphonse Ratisbonne decided to build a convent in the Old City of Jerusalem. When he bought the ruins adjacent to the arch associated with Ecce Homo, he believed the convent would be located on a Christian holy site associated with the suffering of Jesus. And this was of immeasurable importance to Ratisbonne, a French Jew who had converted to Catholicism and had helped found the Fathers and the Sisters of Zion.

When the rubbish was cleared away before construction of the Ecce Homo Convent, what appeared to be the famous *lithostratos* pavement came into view. How exciting it must have been to discover that the stone markings were carved by Roman soldiers! The games on the pavement seemed to correspond

Powerful illustrations at the Church of the Flagellation

perfectly to those mentioned in the New Testament. It certainly must have been the site at which the Roman soldiers had mocked Jesus!

This assumption was given wide credence until the middle of the 20th century. At that time undisputed archeological evidence revealed that the pavement — and the Ecce Homo arch — were built more than a century after the crucifixion. In fact the arch was part of a victory gate built by the Emperor Hadrian in 135. The Emperor had just completed a successful three-year campaign in which he suppressed a last-ditch Jewish effort to obtain independence from Rome, and he decided to provide the world with visible confirmation of his triumph. The pavement belonged to the Roman forum that he constructed at just about the same time.

Nonetheless, pilgrims continue flocking to the arch, where they can recall the confrontation between Jesus and Pilate and examine the flagstone games that are on view inside the convent.

To reach the third and fourth stations follow Via Dolorosa Street to the very bottom and turn left. This is called both Via Dolorosa Street and HaGai (or El Wad) Street. You will see Station III on the corner immediately after you turn.

Station 3: Jesus Falls for the First time — Crowned with thorns, lugging the cross or crossbeam, Jesus attempted to walk forward. Tradition holds that this is where Jesus collapsed under the heavy load.

Two ancient pillars are incorporated into the iron gate in front of Station Three and a powerful bas-relief of Jesus' fall is located over the door to the Armenian chapel established on the site.

The fourth station is located only a few dozen meters from the third, on the same side of the street.

Station 4: Jesus encounters his mother — It is believed that Mary was standing nearby when Jesus collapsed and that she broke through the crowds to reach him. They are said to have met at about this spot, today the fourth station. A poignant relief above the entrance to the oratory shows Jesus holding a cross, his head and Mary's so close together that they could almost have been touching.

To reach the next station, turn right at the first opportunity — a continuation of Via Dolorosa Street. On the corner to your left, immediately after you turn, you will see the Franciscan chapel that marks the fifth station.

Station 5: Simon is instructed to carry the cross — It became obvious that Jesus wasn't going to be able to finish the march. At this point the Roman soldiers looked into the crowd. *"A certain man from Cyrene,* [today's Libya], *Simon, the father of Alexander and Rufus, was passing by on his way in from the country, and they forced him to carry the cross"* (Mark 15:21).

Above the chapel door a Latin inscription reads "Simoni-Cyrenaeo Crux Imponitur" — Simon Takes Up the Cross. Simon helped Jesus bear the cross, assisting him all the way to the foot of Calvary — the site of crucifixion. A Jerusalem Cross is carved into the stone on either side of the lintel.

If you look to the right of the door you will see a depression in the wall. According to Christian tradition, Jesus rested a palm here to gain a small moment of respite. **To reach the next station continue ascending Via Dolorosa Street. Pass under a series of flying buttresses, parts of arches employed as building supports or reinforcements. Then walk under a long arched roof. The phrase "VI Statio" is written on a closed door which you will see immediately afterwards to your left.**

𝖘𝖙𝖆𝖙𝖎𝖔𝖓 𝟔: 𝖁𝖊𝖗𝖔𝖓𝖎𝖈𝖆'𝖘 𝖍𝖔𝖚𝖘𝖊 — The walk probably seemed never-ending and Jesus was tired, dusty, injured and covered with blood. At this point, it is said, a woman holding a cold, wet cloth rushed to Jesus' side and washed his face. Looking down at the cloth, she found that an impression of Jesus' features had remained on the fabric. Because the Greek word for true is "vera" and "icone" means image, tradition has named the woman Veronica and implies that this is where she lived.

> Some people believe that long before Jesus was crucified, Veronica was very ill. According to this tradition she was healed after touching one of Jesus' garments and subsequently followed him everywhere he went. A legend relates that after Jesus was crucified, Roman emperor Tiberius summoned Veronica — and the cloth — to his palace. One look at the imprinted image and Tiberius was cured of leprosy.

At the end of the 19th century, the Greek Catholics who own this site built a small house of worship over a Byzantine monastery erected here in ancient times. The lovely chapel is accessible from the door next to the station and the ancient monastery's large, vaulted crypt is also open to visitors. When Pope Paul VI paid his historic visit to the Holy City in 1964, he stopped here and prayed in this sanctuary.

Continue along the steep ascent on which you are walking. Station Seven is located immediately across from you at the junction where Via Dolorosa Street intersects Khan El Zeit (Beit HaBad Street). Khan El Zeit was part of the Roman Cardo laid out by Emperor Hadrian in the year 135.

𝕾tation 7: 𝕵esus 𝕱alls a second time — After the Last Supper, Jesus had returned to Gethsemane on the Mount of Olives and spent the night in prayer. Early in the morning he had been arrested and taken first to the house of Annas, then to High Priest Caiaphas and finally to the Roman governor's palace. Now, overcome with fatigue and struggling up the steep ascent, he fell once again as he exited the city. Christian tradition holds that this was the site of the gate through which he passed, the gate on which the Romans posted death sentences for public information. Many call it the Judgment Gate.

Franciscan priests bought the site in 1875 and built adjacent chapels, one slightly above the other. They are divided by a gigantic pillar left *in situ*, which once adorned the Roman Cardo.

To reach the eighth station exit the chapels, turn right and then immediately turn right again. Climb up 16 steps and look at the wall on your left.

𝕾tation 8: 𝕵esus talks to the women of 𝕵erusalem — It is here that Jesus is believed to have stopped to speak to the women of Jerusalem. *"A large number of people followed him, including women who mourned and wailed for him. Jesus turned and said to them, "Daughters of Jerusalem, do not weep for me; weep for yourselves and for your children"* (Luke 23:27-28).

All that is visible at Station Eight are a cross and the Greek word "NIKA" engraved in a stone. NIKA means "Jesus Christ conquers." The wall on which they are found belongs to a large Greek Orthodox monastery that blocks the continuation of the Via Dolorosa. As a result you will have to turn around and go back in order to continue along the Way of the Cross.

To reach the next station descend the 16 stairs you just climbed and return to Khan El Zeit. Turn right. You will be walking in a market whose stone arch coverings were built by the Crusaders. Continue until a sign on your right leads to the Coptic Orthodox Patriarchate, then ascend the stairs.

On the wall to your right you see the Russian Orthodox symbol. The wall and the symbol belong to the St. Alexander Nevsky Russian Orthodox Church located right next to the Church of the Holy Sepulchre.

During 19th-century excavations at St. Alexander's Church a Roman-period gate was discovered. Unlike many Christians, who believe that the Judgment Gate stood at the site of the today's seventh station, the Russian Orthodox contend that the gate uncovered within the confines of their church

Jesus falls for the first time — Station 3.

was the true Judgment Gate. **At the top of the steps follow a wide stone walkway to the Coptic Patriarchate.**

Station 9: Jesus Falls for the third time — A pillar is encased in the wall just outside the Coptic Patriarchate and directly across from the Coptic Church of St. Anthony. This column marks the spot at which Jesus faltered and fell one final time.

Walk through the gate to your left onto the rooftop terrace. Ethiopian Christians live in the humble dwellings you see around you. A large cupola on the terrace covers the underground Chapel of St. Helen, located within the Church of the Holy Sepulchre. Just beyond the terrace is the impressive dome that covers the church basilica.

***The last five stations are all located inside the Church of the Holy Sepulchre.* Walk to the far end of the terrace and duck under the low ceiling of an unmarked entrance to St. Michael's Ethiopian Chapel. Stop to look at this interesting house of worship, then descend the steps at its far end.**

You have reached the courtyard that belongs to the Church of the Holy Sepulchre. On your right you may see a number of crosses leaning against a wall: after carrying a cross along the Via Dolorosa, pilgrims deposit them here while they explore the interior of the church.

Of some 300 churches erected under the Byzantines, the Church of the Holy Sepulchre was the largest, the most elaborate and the most important. Destroyed during the Persian conquest in 614, rebuilt and then ravaged again by later Moslems, the church underwent repeated cycles of destruction and repair. What you see before you today is the Romanesque church constructed by the Crusaders. It is far smaller and much less ornate than the original Byzantine basilica but still most impressive to behold!

Enter the church, then immediately climb the stairs to your right. You have reached the site of Calvary. From this point on there will be no numbers on the stations, all of which are found inside the church. To reach Station Ten, stop at a window to your right.

Tradition holds that Jesus and his mother met at the Fourth Station.

Station 10: Jesus is stripped of his garments — You are standing right next to the site of crucifixion. According to the New Testament, *"When the soldiers crucified Jesus, they took his clothes, dividing them into four shares "* (John 19:23); *"And they crucified him. Dividing up his clothes, they cast lots to see what each would get"* (Mark 15:24).

The window to your right overlooks a chapel marking the spot at which Jesus was disrobed and humiliated before being nailed to the cross. Above the gilded altar and couched in an elaborate golden frame is a touching picture of women weeping at the crucifixion site.

To reach Station 11, pass by the window and stop in front of the Latin (Catholic) chapel.

Station 11: Jesus is nailed to the cross — If you try to imagine the scene you will understand the sorrow and gravity with which pilgrims pray at this site. They can almost hear the sound of women wailing ... the thud of the hammer pounding in the nails ... the screams of the other men ...

A striking altar designates the site at which Jesus was nailed to the cross. The altar, made in Florence, Italy, is a fine example of Renaissance art. Ringed by six panels of hammered silver, it was created in 1588 and donated by Cardinal Medici a few decades later. An intensely moving painting that hangs above the altar depicts Jesus lying prone at his mother's feet.

The next station is located at the Greek Orthodox chapel on the other (left) side of the room. To get there pass under an ornamental arch.

Station 12: Jesus dies on the cross — Built over the exact spot on which Jesus is believed to have been crucified, the Greek altar with its small marble pillars is far more elaborate than its Latin counterpart at Station 11. Beneath the stand is a large silver disk. Pilgrims often thrust their hands through the hole in the middle to touch the rock that held the cross on which Jesus was crucified.

Matthew wrote *"...when Jesus had cried out again in a loud voice, he gave up his spirit. At that moment the curtain of the temple was torn in two from top to bottom. The earth shook and the rocks split"* (Matthew 27:50-51). You can clearly see a crack in the rock. It may have been formed at that awful moment when the earth shuddered with anguish.

Station 13 is situated between the Greek Orthodox and the Catholic altars.

Station 13: Jesus is taken down from the cross — According to tradition it was here that Mary took Jesus' body into her arms after he was removed from the cross. A statuette representing Mary is enclosed in glass and situated above an altar. Adorned with jewelry that was donated by thankful pilgrims, the figure is made of painted wood and appropriately called Our Lady of Sorrows. It was presented to the church in 1778 by the Queen of Portugal.

You will note that the figure is pierced with a sword. When Jesus was still a baby the righteous Simeon told Mary that " *...This child is destined to cause the falling and rising of many in Israel, and to be a sign that will be spoken against, so that the thoughts of many hearts will be revealed. And a sword will pierce your own soul too*" (Luke 2:34-35).

To reach Station 14 leave Calvary by a second set of stairs. Turn left. As you walk to the rotunda where the station is located you will see a reddish marble slab. Called the Stone of the Anointing, or Unction, it marks the traditional spot on which Jesus was prepared for burial (embalmed). "*Later, Joseph of Arimathea asked Pilate for the body of Jesus...He was accompanied by Nicodemus... Taking Jesus' body, the two of them wrapped it, with the spices, in strips of linen. This was in accordance with Jewish burial customs*" (John 19:38-40).

Behind the slab you will notice a brilliant wall mosaic illustrating the events which followed the crucifixion: Jesus' removal from the cross, preparation for burial and Joseph of Arimathea carrying Jesus to the burial cave.

Now continue on to the rotunda.

Station 14: Jesus is entombed — Jesus' tomb, the Holy Sepulchre, is the oldest and the most important section of the church. It is located in an impressive rotunda whose magnificent cupola is supported by massive pillars. The tomb is encased in a rectangular edifice, rebuilt in 1810 after a terrible fire destroyed much of the church.

Within the encasement are two halls. The atrium is called the Chapel of the Angel: "*After the Sabbath, at dawn on the first day of the week, Mary Magdalene and the other Mary went to look at the tomb. There was a violent earthquake, for an angel of the Lord came down from heaven and, going to the tomb, rolled back the stone and ... said to the women, "Do not be afraid, for I know that you are looking for Jesus ... he is not here; he has risen, just as he said ..."* (Matthew 28:1-6).

A piece of the rolling stone is on display in the Chapel of the Angel. It is locked inside a glass podium for safekeeping, for when it was exposed pilgrims chopped off chunks of the rock to take back home.

Only a very few people can fit into the second chamber at one time. When it is your turn to enter be careful not to bump your head. Inside, the tomb is covered with a marble slab and decorated with bas-reliefs.

This completes the Via Dolorosa. Christians who have followed this sad route may have found it an enormously emotional ordeal. Not only do they contemplate the agony of Jesus, but during the walk many a pilgrim also makes the connection between Jesus' many sorrows — and his or her own.

Hours: (of those churches and chapels that are open without regard to the Friday procession)
FLAGELLATION AND CONDEMNATION [628-2936]: Daily, 8:00-12:00; 14:00-17:00
ECCE HOMO (SISTERS OF ZION) [627-7292]: Mon.-Sat., 8:30-14:00; 14:00-17:00; No fee for viewing the chapel from its picture window; fee to visit the Roman ruins
CHAPEL AT STATION VII: Open all day
CHURCH OF THE HOLY SEPULCHRE [627-3314]: Open from dawn to dusk

Note: The Friday procession leaves the Omariyah School at 15:00, solar time, for this is the hour at which Jesus is believed to have died. Thus when Israel goes onto daylight saving time it begins, instead, at 16:00

A brilliant mosaic dominates the wall above the Stone of the Anointing.

The American Colony retains its gracious aura.

American Colony Hotel

• Sheikh Jarrah Neighborhood, near Mount Scopus   • Bus: 23, 27

One of the first houses to be built outside of the Old City walls was a fabulous villa replete with splendidly decorated rooms. At first completely isolated in the wastelands, the dwelling was incorporated into the aristocratic Arab neighborhood of Sheikh Jarrah that grew up around it.

The palatial residence included beautifully fitted chambers for the rich effendi who owned it and for each of his four wives. A splendid inner courtyard provided privacy and a measure of protection from outside attack.

When the effendi died he left not a single male heir to take over the historic villa. It stood empty for decades until rented out to a communal group of Protestants originally from Chicago. Known as the American Colony, the group was led by Anna and Horatio Spafford, a couple who had experienced horrendous personal tragedy.

Before they came to Jerusalem the Spaffords lived in a beautiful home in

Chicago. One day in 1873 Anna and the four Spafford daughters took a trip to Europe. Their ship collided with another vessel and, although all four girls perished, Anna was miraculously saved. More children were born to the Spaffords after this catastrophe, but one of them died tragically of disease. The family moved to the Holy City hoping to find respite from their sorrows.

The pioneer group reached the Holy Land in 1881 and moved into lodgings within the Old City walls. But when dozens of Swedes joined the Colony in 1896 the living quarters became far too crowded for comfort. That's when the American Colony relocated to the late effendi's splendid villa outside the walls.

At first it had been quite a struggle to find financing both for the Colony's modest daily requirements and for the help the group proffered to needy Jerusalemites. Once joined by Swedish farmers, blacksmiths and expert crafts-men, however, the Colony finally became solvent — and even began to prosper! With a new bakery, blacksmith shop, dairy and other enterprises, it was al-most completely self-sufficient. And eventually new vistas opened up ...

When Emperor Wilhelm II came to Jerusalem in 1898, Swedish members of the Colony shot some excellent photos of his visit. The photographs were so unique and historic that they were in great demand. Photographs taken by Colony members of Swedish background are among the best documentation we have of the city's milestone events. A few of these pictures are on display at the Four Sephardic Synagogues in the Old City's Jewish Quarter.

The Colony began taking in paying guests at the beginning of the 20th century, doubling up to make room for these out-of-town visitors. Little by little the American Colony Hotel became famous for its combination of Euro-pean and Middle Eastern hospitality and ambience. To this day, descendants of the original Colony own the hotel and the aura remains.

Located as it is between old and new Jerusalem, not far from Mount Scopus and Damascus Gate, the hotel sustained heavy damage in both the War of Independence and the Six-Day War. Fortunately, the building has been completely restored and much of it looks exactly as it did when designed for the wealthy effendi. Visitors are welcome to view the beautiful, original stone floors and to enjoy unique and touching exhibits. My favorite display is a placard from the period of 1938-1939, when the Jews — and the Arabs — were in revolt against Palestine's British rulers. The notice reminds you not to dis-cuss military matters in public, as you never know who might be listening!

The second story features an open sitting room from which you can gaze up at the exquisite painted wooden ceiling. You may walk onto the terrace for a birds-eye view of the splendid landscaped courtyard: luxurious gardens surround a fountain and a goldfish pond. **Phone:** 627-9777

The Garden Tomb

• Conrad Schick Street, north of Damascus Gate   • Bus: 23, 28

"Finally Pilate handed him over to them to be crucified. So the soldiers took charge of Jesus. Carrying his own cross he went out to the place of the Skull (which in Aramaic is called Golgotha)" (John 19:16-17).
"At the place where Jesus was crucified, there was a garden, and in the garden a new tomb, in which no one had ever been laid" (John 19:41).

Two years after Byzantine Emperor Constantine openly adopted Christianity in 324, his mother Helena traveled to the Holy Land in search of sacred sites. With the help of Jerusalem patriarch Bishop Macarius, Helena was able to discover the site she believed to be Calvary (the place of Jesus' crucifixion) and the Holy Sepulchre (Jesus' tomb). Both were located outside the then-known Jerusalem city walls.

Roman shrines had been built atop the holy sites and Queen Helena directed that these pagan temples be razed to the ground. She then ordered construction of a magnificent Christian monument — the Basilica of the Holy Sepulchre. Destroyed by Persian invaders in 614, the church was partially reconstructed by the Crusaders about 500 hundred years later and is still standing today.

While much of the Christian world believes that Helena did, indeed, uncover the site at which Jesus was crucified and later entombed, there have always been some skeptics. The most prominent was British General Charles George Gordon, a courageous soldier, devout Christian and student of the Bible. Gordon was to die a hero's death in 1887 defending the British-Egyptian enclave at Khartoum from attack by Sudanese rebels.

Gordon spent one of the last years of his life roaming around Jerusalem. Thus it was that on a day in 1883 his eyes caught sight of a rocky knoll just a few hundred meters north of today's Old City walls. It looked to him so much like a skull that he believed it to be *Golgotha* (Calvary), the site of Jesus' crucifixion. Near the hill there are both an ancient tomb and a garden, each admirably suited to the biblical description of Jesus' burial place.

What made the discovery even more significant was its location outside the walls of Old Jerusalem, as Jews traditionally bury their dead on the edge of their cities. What was to become known as Gordon's Calvary was eventually taken over and is operated by an English organization called the Garden Tomb Association.

Within the burial cave are a hall and two bench-like stone slabs, only one of which was ever completed. Light from a window which early Christian pilgrims cut into the ceiling of the cave shines directly upon that bench — making this perhaps the world's earliest spotlight! Other evidence of Christian pilgrimage to this shrine includes a cross carved into an inside wall of the cave. An anchor, one of the earliest Christian symbols, is engraved on its exterior.

The Garden Tomb was discovered by General Charles Gordon in 1883.

Many visitors are impressed with the atmosphere of prayer and meditation found at the Garden Tomb, which is much quieter than the crowded and bustling Church of the Holy Sepulchre. Within the site are a charming garden, the rock-hewn tomb and Skull Hill.

Phone: 627-2745

Hours: Mon.-Sat., 8:30-12:00; 14:30-17:00. Protestant service on Sun. morning; There are no regular guided tours of the Garden Tomb. However, you can join a group that is being guided around the site

St. George's Cathedral

• #20 Nablus Road   • Bus: 23, 27

One of Jerusalem's most distinctive landmarks, St. George's Cathedral is a magnificent neo-Gothic edifice that would fit easily into traditional English countryside. Jerusalem's fourth Anglican Bishop, George Francis Popham Blythe, canvassed the world to find funds for the extraordinarily impressive buildings that make up the cathedral enclosure.

St. George's Cathedral opened in 1898 and serves as the center for the Anglican Church in the Middle East. Completely surrounded by a wall, the compound is located only a few hundred meters north of Jerusalem's Old City and is a lovely and peaceful site.

Walk into the courtyard, which is dominated by vaulted arcades. A lone Byzantine pillar stands in the center. Capped with a cannonball and surmounted by a cross, it represents the victory of Christianity over war. Positioned around the courtyard are the Bishop's residence, a delightful guest house, the cathedral and a splendid tower that was completed in 1910. The latter was named for King Edward VII, a genial patron of the arts who died that same year.

Interestingly, the 33-meter high square tower with its four pointed turrets was purposely not attached to the church. It was planned that way by the architect, who feared the consequences of interdependence should there be an earthquake. The tower's three bells are sounded for the daily Angelus (a historic call to prayer), as well as on solemn occasions.

The cathedral's uplifting ambience is created by a combination of stone walls, arches and by the warm, dark woodwork especially apparent in the ceiling and the pulpit. An Austrian organ is housed in a beautifully carved wooden structure at the rear of the church.

Near the organ are two baptismal fonts. The traditional font with a fine canopy made from Jordanian oaks was a gift from Queen Victoria. The other font is for total immersion.

Take a good look at the Dean's Stall. The prayer desk holds a beautiful wood carving of Moses with his hands upheld by Aaron and Hur. This, of course, reflects the biblical scene in which the Israelites and the Amalekites fight a desert battle.

Israel prevailed only while Moses held up his hands. But, obviously, Moses couldn't keep them up indefinitely. Thus, *"When Moses' hands grew tired, they took a stone and put it under him and he sat on it. Aaron and Hur held his hands up*

— one on one side, one on the other — so that his hands remained steady till sunset" (Exodus 17:12).

The Bishop's cathedra is a copy of the chair that belonged to Paschal I, an early 9th-century pope. Located in the catacombs of Rome's St. Calixtus, the original is the oldest episcopal throne still in existence. An old Saxon cross, found at Canterbury, is attached to a pillar on one side of the throne. On the walls of the nave hang four beautiful banners in Palestinian needlework depicting the four evangelists: Mark, Luke, Matthew, and John.

As you leave the cathedral visit the side chapel of St. Michael and All Angels. It is a study in tranquility and is always open for private prayer. A beautifully carved wooden Madonna from Bethlehem graces the wall.

St. George's College, surrounded by a serene biblical garden, is also located within the complex. The garden was designed by Nigel Hepper, who was curator at England's famous Kew Gardens for over half a decade.

The guest house at St. George's Cathedral contains 25 tastefully renovated rooms whose charming stone walls give them an ancient aura. Visitors relax with coffee in a garden next to a "hooshhoosh" tree. The "hooshhoosh" is a strange-looking wrinkled fruit, a cross between a grapefruit and lemon. Its skin is used for making a marvelous marmalade.

Hours: All day, every day

The Supreme Court

• Givat Ram   • Bus: 9, 24   • *Wheelchair accessible*

'The most important trial in Israeli history was [that] *of a non-Jew, a nonresident, and a man whose crimes were committed before the State of Israel even existed. Yet few people, save anti-Semites, disputed Israel's right to try Adolph Eichmann, the chief administrator of the Nazi Final Solution.'* (Rabbi J. Telushkin in **Jewish Literacy**)

Due to the enormous public interest generated by the case against Adolph Eichmann, the trial was heard in a special venue — Jerusalem's Binyanei Ha'uma (National Hall). It ended when District Court judges passed the first and only death sentence in the history of the State — a sentence upheld by Israel's Supreme Court.

Many years later this same Supreme Court reversed the conviction of Wachman Ivan Demjanjuk on the basis of reasonable doubt that he was the sadistic and murderous guard Ivan the Terrible from Treblinka. And in the 1990's the Supreme Court delivered another significant decision: its judges determined that women have as much right as men to compete for the position of pilot in the Israeli Air Force!

Israel as a Jewish State grants the right of citizenship to any Jew who wishes to return to the land of his forefathers. Under the Law of Return statute all that a Jew must do upon immigrating to Israel is to request citizenship. It is granted automatically unless there are specific prohibitions in his case.

The issue of Brother Daniel was brought before the Israeli Supreme Court in 1962. Brother Daniel had been born as the Jew Daniel Rufeisen. During the Holocaust he was hidden by Catholic priests and later not only converted to Catholicism but eventually became a priest himself. Upon entering Israel he asserted that his birth as a Jew entitled him to automatic citizenship despite the fact that he was a Catholic priest.

In denying Brother Daniel's right to citizenship under the Law of Return, the Supreme Court held that the saying "Once a Jew always a Jew" does not apply to a Jew who has abandoned his Jewish status by converting into another established religion. Brother Daniel accepted the ruling with good grace. He then became a citizen under the State's naturalization process, remaining in Israel and performing good deeds.

Israel's Supreme Court judges are constantly being called upon to make weighty decisions. Yet until the current majestic edifice on Givat Ram was completed in 1992 the Supreme Court convened in an almost primitive structure inside the Russian Compound. In winter the kerosene heaters that were used to warm the otherwise unheated building gave off a horrible smell. But when the windows were opened to air the rooms, the cold rushed in to freeze judicial fingers and toes! With the Court's relocation the judicial branch joined the legislative (Knesset) and administrative departments of the government on Givat Ram.

In its design the magnificent Supreme Court attempts to make a statement about its purpose. Architects Ram Karni and Ada Karni-Melamed, a world-renowned brother and sister team, combined unique materials, lines and light to interpret 'truth', 'justice' and 'mercy' as reflected in biblical references.

Stop in at the small museum located at the end of the Courtyard of the Arches. Here you can follow a short summary of the history of the Supreme Court and view footage from some of the Court's major cases.

Phone: 675-9666
Hours: Sun.-Thurs. 8:30-14:30; Daily guided tour in English at 12:00

The garden at St. George's Cathedral and the view from Israel's Supreme Court.

The Knesset — Israel's Parliament

• Givat Ram   • Bus: 9, 17   • *Wheelchair accessible*

Following the destruction of the First Temple most of Jerusalem's Jews were exiled to Babylon. When they returned half a century later under the leadership of Zerubbabel, they formed a body of 120 sages to decide on issues crucial to the continued existence of the Jewish people. This body was known as Knesset Gedola or "large gathering."

It is no wonder, then, that the parliament which governs the State of Israel is called the Knesset. Charged with continuing the legacies of those early sages, the Knesset is the legislative body that gathers to vote on national policy.

Knesset members are not selected by direct vote as is the case in many democracies. Instead, they appear on the list of a certain political party. Whether or not they are chosen for parliament depends upon their position on the list and how many votes their party garners.

Beginning in 1949 and for most of the next 17 years, the Knesset met in a modest building on King George Street. That building is still remembered by tourists who received a shock when Knesset workers ordered them to "take off their clothes" before entering the gallery. The workers, who were recent immigrants to Israel, really meant to say "coats!"

This older Knesset saw some fiery moments. In 1952, for example, former Jewish Underground leader (and later Prime Minister) Menachem Begin led a march upon the Knesset to protest the acceptance of reparations from Germany. In his wake came thousands of Holocaust survivors and the families of those who had perished in German concentration camps. Held back by Knesset guards, Begin roared that "A Jewish government that negotiates with Germany can no longer be a Jewish government!" and Prime Minister Ben-Gurion screamed "Hooligans!" at the marchers. Guards sprayed tear gas at the crowds, who responded with stones that broke the Knesset windows. (The Knesset voted to accept the reparations, badly needed by the brand-new State of Israel).

The 120-member parliament moved to new premises in 1966, on a high plateau called Givat Ram — "the lofty hill." There it stands today, together with buildings that house Israel's Government offices, the Bank of Israel, the SUPREME COURT and the ISRAEL MUSEUM. Israel's parliament was the site of a historic visit by former Egyptian president Anwar Sadat in 1977. Standing at the podium he told the people of Israel — and the entire world — that the war between his country and the Jewish State had finally reached an end.

Visitors to the Knesset can enjoy some spectacular art, sculpture and architecture. Opposite the main gate stands a large bronze *menorah*, chosen as a symbol of the State and reminiscent of the candelabrum that illuminated the interior of the Temple sanctuaries. You will want to examine the *menorah* more closely: the beautifully crafted bas-reliefs that cover its seven branches depict over two dozen of Israel's most significant historical events.

A few of Marc Chagall's most extraordinary works are on display in a hall named for that famous Russian-Jewish artist. They include wall and floor mosaics of rare beauty as well as three tapestries depicting the history of the Jewish people.

If the Knesset is in session you will be able to sit in the visitors' gallery and watch parliamentary proceedings in Plenary Hall. Israeli parliamentarians can be extraordinarily volatile, cantankerous, loud and flamboyant — so if there is a hot debate taking place you are in for an experience!   **Phone**: 675-3333

Hours: Sun. and Thurs., 8:30-14:30; Bring a passport or identity card to present at the entrance. You may not take in cameras or any form of weapon. Small bags can be deposited at the security desk when you enter. All visitors join a (free) guided tour. There are tours in English approximately every half-hour. *If you use a wheelchair, call in advance so arrangements can be made for your visit.*

Israel Museum

• Givat Ram   • Bus: 9, 17, 24, 28   • *Wheelchair accessible*

Until the Israel Museum was established in 1965, Jerusalem's art, archeology and Judaica collections were dispersed all over the city. Surprisingly, however, when these assorted items were finally combined into one large complex there wasn't very much to see!

But museum founders did not despair. They were absolutely certain that some day, and in the not-too-distant-future, their museum would become the world-famous institution that it is today.

All of which explains the museum's unusual exterior design: a series of squarish buildings with temporary outer walls that allow for future expansion. And, indeed, once open, the Israel Museum soon began to grow by leaps and bounds. It wasn't long before new buildings were added to the complex.

Outside the Museum

THE SHRINE OF THE BOOK. Here you can inspect the celebrated Dead Sea Scrolls and learn more about the unique Essene community, its daily lifestyle and the art of copying scrolls. Samples of the original Dead Sea Scrolls are housed beneath the famous white dome. Most of these scrolls predate the last-known biblical text — the Aleppo Codex, also on display — by at least 1,000 years!

THE BILLY ROSE ART GARDEN. Studded with sculptures dramatically placed along the museum's beautifully landscaped slopes, the Billy Rose Garden was designed to offer visitors a truly superb, bird's-eye view of Jerusalem.

Inside the Museum

THE BRONFMAN ARCHEOLOGICAL WING. Most prestigious museums send teams to other lands in search of artifacts for their collections. Here in Israel, however, archeologists often have to look no farther than their own back yards to come up with amazing discoveries. In fact, almost every item in the museum's vast archeological wing — including finds of enormous religious and historical significance — was unearthed somewhere within this country.

When you were at the OPHEL GARDENS you saw a copy of an inscription at least 2,000 years old. Carved onto a rock, it read "To the house of the trumpeting to procl [aim the Sabbath?]." Here at the Israel Museum you can view the original inscription. You may find a pillar from Caesarea of special interest as well. Its inscription mentions Pontius Pilate, the Roman Procurator of Judea at the time of Jesus' crucifixion.

THE JUDAICA AND JEWISH ETHNOGRAPHY WING. This is the section in which to observe handsome Jewish ceremonial objects, including the most fabulous Torah scrolls, Hanukkah lamps and Havdalah sets in the world. You can also walk through three completely reconstructed synagogues — from India, Italy and Germany — each situated in side-rooms off the main display hall.

BEZALEL ART WING. In this part of the museum you can view collections of fine art from the 17th century to present. Here special emphasis is placed on the contributions of contemporary Israeli artists.

RUTH YOUTH WING. Many an Israeli parent learns to enjoy museums after an unforgettable school trip to the Israel Museum's youth wing. Intended mainly for young visitors, this is always my first museum stop. Its two floors provide wonderfully innovative and imaginative displays whose ever-changing themes are unfailingly creative.   **Phone**: 670-8811

The Israel Museum is often identified by this symbolic cover above the Shrine of the Book.

Hours: Sun., Mon., Wed., Thurs., 10:00-17:00; Tue., 16:00-22:00
Shrine of the Book: 10:00-22:00; Fri., 10:00-14:00; Sat., 10:00-16:00; During vacations the hours may be extended. Free guided tours available in English. Call for details. **Entrance fee**. Leave cameras and small bags at security.

Jerusalem Botanical Gardens

• Access from Burla Street   • Bus 17   • Partially *wheelchair accessible*

On a late afternoon one August I took a leisurely stroll through some beautiful botanical gardens. When it came time to rest I stopped alongside a shimmering pool studded with flowering water lilies and watched the antics of the pond's playful ducks and swans.

Believe it or not, I was not on vacation in Paris and this was not the Tuileries Public Garden. Rather, I was in the very heart of Jerusalem, only minutes away from a plethora of shopping centers and high-rise apartments. And I was enjoying every minute of a visit to the Jerusalem Botanical Gardens.

Located right next to the Hebrew University's Givat Ram campus, the Jerusalem Botanical Gardens is one of the city's most refreshing spots. Indeed, it is rare in Jerusalem to find such a pastoral atmosphere, in which blackbirds chirp amidst fields of blooming flowers and woodpeckers noisily bob their heads on the tree trunks. Visitors of all ages vie for the attentions of the swans and throw pita bread to the fish.

Actually, there are two Jerusalem Botanical Gardens, both affiliated with the Hebrew University. (See MOUNT SCOPUS, p. 99.) The Scopus gardens are less than a quarter of the size of those in Givat Ram and feature strictly native Israeli plants and flowers. In the Givat Ram botanical gardens you find flora from almost every region in the world.

Rather than sorting the foliage by plant groups, a common procedure in numerous other international botanical gardens, the plants here are arranged by geographical region. For many of us a walk through the North American

A shimmering lake in the middle of the Jerusalem metropolis.

region will be a stroll down memory lane. And a South African passing through the Garden's Cape region will undoubtedly recall his native country.

Flowers do not blossom all year long in the Botanical Gardens. That's why Exhibition Loop is such a surprise. Aware that many people are interested more in beauty *per se* than in studying botanical strains, Exhibition Loop includes many cultivars (domestic, commercial blooms) as well as foreign flowers. This particular area is constantly recycled so that even winter visitors can view some delightful blooms. Indeed, in late winter and spring you will find varieties of mint and flowering thyme, gorgeous purplish-blue mountain lupin, domestic anemone, irises, peonies, and yellow-green Jerusalem spurge.

Look for another unusual touch — but one so typical for Jerusalem! While landscaping the site the university uncovered Second Temple period Roman burial caves which have become part of the garden experience. You and your youngsters can climb inside and explore to your hearts' content.

One plant is called, in Hebrew, *pegam.* This is rue, a plant thought to have medicinal powers and to be able to cure just about any ills. In the New Testament Jesus speaks of rue when chastising the Pharisees: *"Woe to you Pharisees, because you give God a tenth of your mint, rue and all other kinds of garden herbs, but you neglect justice and the love of God ..."* (Luke 11:42).

When you step into the conservatory you will feel as though you have entered a tropical wonderland. In the center you will see members of the palm family. On each side are aerial orchids — orchids that grow above the ground. They have a nutritional system that allows them to extract all the goodies they need from the air around them, a quality that frees them from dependence on the soil.

Following these are crop plants, commonly cultivated in the tropics, which have nutritional value (or questionable value, like tobacco). These include a vanilla vine, which is a climbing orchid whose sweet vanilla aroma is extracted from fermented seedpods. There are papayas and bananas, both of which bear fruit.

The European region is near the lake. And it is a picture that could have jumped out of any European guide-book: a glistening green lake smothered in water lilies, charming foot bridges, the impressive glass-and-stone Visitors' Center and a Swiss chalet with sustenance for the hungry.

Phone: 679-4012
Hours: Daylight, seven days a week. The conservatory is open Sun.-
              Thurs., 10:00-14:00; Sat., 10:00 -18:00; closed Fri.; **Entrance fee**

Bible Lands Museum

• Givat Ram   • Bus: 9, 17, 24, 28   • *Wheelchair accessible*

For over seven years the building site next to the Israel Museum remained a mystery to the Jerusalemites who passed it by. Finally, in 1992, a white stone edifice with a striking green entrance opened to the public. Since it was called the Bible Lands Museum Jerusalemites naturally assumed that the artifacts would share one common denominator: the land and the people of Israel.

But the contents of the museum turned out to be a complete surprise. For the items on view were discovered not only in the Holy Land, but in countries whose ancient cultures preceded our own! And the explanations related to the peoples who influenced Father Abraham, whose merchants traveled back and forth across the tiny strip that would become the land of Israel, and whose customs and traditions provide the backdrop to the Jewish religion, the Jewish spirit and the Jewish homeland.

Unlike many other museums, this one takes you through time in chronological order. You begin by descending a wide staircase whose purpose is to lead you "down" into the past, just as the archeologist digs deep in the earth to find the answers.

Three glass-enclosed displays will catch your attention as you enter the introductory gallery at the bottom of the steps. These little figurines and statuettes are samples of artifacts from the lands where Ham, Shem and Japhet wandered after the flood. Here museum curators emphasized the fact that we are all descendants of Noah.

As you follow the galleries clockwise around the museum, enjoy the quiet elegance of the design and the excellent Hebrew, English and Arabic explanations. The walls never reach the ceiling, providing an open and spacious ambience. Green foliage contrasts deliciously with the white walls and ceilings.

The first quote in Gallery One is from Genesis, and the room contains displays from the period when Adam and Eve lived in the Garden of Eden. At that time man began to manipulate his surroundings: he learned to domesticate animals, began cultivating the soil, invented tools and used clay to create artistic utensils.

Once he had become master of his environment man became interested in fertility. The bull figurines you see before you have been signs of fecundity for thousands of years and so has the form of a woman as you see it here, with heavy breasts and wide hips.

A poster depicting the village of Hacilar in southwestern Anatolia (Turkey of today) offers an interesting picture of man's progress over a period of a thousand or so years. The village grew from a settlement whose little houses had no doorways, to a sophisticated wall-enclosed town with a central square, residential districts, a well and a shrine.

One gallery emphasizes weapons used in the ancient Near East; another displays statues, inscriptions and musical instruments found in Mesopotamian temples from the 6th century B.C.E. You will see a scale model of the royal burial ground at Giza (in Egypt) shortly after completion of the third pyramid. A graphic illustration of circumcision in Ancient Egypt covers a nearby wall.

Enjoy the gallery exhibiting the fleshpots of Egypt during the period prior to the Hebrew exodus. The era during which Rome ruled Judea is covered as well: on view are a Jewish sarcophagus of that time and an elaborate Christian sarcophagus from 4th-century Rome.

Seals are given a lot of attention in the Bible Lands Museum. That's because seals can provide us with important information about ancient times. Often, they also verify biblical sources.

One of the seals on display is a stamp seal from 6000 B.C.E. used for printing a design on fabric. Stamp seals (and later cylinder seals) are made by taking an imprint of clay and putting a design in the negative so that the positive will be stamped on the product.

In Gallery Three virtually anyone — even a person with absolutely no computer skills whatsoever — can delve into the fascinating world of the seal. The interactive program that this gallery provides is superb: even the most computer-phobic people will find it difficult to tear themselves away!

Phone: 561-1066
Hours: Sun., Tue., Thurs., 9:30-17:30; Wed. (April-Oct.), 9:30-21:30; Wed. (Nov.-Mar.), 13:30-21:30; Fri., 9:30-14:00; Sat., 11:00-15:00; **Entrance fee** includes audio guide

Bloomfield Science Museum

• Givat Ram   • Bus: 9, 24, 28   • *Wheelchair accessible*

Sometimes it seems as if Jerusalem is famous only for its ancient and holy sites. However while the essence of the city may be found within its old and hallowed stones, Jerusalem has plenty to offer visitors who are looking for some old-fashioned family entertainment: a fantastic zoo, two botanical gardens, a water walk, terrific parks, a natural history museum and the Bloomfield Science Museum.

You don't have to be either a science buff or a youngster to have a great time at Bloomfield. The fun begins at the entrance, where an odd-looking sphere will catch your eye. Walk up to it and read the explanation: "Money makes the world go round … or can be used to describe why the world revolves around the sun."

Confused? Try taking a coin of any denomination and rolling it down the tiny ramp. Watch as it falls into the "Gravitational Saucer." Your tension rises uncontrollably as the coin circles around at an agonizingly slow speed, speeds up into an ever-accelerating spin and then drops into the tank. Now, finally, the connection becomes clear!

You have entered a world in which a strange gravitational pull of uncontrolled curiosity draws you from one exciting museum display to the next. Hands-on displays portray different aspects of the nature of electricity, air, water and a variety of metals and machinery. Innovative exhibits developed by scientists at the museum utilize computer and video technology of the highest level to enlighten and amuse the entire family.

The museum is constantly offering new exhibits. Depending on when you visit you may be able to explore a House on Mars, learn about communication in a new millennium, or watch whatever riveting new show is being offered at the multi-media auditorium.

Phone: 561-8128
Hours: Mon., Wed., Thurs., 10:00-18:00; Tue., 10:00-20:00; Fri., 10:00-13:00; Sat., 10:00-15:00; closed Sun.; **Entrance fee**

Yad VaShem Holocaust Memorial

Hill of Remembrance, on the western slopes of Mount Herzl
Bus: 13, 17, 18, 20, 23, 26, 27
Wheelchair accessible

In the middle of the 20th century the Jewish people suffered an appalling holocaust of inconceivable dimensions: six million men, women and children were hounded into cattle cars, thrust into death camps and slaughtered by the Nazis for the "crime" of being Jews.

Five years after the establishment of the State of Israel its leaders resolved to build a memorial so extraordinary that future generations would learn about the Holocaust — and never, never forget. That memorial is called Yad VaShem, for the verse in Isaiah: *"And to them will I give in my house and within my walls a memorial [YAD] better than sons and daughters: I will give them an everlasting name [SHEM], that shall not be cut off"* (Isaiah 56:5).

Inaugurated in 1957, Yad VaShem has grown immensely over the years as impressive and creative monuments to the massacred six million are added to the complex. The grounds are covered with numerous sculptures, each portraying a theme connected with the Holocaust.

Pick up a site map before you enter, then walk in and out of the memorial's haunting displays. A belt of trees, called the Garden of the Righteous, rings the entire compound and honors those Gentiles who endangered their own lives in order to save the life of a Jew.

The Historical Museum: This series of buildings follows the story of the Holocaust from the rise of the Nazi Party to power through life in the forced ghettos, mass murders, the Jewish Resistance, the liberation of the concentration camps and the aftermath of the war.

The Hall of Names: By the end of the 20th century, over three and a half million names had been collected and immortalized in this chamber. You, too, can add a name by filling out a Page of Testimony and thereby preserving the memory of a victim of the Holocaust.

The Hall of Remembrance: Designed to resemble the tent in which the ancient Israelites carried the Ten Commandments through the desert, this site hosts somber memorial gatherings. Especially moving are the thin spirals of smoke which rise heavenward from an eternal flame.

The Children's Memorial: One and a half million children were ruthlessly cut down during the Holocaust. Just beyond the entrance a system of mirrors reflects and multiplies candle flames to infinity, while the names, ages and place of birth of children who died in the Holocaust are read out in Hebrew, English and Yiddish. The total effect awesomely conveys the incomprehensible magnitude of this tragedy.

The Valley of the Communities: The huge maze dug into the slope of the mountain is designed to look like a map of Europe, but when viewed from the top it resembles a series of mass graves. Symbolic of what happened to European Jewry during the Holocaust, this complex commemorates the thousands of thriving Jewish communities that were ruthlessly destroyed. On one of the stones near the entrance is a phrase from the Bible: *"so the next generation would know them, even the children yet to be born, and they in turn would tell their children"* (Psalms 78:6).   **Phone**: 644-3400

Hours: Sun-Thurs., 9:00-17:00; Fri., 9:00-14:00; Closed Sat. Workshops and English guided tours available by prior arrangement. **No entrance fee but there is a charge for the site map**

Mount Herzl

• Herzl Boulevard   • Bus: 13, 17, 18, 20, 23, 26, 27   • *Wheelchair accessible*

Until the assassination of Prime Minister Yitzhak Rabin in 1995, many people who visited Mount Herzl left as soon as they finished touring the Holocaust memorial situated on its western slopes. But all that changed when the world-famous Israeli leader was murdered during a peace rally in Tel Aviv. Today almost everyone who visits Jerusalem makes a pilgrimage to Rabin's grave on Mount Herzl, inevitably passing the tombstones of *other* notable figures as they walk.

Foremost among them, of course, is Theodore Herzl, the visionary who organized and chaired the First Zionist Congress in 1897 and who coined the phrase "if you will it, it is no dream." Thousands of people gather together on the plaza next to Herzl's grave every year as a sad and solemn ceremony brings Memorial Day to a close. Then, as the first evening stars appear in the sky, the festivities marking Independence Day begin.

Mount Herzl is unlike any other site in the world. Its western slopes hold an extraordinary memorial to six million murdered Jews — YAD VASHEM. A unique military cemetery to the north, interspersed with stirring monuments to their valor, holds the remains of courageous men and women who died while serving their country. And in Mount Herzl Park, at the center of this exquisitely landscaped mountain, a section called Leaders of the Nation was set aside as a burial site. Among those luminaries lying here at rest are former Prime Ministers Golda Meir and Levi Eshkol, former President Chaim Herzog, founder of the Revisionist Movement Ze'ev Jabotinsky, and Ophira Navon, beloved wife of former President Yitzhak Navon.

Take your time and read the signs near the monuments and on the tombstones. The body of sensitive poet Hannah Senesh is buried in one plot, together with other young paratroopers who jumped into Hungary on a rescue mission during World War II. Caught by the Nazis, Senesh was tortured and then executed by a firing squad.

Walk through a stone tunnel that commemorates defenders of the Old City's Jewish Quarter, lost to Jordan in 1948. You can read the soldiers' names —

Prime Minister Yitzhak Rabin was assassinated at a peace rally; memorial ceremony on Mount Herzl.

including that of the youngest, a 10-year-old boy. Then descend to an underground memorial to 69 sailors who drowned in the submarine Dakar. Finally located in 1999, the Dakar had disappeared in 1968 while on route from England to the Haifa Port.

Victims of Arab terrorist attacks are buried in cemeteries around the country. In 1999 a stunning memorial site for their families was erected on the slopes of Mount Herzl. Its plaza overlooks the hills and vales of Jerusalem — the capital of a Jewish State that Theodore Herzl helped bring into existence.

Phone: 651-1108
Hours: Mount Herzl Park: Sun.-Thurs., 8:00-16:45; Fri., 8:00-13:00; Sat., 9:00-16:45. Military Cemetery — separate entrance — open 24 hours a day, seven days a week
Restrooms: Mount Herzl Park

Second Temple Model

- HaRav Uziel Street in Bayit Vegan, adjacent to Kroch Square
- Bus: 21, 21a   • *Wheelchair accessible*

In the middle of the 1st century Jerusalem was a thriving metropolis graced with royal palaces, spacious mansions and ordinary dwellings. Like many other cities under Roman rule it also boasted impressive public marketplaces, a large forum, a theater and even a hippodrome. Yet despite the somewhat Roman flavor of Jerusalem, the city's focus — and the jewel on the Jewish crown — was always the sacred Temple.

To truly understand the glory of ancient Jerusalem, visit the city's extraordinary Model of Jerusalem in the Second Temple Period. Planned by archeology professor Michael Avi–Yona, the model's unique design is based on historical sources and archeological finds from inside and around the Old City. The model is a 1:50 scaled-down version of Jerusalem around the year 66, just prior to the outbreak of the Jews' Great Revolt and before the city's destruction by the Romans four years later.

Pick up a pamphlet at the entrance to the complex, then start your tour of ancient Jerusalem on the northern side of the "city." From here you can view all of ancient Jerusalem at a single glance: the city's hills and vales, water systems and springs, neighborhoods and public institutions. Try to identify the ridge on which David's City was originally situated, then follow the city's expansion northward to a time when it encompassed Mount Moriah — site of the First and Second Temples.

Follow its development westward to the Lower and then to the Upper Cities. Over time, houses were built outside of the city boundaries: look for the first, the second and the third walls — all built to envelop these new neighborhoods.

An arrow points to the location of the Western Wall. Actually only a small section of the western supporting wall which surrounded the Temple Mount, the Western Wall has been a center of Jewish prayer for centuries. From the east you can see into the Temple enclosure, and observe its various inner courtyards and structures.

Having experienced for yourself the splendor of ancient Jerusalem, you will no doubt appreciate the sages' sentiments when they exclaimed:

"He who has not seen Jerusalem in its glory has not seen a beautiful city" (Talmud, Succa 51b).

Phone: 643-7777
Hours: Daily, 8:00-22:00; **Entrance fee**

The Tisch Family Zoological Gardens (Jerusalem Zoo)

• Manahat (Malha) neighborhood   • Bus: 26, 33   • *Wheelchair accessible*

When Jerusalem's Hadassah Hospital moved to new quarters in the 1930's, its former courtyard in downtown Jerusalem was taken over by a rather different set of occupants. The newcomers were a desert monitor, two rhesus monkeys and a hyena … and the Jerusalem Biblical Zoo was born!

The Zoo developed so fast that the neighbors began to complain but fortunately the Hebrew University on MOUNT SCOPUS offered to take it in. Cages were prepared and the animals were moved to Mount Scopus in early 1948. However it soon became too dangerous to take the road to the mountain: vehicles traveling to both the University and the Hadassah Hospital were repeatedly ambushed by hostile Arabs.

Jerusalem was under Arab siege until June of 1948 and most of the animals not slain by Arab bullets died of hunger. Even after the city was divided, with Mount Scopus remaining part of Israel, the road to Scopus was too hazardous to travel. Thus in 1950 the Zoo was evacuated to new lodgings in Romema. Of the Zoo's original 200 animals only 18 remained ...

In 1993 the Jerusalem Zoo moved to its permanent home in the suburb of Manahat (Malha). Happily, the wide-open spaces of western Jerusalem replaced restrictive, old-fashioned enclosures used when the Zoo was located well inside the city. Tastefully landscaped and easily maneuvered, the Jerusalem Zoo is a delightful treat for the entire family.

Among the Zoo's many attractions is the small animals' building — a trip around the world in which visitors wander from desert to jungle. Another is a stunning 5-dunam lake filled with waterfowl. Search one of the islands for rare apes called siamangs: they will probably be busily climbing trees. Indigenous to the Far East, these fascinating apes have bags under their throats. When agitated, courting, looking for food or during a fight they communicate by blowing up the bags and emitting loud whoops!

On weekdays a little train takes you through most of the zoo. You can get on and off the train to visit the bears and the swamp fowl. The antics of the primates are great fun to watch. Then look for a very special display that contains birds of prey. This is a rare opportunity to closely observe eagles and vultures.

You won't want to miss the exotic tropical birdhouse. Here you should stand quietly in one place for several minutes, watching as the enclosure's 150 brilliantly colored birds fly through the trees or become visible on the branches.

The Biblical Animal Area is a rare treat. Stand on a bridge to view 40 dunams occupied by oryxes, gazelles, fallow deer, ibexes and wild sheep. Or gaze over at the African lake to see giraffes, rhinoceroses and other large mammals. A life-size model of Noah's Ark serves as an inviting Visitors' Center.

Don't pass up the lemur exhibit. On our last visit we had the opportunity of getting a really close look when beautiful lemur monkeys crossed the sidewalk only a few centimeters from where we were standing! Then continue on to the area known as the South American Yard to see interesting tapirs and other animals otherwise unknown in this part of the world.

Phone: 675-0111

Hours: Sun.-Thurs. 9:00-17:00; Fri., 9:00-16:30; Sat., 10:00-17:00; Hours are extended in summer, call for details; **Entrance fee, extra fee for train.** *Wheelchairs available upon request*

Monastery of the Cross

• Greek Orthodox   • The Valley of the Cross   • Bus: 19, 22, 24, 31, 32

According to local tradition, the wood for the cross on which Jesus was crucified came from a tree that grew in a local valley. King Tatian of Georgia, whose country had embraced Christianity during the early Byzantine period, determined to build a church over the stump that remained after the tree was cut down. That 5th-century church, and the cloister in which it was located, eventually became known as the Monastery of the Holy Cross.

For hundreds of years the isolated monastery was situated several kilometers west of Jerusalem in a veritable wilderness. Once Jerusalem had spread outside of the Old City walls, however, the Monastery of the Holy Cross found itself situated in the middle of a metropolis. Indeed, it is located in the very heart of modern Jerusalem right between the prestigious REHAVIA neighborhood and the world-renowned ISRAEL MUSEUM. Restored and repaired in the late 1960's and early 1970's, the distinctive dome-topped church has become a favorite attraction for tourists and Israelis alike.

The early monastery was laid waste during the Persian conquest of 614 and probably abandoned until a Georgian monk rebuilt the abbey about 400 years later. It was again at least partially destroyed in the 13th century and the fanatic Moslem who sacked the church personally slew the monks within. The property was returned to the Georgians a few decades later.

In the late 17th century the Georgian Church ran up heavy debts and was forced to sell most of its Jerusalem properties. To prevent having the monastery fall into the hands of the Turks or some other non-Orthodox group, it was transferred to the Greek Orthodox Church. In 1858 the Greek Orthodox established a theological seminary in the compound.

Considering its vulnerable position over so many centuries it was only natural that the monastery would require heavy fortifications. Thus the Monastery of the Cross resembles a fortified city more than it does a cloistered sanctuary. Indeed, it contains very few windows and is rectangular in shape, with many of its buildings part and parcel of the compound's solid surrounding wall. Inside the complex are monks' quarters, rooms for study, a lecture hall, office and archives, a kitchen, bakery and meeting halls. At one time, when clergy preferred not to open the gate, a basket descended from an upper room to collect food and mail from the outside world!

Only one door opens into the complex and the entrance is so squat and narrow that you feel you are entering a cave rather than walking into an inner courtyard. Only after making it through that courtyard do you finally reach the church.

Unmistakably eastern, the church was built in basilica style. The prayer hall and the altar area are divided by a richly decorated iconostasis. Several of the sanctuary's square pillars are covered with dark frescos, mostly depicting the apostles and Greek Orthodox saints.

One of Jerusalem's most remarkable mosaic floors is located near the iconostasis. Part of it dates back to the 6th century, with the rest of it about 300 years old. On its stones you can make out geometric shapes, plants and fish — an early Christian symbol. The stone ceiling and walls bestow a Crusader aura upon the church.

Tradition holds that Abraham gave his nephew Lot shoots from cypress, cedar and olive trees and suggested planting them as penance for the sins he had committed after fleeing with his daughters from Sodom. Lot cared tenderly for the shoots. Each morning he took his donkey to the Jordan river and, laden with its holy water, he went back to the fertile valley in which he had planted his sprouts.

One day a traveler accosted Lot on his return from the Jordan River. The traveler asked for water, and Lot gave him a drink. Soon afterwards he appeared again, and again Lot fulfilled his request. The third time the thirsty wayfarer drank up all that remained of the precious liquid and there was nothing left for the tree. Lot was sorrowed by what had happened but the traveler — really an angel — told him not to worry. His good deed had compensated for his earlier sins. And the tree had an important future in store for it ...

Eventually the twigs combined into a special three-crested tree. Then, one day, it was cut down — its wood to be used in fashioning the cross on which the Romans crucified Jesus.

Just underneath the altar there is a silver disk with a recessed center, covering the spot on which Lot's tree once stood.

Phone: 679-0961
Hours: Daily, 10:00-13:30; **Entrance fee**

Haas-Sherover Promenade

- Armon Hanatziv — East Talpiot   • Bus 8
- The Overlook and part of the Promenade are *wheelchair accessible*

"Some time later God tested Abraham… He said to him, 'Take your son, your only son, Isaac, whom you love, and go to the region of Moriah. Sacrifice him there as a burnt offering on one of the mountains I will tell you about.'" Early the next morning Abraham got up and saddled his donkey…. [and]… set out for the place God had told him about. On the third day Abraham looked up and saw the place in the distance" (Genesis 22:1-4).

The mountain range from which Abraham probably got his first glimpse of Mount Moriah is, today, a spectacular promenade with breath-taking panoramic views. Financed largely by the generous Sherover and Haas families in the 1980's, it is open all day, every day. You can either content yourself with what you see from the main lookout near the parking lot or you can stroll a kilometer of beautiful walkways, landscaped gardens and creative balconies. Because this is not a circular route you get to enjoy the view twice — coming and going!

From the promenade's observation points it shouldn't be hard to pick out Mount Moriah, which in biblical times was only a barren hill. Today it is topped by the golden Dome of the Rock, built in 691 on the site where the First and Second Temples once stood. A silver-gray dome covers the El Aksa Mosque.

Look for a narrow ridge that descends in your direction. It is delineated by the precipitous Kidron Valley to the right and a distinct asphalt road running parallel on the left. You are looking at the boundaries of the ancient Jebusite city conquered by King David and made into the political and spiritual capital of Israel over 3,000 years ago.

Over the millennia Jerusalem has expanded and contracted, and the city walls have been repeatedly destroyed and rebuilt. The walls before you were constructed in the 16th century by Suleiman the Magnificent.

This is a great family outing! If you have them, bring roller blades, skateboards or bicycles.

Restrooms: at both ends of the promenade

L.A. Mayer Museum of Islamic Art

• Talbieh Neighborhood, 2 Palmach St.   • Bus 15   • *Wheelchair accessible*

Although it consists of less than a dozen galleries, Jerusalem's Museum of Islamic Art is one of the city's most enchanting museums. Its exhibits include thousands of everyday articles used in Moslem life over the centuries. So elegant, elaborate or decorative are these items that experts consider them to be functional art.

A gorgeous painted jar in luster on a white background dating back to 10th-century Egypt, fabulous Iranian glassware from the 9th and 10th centuries, and even ornamental horse trappings from India in the 1700's are just a few of the fascinating pieces in the jewelry exhibit. Other items on display include a 9th-century green and yellow Egyptian dish with a splashy design and an Iranian pomegranate drinking vessel about 1,500 years old.

They may be unrelated to Islamic art, but the museum offers a splendid collection of clocks that is a lot of fun to visit. Look for gold watches from Paris, watchmakers' tools, a musical bracket clock dating back to the 1700's, a rolling ball clock and dozens of others. There is also a small collection of firearms on display in this part of the museum.

Phone: 566-1291
Hours: Sun., Mon., Wed., Thurs., 10:00-15:00; Tue., 10:00-18:00; Fri., Sat., 10:00-14:00; **Entrance fee**

Index

Favorite Sites

Notes